# Tiger Wars

# TIGER WARS

## JOE EXOTIC vs. THE BIG CAT QUEEN

AL CIMINO

First published in 2020 by Ad Lib Publishers Ltd
15 Church Road
London, SW13 9HE

www.adlibpublishers.com

Text © 2020 Al Cimino

ISBN 978-1-913543-79-2

A CIP catalogue record for this book is available
from the British Library.

Every reasonable effort has been made to trace copyright-holders
of material reproduced in this book, but if any have been
inadvertently overlooked the publishers would be glad to
hear from them.

Printed in the UK

10 9 8 7 6 5 4 3 2 1

# CONTENTS

# INTRODUCTION: King of the Jungle

The movie *The Lion King*, released in 2019 and starring the voice of Beyoncé, was the highest-grossing animated film of all time, the highest-grossing musical film of all time and the highest-grossing remake of all time. The original movie, released in 1994, was the highest-grossing motion picture of 1994 worldwide and the second highest-grossing film of all time worldwide, behind *Jurassic Park*. It spawned a direct-to-video sequel, a spin-off movie, a television film sequel, two spin-off television series, three educational shorts, several video games, merchandise and, with songs by Elton John and Tim Rice, the third longest-running musical in Broadway history. It won six Tony Awards including Best Musical. The franchise, led by the musical's box office receipts of $8.1 billion (as of December 2017), is the world's highest-grossing entertainment property.

*The Jungle Book*, which came to the silver screen in 1967, also featured big cats – in that case a black panther and a Bengal tiger. During its initial run, it was the most successful animated film ever released. It was re-released theatrically three times and various video releases made millions. There was a live-action adaptation in 1994, an animated sequel, *The Jungle Book 2*, in 2003 and a live-action remake in 2016. Rudyard Kipling's book, *The Jungle Book*, has never been out of print since its publication in 1894.

The world of Winnie the Pooh also featured a tiger, called Tigger, who has been bouncing in the Pooh books and movies since 1928. He got his own film in 2000, *The Tigger Movie*. Then in 1968, there was *The Tiger Who Came to Tea*, a popular children's short story that came onto the small screen in 2019 over fifty years after it was written. Which goes to show that everybody loves big cats, particularly tigers.

And no one loved big cats more than Joe Schreibvogel, aka Joe Exotic – the self-styled Tiger King. He ran a roadside zoo in Wynnewood, Oklahoma, which featured at its height 187 big cats. Or, at least, Joe said he loved them. Carole Baskin disagreed. She was the CEO of Big Cat Rescue in Citrus Park near Tampa, Florida, which claimed to be the world's biggest accredited animal sanctuary. Baskin said that Joe Exotic was cruelly exploiting the animals in his care to make money. He said that, by selling tickets to visitors, she was in the same business.

And big cats are big business in America. In the 1930s, the world's biggest private zoo was owned by legendary newspaper publisher William Randolph Hearst, who filled his estate at San Simeon, California, with hundreds of wild animals, including leopards and grizzly bears. Escaped zebras still roam on the coast nearby.

Some of America's most reputable zoos are actually privately owned, such as the award-winning, non-profit Phoenix Zoo, which is accredited by both the Association of Zoos and Aquariums and the World Association of Zoos and Aquariums. But fewer than ten per cent of the animal exhibitors licenced by the US Department of Agriculture (USDA) are accredited by the AZA who check on animal welfare.

This is a vast problem. There are some 2,400 zoos in the US, the vast majority of which are considered "roadside zoos" like Joe's. The term is contested, but they're generally private and unregulated, with little or no research function. Their conditions are poor even to untrained eyes and many house big cats.

Visitor Sean Williams, reporting for *The Daily Beast*, said: "Among the many roadside zoos I visited… Joe's old park was the worst. When I went, it had rained, and tigers sloshed back and forth in ankle-deep slurry. A man-made lake was neon green and stagnant. A brown bear sat in its own faeces while a man fed it potato chips. Tenpins were scattered about the cages and one monkey enclosure featured a child's kitchen play set."

The AZA don't allow any physical interaction with dangerous animals.

"It's dangerous for the animals and dangerous for the people," said AZA president Dan Ashe. Interactions where a dangerous animal is restrained so the public can pet or hold it are unethical.

"It's restrictive and potentially abusive to the animals," Ashe says. "In order to be in direct contact with humans, humans have to be in control of the animal."

Unaccredited zoos such as Joe Exotic's Greater Wynnewood Exotic Animal Park, formerly known as Garold Wayne Exotic Animal Memorial Park aka G.W. Zoo, allowed visitors to cuddle a tiger cub or pet a lion. An analysis by New York University researchers identified seventy-seven facilities offering public contact with baby animals in late 2015 and early 2016, mostly big cat cubs. The practice was legal, but the USDA said only cubs between the ages of four weeks – when they are no longer consider neonatal – and twelve weeks – when they become "too big, too fast, and too strong" – should be used. At many parks, cubs are caged, sold, or shot when they get too old.

That creates an incentive for breeders such as Joe Exotic to pump out cubs to replace those too old to be safely cuddled. It also means there is a constant supply of hundred-day-old tigers that have outgrown their use.

David Stanton, who ran Joe's video operation in 2012 and lived at his zoo for eight months, said newborn tigers were sometimes removed from their mothers within twenty minutes of birth to be raised by hand for use in petting or the road show, or simply sold.

"Baby tigers are like money in the bank," he said.

According to Joe Exotic: "There are more captive tigers in the US today than there are in the wild throughout the world."

And Joe should know as he bred them to sell to other collectors. Leaving aside zoos, there appears to be more tigers in American backyards than anywhere else on earth. There are only some 4,000 tigers at large in Asia, while it is estimated that there are between 5 and 10,000 tigers in captivity in the US. The wildlife trafficking is a $19 billion industry.

Since 2013, Oklahoma veterinary records show that Joe's zoo shipped out more than a hundred tigers as young as a week old. Cubs could go for as much as $5,000. Dozens were sent to private zookeepers and animal owners in Florida, Indiana, Colorado and beyond. In 2015, he obtained an export permit to ship a lion-tiger hybrid to the United Arab Emirates.

The Lacey Act Amendments of 1981 sought to stem the trading of wild animals as pets across state lines and national borders. However, the regulatory system is porous. The USDA employs around 110 relevant inspectors to oversee 10,000 locations countrywide and the paperwork is easily faked.

Joe Exotic also took flack for taking his animals on the road as part of a carnival that he put on in shopping malls. And he was condemned for breeding the lion-tiger hybrids to bring in the crowds. These animals suffer from genetic abnormalities that require specialised care that many of these facilities are unable to provide. But questionable animal interactions and breeding practices are common at the private zoos. At Joe Exotic's G.W.

Zoo, guests paid $80 per couple for a twelve-minute Deluxe Private Playtime with animals that include ligers and tiligers, hybridised offspring of lions and tigers that do not exist in the wild.

The flamboyant, "gay, gun-toting cowboy with a mullet," as Joe Exotic likes to call himself, became the central figure in a war between the private zoos and animal rights activists. He used the media to defend these practices against such pressure groups as People for the Ethical Treatment of Animals, the Humane Society of the United States, the American Society for the Prevention of Cruelty to Animals, the AZA, the American Sanctuary Association, a number of government agencies and Congress itself. Joe picked out for particular vitriol Carole Baskin, who fought back, winning a $1 million lawsuit against Joe which eventually forced him out of business. In response he accused her of killing her husband.

As the Tiger War escalated it became a fight to the finish with Joe Exotic ending up in jail – and plastered across TV screens worldwide during the coronavirus lockdown of 2020, while Hillsborough County Sheriff's Office re-examined the file on the disappearance of Carole Baskin's husband. The war ain't over yet.

# ONE: Joe Exotic

Born on 5 March 1963, Joseph Schreibvogel was brought up surrounded by animals on a farm in Kansas. These animals were not just of the domestic or barnyard varieties – dogs, cats, horses, cows, chickens. The farmhouse was also home to a range of prairie varmints such small American antelopes, raccoons and porcupines brought home by Joe's two brothers and two sisters.

Their parents were German heritage and, though they were comparatively wealthy, did not pamper their children. Rather they used them as unpaid farmhands. The kids were also hauled to Catholic church every Sunday. It was not an affectionate household. Joe's father Francis – or Francie as he was known – was a Korean war veteran who smoked heavily and rarely spoke. His mother, Shirley, was short and round-faced with a softer side, but Joe could not recall his parents ever saying, "I love you."

At the age of five, Joe recalled, he was repeatedly raped by an older boy in his own home. He said he vividly remembered how a drawer could be opened to jam the bathroom door shut. As humans proved to be the cruellest of creatures, Joe decided to give his love to animals. He brought home ground squirrels, raccoons and ferrets that he kept in cages on the back porch. There were so many that his mother could barely get through the back door. She called a halt to this when he began bringing home snakes. However, she was proud when he won school-fair awards for his knowledge of horses, poultry, rabbits and crops.

Joe shared his love of animals with his older brother Garold Wayne. They watched nature documentaries on TV. Garold dreamt of one day living in Africa so that he could see big cats running free, while Joe set his heart on being a veterinarian. He turned his sister Pamela's playhouse into an animal hospital. On his afternoons off from pulling weeds or other chores around the farm, he would take his BB gun and shoot sparrows. Then he would inject the birds with coloured water he stored in used medicine bottles left over from treating the cows in the vain hope of reviving them.

When Joe was eleven, his mother says that his father, Francie, decided that he would rather tend racehorses than crops and moved the family to a ranch in Wyoming. There Joe stuck a flashlight on the top of an old Buick and pretended to be a cop.

Three years later, the family moved on to Texas, settling in an eight-bedroom house on a large ranch in the small town of Pilot Point, north of Dallas. Joe was fourteen. The moves disrupted Joe's schooling. Few of Joe's classmates from those years remember him, and his photo is often missing from his junior high school yearbook. In high school, he got bullied by the jocks because he preferred to hang around with girls. In retaliation, he said he sprinkled roofing nails all over the school parking lot that popped the tyres of a hundred cars.

"I had to get a job and pay for them all," Joe said. "But they never fucked with me again. Never."

People who knew Joe at the time, including the school principal, did not recall this. But then, Joe always cultivated a fantasy life.

Although he was a member of the Future Farmers of America, he did not stay on the farm after graduating from high school in

1982. Instead he went to work at a local nursing home, where he wore full scrubs, with a fanny pack and stethoscope. On a break he told a convenience store clerk he'd emerged from successful surgery.

In 1983, Joe began a three-year stint as a policeman in nearby Eastvale, an outer suburb of Dallas. It only had a small police department and, at nineteen, Joe became police chief. Serious crimes were rare and he had only a few officers working under him.

Joe lived with a girlfriend named Kim and they had a son named Brandon. But while they played house in Eastvale, Joe was also exploring Dallas' gay nightlife as he came to terms with his own sexuality. Although homosexuality was still illegal in Texas, his colleagues broadly accepted this. But in 1985 – "the bad year," Joe called it – his brother, Yarri, outed him to his father, who made Joe promise not to attend his funeral, sealing the deal with a handshake. Overcome with shame, Joe said he tried to commit suicide by crashing his police cruiser into a concrete bridge parapet at high speed, nearly plummeting over the edge.

There is no record of this incident and neither Joe's family nor the residents of Eastvale remember it, though Joe does have a photograph of the damaged vehicle which he offers as proof. Joe said he ended up with a broken back, spending fifty-seven days in hospital in traction before moving down to West Palm Beach, Florida, to join in an experimental saltwater rehabilitation programme. His boyfriend at the time remembered only that Joe had a broken shoulder and said the only saltwater treatment he underwent was snorkelling.

Joe lived with his boyfriend and, indulging his love of animals, got a job in a pet shop called Pet Circus. The manager, Tim, had a friend who worked at a drive-through safari park where visitors could see lions and other wild animals roaming more or less free. He would often come home with baby lions and monkeys that he would let Joe bottle-feed. They would roll on the floor together and Joe was hooked.

After a few years, Joe returned to Texas, got a job as a security guard at a gay cowboy bar called the Round-up Saloon, where he sometimes performed in drag as Dolly Parton. It was there that he met his first 'husband', Brian Rhyne, a slim, sassy nineteen-year-old cosmology student at the University of Texas. They moved into a trailer together in Arlington, where they shared a bed with a pack of poodles. This is when Joe adopted his distinctive look with a bleach-blond mullet, horseshoe moustache, jeans and cowboy boots, complete with a ten-gallon hat and side-strapped six-shooter. He wore spurs on his boots, even when shopping for groceries. It was a look they shared as Brian wore the same.

On Saturdays, they would snort strawberry meth and hang out in bars. Sundays would be spent lazing around at home, watching westerns on TV. Joe and Brian eventually got married in an unofficial ceremony at the Round-up. Gay marriage was far from legal then.

Down the street from the trailer park where Joe and Brian lived was a pet store called Pet Safari. Joe got a job there and in 1986 Joe, Brian and Garold bought the shop. For the first few years they sold small animals – reptiles, birds and fish. To attract a gay clientele, Joe hung rainbow banners outside and stocked the shelves with rainbow doggy T-shirts.

Joe was a smooth talker and a great salesman, but still the store was not profitable. So he and Garold set about finding ways to make money. Garold would dumpster dive behind furniture and carpet stores. Then they would turn the trash into doghouses and cat playgrounds which they would sell. Then they used the money to expand the range, buying bigger cages for exotic pets, such as three-banded armadillos and four-eyed opossums.

With a $50,000 loan they bought a new site, calling it Super Pet, and added a lawn, a garden centre, a 30,000-square-foot dog obedience training area, a wildlife rescue centre and a petting zoo. It was the largest venue of its kind in the state, Joe told people. Super Pet thrived despite complaints about dirty cages.

Garold got married and had two kids. He coached soccer across the state line in Ardmore, Oklahoma, while Brian and Joe built a marital home in Fort Worth.

"We worked together, lived together: the whole nine yards," Joe said.

Around 1995 Joe and Brian travelled to Palm Springs, California and drove across the dunes of the Coachella Valley in a Jeep. Soon after they returned, Brian fell ill. Doctors diagnosed him with a life-threatening fungal infection. He was also HIV positive.

The business was going well when, in October 1997, Garold was driving in the rain near Dallas with his sister Tamara, when a semi truck hydroplaned and ran into his vehicle, crushing him in his chassis. He was cut out of the car and airlifted to hospital. A week later, the family switch off his life support. Joe claimed he pulled the switch. Others deny it.

Joe also claimed that the truck driver who killed Garold was drunk, though this does not appear to be the case. Nevertheless that family were awarded $140,000 damages from the trucking company. Joe's father, Francie, refused to have anything to do with the cash, dismissing the settlement as "blood money". Garold's wife and kids wanted to use it to build a soccer field in his honour, but Joe had another idea. He reminded the family of his brother's dream to go to Africa to see lions and spend time with "people with bones in their noses and shit".

Since Garold never got to travel to Africa and see the wild animals there, Joe suggested that they bring the wild animals of Africa home so that people like Garold could see them. He persuaded them to ditch their plans for the soccer field, and instead spend the settlement on an animal park which they would name after Garold. Not everyone was happy with this.

"He's a goddamn – what do you call it – a Charles Manson," said his brother Yarri. "They were still grieving, still grabbing at anything. He's just got a way of brainwashing them."

Sister Pamela was equally forthright: "Joe used [Garold] and his memory to just get what he wanted."

Joe sold the shop for $70,000 and, with the compensation, bought an old horse ranch with eleven acres of land off the I-35 outside Wynnewood, Oklahoma – population 2,000. The site was separated from the one-stoplight town by the meandering Washita River. They poured cement for sidewalks and built a row of nine cages. The Garold Wayne Exotic Animal Memorial Park opened two years to the day after his death. Joe wanted Garold's grave moved to the G.W. Zoo, as everyone called it, but his wife and children refused. They have barely spoken since. Instead Joe built a shrine to Garold, who Joe described as "the best friend I ever had".

Two of Garold's pets, a deer and a buffalo, were the zoo's first residents. Then came a mountain lion and a bear. Once word got round that Joe had opened an animal sanctuary, people began dropping off exotic animals that they no longer wanted, or had grown too big to cope with. Lions, tigers, monkeys, birds and other rare creatures arrived at its gates. Joe and Brian moved into the ranch house, where they nursed baby animals born in the zoo. Brian also looked after the finances, as he had done in Texas, while Joe told visitors Garold dreamt of seeing exotic animals in Africa – something his siblings deny.

In 2000, Joe got a call from a game warden telling him that someone had abandoned two tigers in a backyard thirty miles away near Ardmore. Joe collected them and brought them back to his animal park. Named Tess and Tickles, these were his first tigers. They bred and Joe raised their cubs. Joe built more cages and fences all around the house, which he filled with lions and tigers. These beautiful beasts were hardly running free, but visitors could see them up close and Joe said Garold would have loved it. Almost without noticing, Joe the showman became just another exotic animal living in a cage inside the zoo.

By then the trouble had already started. In 1999, while the park was still under construction, Joe agreed to collect a flock of starving emus from a ranch in Red Oak, some twenty miles south of Dallas. The emu craze had hit Texas hard in the early 1990s. Thousands of ranchers began breeding them, convinced that low-cholesterol emu steaks would replace beef at butchers' counters and on restaurant tables, and that emu oil would fly off of the shelves of health food stores as a miracle cure-all. A breeding pair of birds fetched as much as $50,000.

In 1995 Kuo Wei Lee, a real-estate developer from Plano, Texas, bought dozens of the birds, just as the bubble was about to burst. Consumers did not take to their meat, which was said to be a red-meat version of pork, and the customers of health food stores – even if they were not vegans or vegetarians – did not like the idea of the slaughter of exotic animals. With the craze over, Lee cut back on the birds' feed to save money. When the police raided his property, they found sixty-nine dead emus and over a hundred more feeding on the remains.

The authorities called Joe. He planned to take them back to Wynnewood and turned up with two rescue volunteers and a high school contingent of Future Farmers of America who had no experience of herding emus. The two-day rescue operation went horribly wrong. Fifteen birds died from the stress of the event, largely trampled to death. While they rescued more than a hundred, others escaped and headed for the freeway. Joe borrowed a shotgun and shot six of them. Some dropped instantly. Others, according to local reports, "flopped and jumped, requiring several shots". Joe claimed he'd killed them to prevent them dying of stress.

"We're hurt and we're tired, and now we're responsible," he said. But the police took a different view.

"You can't do something like that and explain it away," said Red Oak Police Chief Doug McHam. "Nobody is that silver-tongued."

Local law enforcement and the American Society for the Prevention of Cruelty to Animals lambasted Joe for his actions, but a grand jury declined to indict him on animal cruelty charges. He did not get to keep the emus either. They were given to a rancher in Tolar, Texas, for safekeeping. Joe then sued the Dallas branch of the ASPCA for defamation, after it released a videotape of the emu round-up to local reporters. This apparently resulted in a loss of business at his Arlington pet store. It was Joe's first fight with an animal rights agency.

Joe sold Super Pet and ploughed the money into the G.W. Zoo, which gradually expanded into neighbouring properties. By 2001, Joe had eighty-nine big cats and 1,100 other exotic animals. His father, Francie, helped dig ponds and build fences, while his mother, Shirley, ran the gift shop and Brian balanced the books. While Brian and Joe didn't kiss in front of his parents, they'd gently brush past each other. But in the park he was out and proud. Joe would put on a cheeky grin and treat his visitors to an expletive-laden, un-PC tour of the zoo.

"This ain't SeaWorld," he would say by way of an excuse.

With the park prospering and drawing in crowds, Joe became a favourite of the local chamber of commerce who invited him to join. He also volunteered as an Emergency Medical Technician and snuck tiger cubs into the local hospital to entertain the patients.

However, for Brian things were going from bad to worse. His weight plummeted. A hospice nurse came by each day, while Joe became Brian's primary carer. By mid-December 2001, Brian was skeletal and couldn't speak. He died due to complications arising from HIV four days before Christmas. Joe was loading him into a pickup to take him home to die peacefully when he breathed his last. It was said Joe screamed loud enough that it made your ears ring. The funeral was held at the zoo and the alligator nursery was named after him as a memorial.

Having lost a brother and a lover within four years, Joe felt that the world was turning against him.

"You tend to wonder what the hell you did wrong," he said. It was a rare moment of introspection.

According to Joe's niece, Chealsi Putnam: "When Brian died, that's when the whole demeanour of everything changed. Something just came over him and he was never the same again... as far as the way he even did business."

Within a year, Joe had a new lover, a hard-drinking, drug-abusing twenty-four-year-old named Jeffrey Charles "J.C." Hartpence, who he met in the gay bar Copra. As an event producer, J.C. took Joe's animal show on the road. Taking his inspiration from magician David Copperfield, Joe donned sequined cowboy shirts and toured as an "illusionist", putting on shows at malls and fairs across the country. He lectured on conservation and let kids pet his tiger cubs – for a modest fee. He used stage names "Aarron Alex", "Cody Ryan" and "Joe Exotic" across Texas, Oklahoma and as far north as Green Bay, Wisconsin, where he was billed in a newspaper advert as "Master Illusionist Joe Exotic".

Given the tale Joe often told about the death of his brother, J.C. decided to swear off drink and drugs while they were on tour. He and J.C. "monkey promised" on the finger of a monkey to stay clean. However, Joe ran into trouble with the authorities for safety violations, allowing kids to enter cages with wild animals. Charm, wit and threats of lawsuits kept him out of harm's way.

But Joe also garnered some good publicity when he rescued three emaciated bears seized from a Russian circus trainer. The newspaper, *The Oklahoman*, launched an appeal and readers donated $17,400 towards the bears' upkeep. Joe spotted another lucrative outlet and asked visitors for donations to sponsor other animals. Memorial plaques sprang up around the park, alongside posters soliciting cash. The self-styled Tiger King was now a local celebrity and was raking in serious royalties. There were questions about where the money went. Particularly sceptical was brother Yarri.

"It was like a con deal from the start," he said. "I think he started right then, like, 'Dude, this is easy. I can eat red lobster every damn day, twice a day, and somebody else is gonna pay for it.'"

Another of Joe's sidelines was breeding hybrid big cats, such as ligers – the offspring of a male lion and a female tiger. Then there were liligers – the offspring of a second-generation male lion and a ligress – and tiligers – the offspring of a second-generation male tiger and a ligress female.

These crossbreeds do not exist in the wild and fetch many times more money than the sale of a regular cat. Staff at the zoo said Joe made between $1,500 and $10,000 for hybrid cubs. The creation of these hybrids drew criticism. They do nothing to help the genetic diversity of big cats and many have exhibited birth defects. But to Joe, creating these creatures made him a demi-god – if not God himself. He said he wanted to reintroduce the sabre-toothed tiger to America, an animal unrelated to modern cats, which died out around 10,000 years ago, though had existed for a long time before.

"Can you imagine how exciting it would be, to see and talk to an animal ambassador that evolved from 360 million years ago, just because of one man's belief?" said Joe. "If the male ligers weren't sterile and could breed with the lionesses, that's the closest thing you can get to a sabre-tooth tiger."

Concerning hybridising, a spokesperson for People for the Ethical Treatment of Animals (PETA) pointed the finger squarely at Joe, saying: "He's the spoke at the centre of the wheel. There are others who breed, but he's the primary one."

The road shows and the sale of hybridised cubs helped fund the further expansion of the zoo. As a result, Joe needed more employees to help run the zoo and the road show. He found most of his staff through the website Craigslist. In general, he picked misfits – ex-cons and others. In the early summer of 2003, a stocky nineteen-year-old named John Finlay answered one of Joe's adverts. He'd graduated high school in Davis, ten miles from Wynnewood, and trained to be a carpenter. But jobs were few and far between, and John didn't hesitate when, the following day, Joe hired him. At first he mucked out cages and carried out other menial tasks with the other misfits. But soon the tigers enchanted him. The park then had around eight-hundred animals and eighteen workers. It was a place where both animals and humans came for a second chance, as Joe said: "Most of the volunteers here are ex-druggies, ex-alcoholics, on prison's doorstep. Why do people turn to drugs and alcohol? Usually because they don't fit in somewhere. Well, here these animals don't judge you."

What's more, John thought his new boss was cool. He was clearly off-the-wall, like a comic-book gunslinger and nothing like anybody John had met in Oklahoma, or Texas, where he'd been born. Joe's treatment of staff could be cruel and vindictive. He fired them just because he liked firing people. But John shared with him a love of animals. Joe took John to the travelling shows in Kansas. These long trips on the road gave them plenty of time to get to know each other.

At the time, John was living with a girlfriend in Pauls Valley, a few miles from the zoo. One night, a month after John began work at Wynnewood, he sent Joe a text message that read simply: "Come save me." When Joe arrived, John's girlfriend was throwing John and his belongings out onto the street. Joe took John back to the park, where he stayed for over ten years. Within a month of Finlay moving in, they were in a relationship and, just below his beltline, Finlay had tattooed: "PRIVATELY OWNED BY JOE EXOTIC."

Joe's relationship with Hartpence was already at breaking point. Turning back to drink and drugs, Hartpence had become disillusioned with Joe's plans for the zoo. He wanted to see it become a sanctuary for animals they had rescued, with large enclosures giving them room to roam where they could be rehabilitated with an eye to possible release. But Joe was no longer interested in rescuing ill-treated or abandoned animals. Instead he was buying in animals from breeders, then breeding more of his own. After the cubs had been used in the photo opportunities visitors paid for, the growing animals were then sold on for profit.

In mid-2003, Hartpence walked into the office and found a photograph on his desk. It showed the zoo's largest tiger, Goliath, baring his teeth menacingly over a big slab of meat. The caption "J.C.'s remains" was typed in white letters over the picture. A Post-it note attached read: "If you don't get your shit together, this is gonna be your reality." The handwriting was Joe's.

One night, Hartpence waited until Joe fell asleep, then pointed a loaded .45 and a .357 Magnum at his head. The click of the guns cocking woke Joe.

"I want out," said Hartpence. "Are we clear?"

Joe talked Hartpence into putting the guns down and called the police. Hartpence was arrested at the zoo and never returned. His life continued on a downward spiral. He was later convicted of "aggravated indecent liberties with a child under the age of fourteen" and put on the sex offenders register. Then he was sentenced to life in prison in Kansas for first-degree felony murder of Curtis Shelton who was found dead in his home with multiple gunshot wounds in 2014. Hartpence ended up in the Larned Correctional Mental Health Facility in Kansas and won't be eligible for parole until 2034, but he is likely to spend the rest of his life in prison.

In the midst of the break-up, John began self-harming. After sleepless nights, he would often lay in bed until mid-afternoon. With Hartpence gone, Joe and John became an item, doing everything together. When parted, they would exchange messages.

"I love that kid so much," Joe said.

Joe found other uses for Craigslist. He often posted ads on the website soliciting young men to join him and John for weekenders in motels in Pauls Valley or Oklahoma City. They returned from the trips bleary-eyed, belligerent and to absolute squalor. Tiger, lion and bear cubs lived in Joe and John's trailer, and defecated everywhere. The smell was appalling. John blames Joe for introducing him to meth, and the pair began lifting weights. John took steroids, which gave him violent mood swings. "At the drop of a dime, I could go off," he told me.

There were sweeteners though. Joe bought John almost anything he wanted, from belt buckles to trucks. But he was possessive, and kept his young boyfriend high on drugs. "[Joe] had it in John's head that if he left, he couldn't go nowhere," one of John's former girlfriends said. "He couldn't do nothing."

Joe's zoo continued to grow in popularity and his travelling show staged more events. But the operation was attracting the attention of the local authorities. There were thousands of dollars' worth of outstanding fines for illegal animal trading. Joe complained that he could not pay because the animals consumed $36,000 a month in food. Local cop, David Steele, told a reporter: "I don't know what his problem is. We didn't force him to take the animals. He wanted them."

The attention he attracted invited more scrutiny from federal regulations and animal rights groups. In July 2004, *The Oklahoman* published an article about a crippled two-month-old lion cub named Angel that had been born at the zoo, possibly a result of inbreeding, against the advice of an Oklahoma USDA expert.

Joe claimed there was a conspiracy against him. The USDA, he said, would "pull some strings out of the air to kill" the cat and frame him. Meanwhile the animal rights lobby kept their eye on the suffering of the crippled lion cub.

"No legitimate animal sanctuary would allow that to happen," said one activist who was quoted in the article.

"If they have a problem with my morals," Joe countered, "then they can write me a cheque so I can build separate cages for my males and females."

The activist had another issue to air.

"I believe he's breeding animals for financial gain," she said. "He's the reason that poor cub was born crippled... People like that know what they're doing."

The name of the activist was Carole Lewis – later Carole Baskin, the Big Cat Queen. This was the first shot in the Tiger Wars.

## TWO: The Big Cat Queen

Carole Baskin, *née* Stairs, was also an animal lover with a childhood dream of becoming a veterinarian. Born on 6 June 1961 at Lackland Air Force Base in San Antonio, Texas, she was brought up in Florida. From the age of nine or ten, she would rescue stray cats which she took for walks in the swamplands around her home. But her ambition to be a vet faded when she learnt that she would have to euthanise animals.

At fourteen, she says she was raped by three men at knifepoint. Getting no support from her conservative Christian family who believed that she must have been asking for it, she quit high school and ran away from home with a member of a rock band who worked at a local roller rink.

For a time, she hitch-hiked up and down the coast, from Florida to Maine. She slept in garages and underneath parked cars because no one would think to look for her there. At one point, she said she broke her neck in a car accident and was paralysed for some time. Later she bought an orange Datsun truck and slept in the back with her pet cat.

She got a job at a discount store in Tampa. Her boss there, Mike Murdock, offered to let her cat stay in his apartment during the day so it would not roast in the truck. Carole moved in too and, though he was eleven years older than her, they got married and had a daughter named Jamie.

Mike turned out to be controlling and incredibly possessive. He would mark the odometer on her car each day to make sure she wasn't sneaking out on him. She wanted to leave but was afraid she wouldn't make it on her own, being just seventeen.

"He was Jamie's father and he was extremely abusive," Carole explained. "But the idea of leaving and having to raise a child on my own was terrifying."

To make extra money, Carole began breeding rare Persian and Himalayan show cats. These were fluffy little freaks, with faces so flat they could barely breathe. For fun, she began taking in injured bobcats, which she would rehabilitate and release. She soon found she preferred them to the domestic variety.

One night Carole and Mike had a particularly bad argument. Fearing that he was going to give her another beating, she threw a potato at this head and ran out of the house barefoot, ducking down between houses to evade him.

As she was walking down a road, a car pulled up beside her. Then nineteen years old with blonde hair and blue eyes, people often thought she was a TV star. The driver wound down the window and asked if she wanted a ride. He was a tall, tanned, older man dressed in shabby clothes. "No thanks," she said.

He drove off, but reappeared a few minutes later. This time he had gun on the passenger seat. He said that, if she did not trust him, she could hold the gun on him. She noted that he had happy eyes and rakish smile, and she got into the car.

With Carole holding the gun on the driver, they drove around for a while. Then he stopped and put his hands around her neck. He said he could strangle her. "I know," she said. But his hands relaxed and he began to massage her shoulders.

They checked into a cheap motel, but just spent the night talking. Eventually she fell asleep wearing a baggy pair of pyjamas he had lent her. Because he had not pressed himself on her, she said she fell in love with him there and then.

He said his name was Bob Martin and, like her, he was married. They would have their trysts in a trailer on the site where he worked. As they pulled into the lot, Bob would make her lie on the floor of the truck so no one would see her. She thought they were hiding from his boss, who he said was a wealthy businessman named Don Lewis.

She would phone him at work, asking for Bob Martin. One day, the phone was answered by a new receptionist who said that there was no Bob Martin working there. Carole was puzzled so she described him – middle-aged with blond hair and blue eyes. The receptionist laughed. "You're describing Don Lewis," she said. Carole was having an affair with the millionaire.

The couple divorced their respective spouses and married in 1991. Again there was a considerable age gap. She was thirty; he was forty-two. But they shared an interest in animals. In 1992, they were, they were at a pet auction in Ohio when a bobcat came up for sale. She overheard another bidder saying that he was going to buy the bobcat, kill it and have it stuffed. Carole cried at the very thought. Don outbid the man and they took the bobcat home.

They called the bobcat Windsong, but she was a handful. She'd chase Jamie around the house and face off with their German shepherd. Or she would lie on top of the refrigerator and, when Don opened it, she would pounce on his head.

Don decided that Windsong needed a companion, so they drove to a bobcat breeder in Minnesota. The place was filthy. The flies were so thick that Carole had to put a handkerchief over her face to keep them from flying into her mouth. The breeder had rows of cages with fifty-six bobcat kittens in them.

"Is there really this big of a market for bobcats as pets?" she asked.

"Oh, no," said the breeder. "We're a fur farm. We'll just raise them until they're a year old and then slaughter them."

Carole then noticed a pile of dead cats with their belly fur already sliced off. Again she burst into tears.

"How much for every cat here?" Don asked, and bought the lot.

He also took a forty-acre tract of land at the end of a dirt road called Easy Street in Hillsborough County, Florida, where they set up Wildlife on Easy Street. Initially they ran it as a small sanctuary. When word got round, people would phone up asking them to take the lions and tigers they could no longer cope with, along with smaller cats such as African wildcats and lynxes. Within a year they had two hundred cats from seventeen different species. They built cages inside and outside the house, including one around Carole's desk so the cats wouldn't pee on her fax machine. The early sexual abuse, the debilitating car crash, the donated animals were all curious parallels to Joe's beginnings in the big cat business. But Wildlife on Easy Street was a not-for-profit venture, staffed by more than a hundred volunteers.

To help fund the sanctuary, Carole and Don turned four cabins into a small bed-and-breakfast operation where guests would pay $75 to spend the night with bobcats and cougars.

"You'd pay that much at Holiday Inn, with no entertainment," said Carole, who played the part of the big-cat hotelier, dressed from head to toe in tiger and leopard print.

Visitors Mary Lou Johnson and Lee Foster wrote on their website: "Once the fold-out bed was securely set up, the three of us seemed ready to settle in for the night. However, before climbing between the covers, we had to coax our overnight comrade out from under the bed.

"Tonga, a member of the African wildcat clan known as servals, was our invited guest for the evening. Although most bed-

and-breakfast establishments entice travellers with big beds and designer decor, Wildlife on Easy Street in Tampa is a B&B that allows you to cuddle with the endangered or exotic young cat of your choice. By cat they mean a baby bobcat, cougar, leopard, serval or caracal. (Guests are required to sign a waiver covering any possibility of injury, but no one has ever been hurt by the cats.)

"A frisky young serval struck us as a good choice of roommate. With his large eyes, tawny colour and lanky build, Tonga resembled a young deer more than a house cat. When he is not sharing a cabin with overnight guests, he roams a sizable enclosed area within the forty-acre facility."

Conditions for the animals were good – not so good for the humans though.

"Wildlife on Easy Street ranks among the most humane habitats we have come across," Mary Lou and Lee added. "In fact, the cats' quarters are quite spacious, filled with grassy areas, trees and shady retreats. By contrast, the rustic cabin where we stayed was rather cramped. The thought of two adults and an energetic serval occupying the cosy cabin was a concern. Don't expect lavish accommodations, but do expect to have a memorable experience."

While Carole was concerned about animal welfare, Don had an eye for business opportunities. He wanted to breed big cats and sell them. Carole thought this was immoral. As cats reared in captivity could not survive in the wild, there was no possibility of releasing them, so breeding big cats would simply mean that there would be more of them spending their lives in cages. Naturally the lachrymose Carole wept at the thought.

Nor did she like the idea of people buying big cats to keep as pets. In interviews, she insisted that visitors' interactions with the animals at Easy Street would make them think twice about owning a big cat.

"I thought, if people could go in a cage with one of those cats and see that they're not affectionate – all they want to do is pee on you – then they won't want them as pets," she said.

But Don saw things differently. He was from a poor background and had clawed his way to becoming a successful businessman by buying and selling scrap metal and machine parts before moving on to renovating run-down real estate. Although he was a multimillionaire, he was also notoriously stingy. He owned private planes, but would go dumpster diving behind the local grocery stores for day-old bread. There was no fancy wedding. They married in a courthouse ceremony with a $14 cubic zirconia wedding ring. Later he refused to pay his stepdaughter's cable bill. He was also unfaithful and Carole knew it. In her diary, she described him as cruel and venomous.

They fought. In June 1997, Don filed a petition for a restraining order on Carole. He told police she had threatened to shoot him if he didn't leave the house – a claim she denied.

"The worst thing I ever did was threaten to report him to the IRS," she said.

Although the petition was rejected, he asked his secretary of eighteen years, Anne McQueen, to keep it safe in case anything ever happened to him.

"I'm probably the only woman he never fooled around with," said McQueen, later one of the beneficiaries of Don's $1.25 million life insurance policy. "I used to say it was the only time in my life that I was glad I was short and fat."

A few weeks later, Don disappeared. Carole said he got up before her that morning, telling her that he was going to Miami. She never saw him again. Two days after Carole reported him missing, his 1989 Dodge van was found at a nearby airport in neighbouring Pasco County, but staff there said they never saw him and there was no record of him taking a flight that day. None of his credit cards were used subsequently. Carole thought Don had either fled to Costa Rica in one of his private planes, or he had been thrown off a plane over the Gulf of Mexico. She said he often flew to the islands for sex when she was menstruating. She also said that their former attorney in Costa Rica told her that Lewis was loaning money to the "Helicopter Brothers", a local organised crime gang.

Detectives have said there was no way one of Don's private planes could have held enough fuel to take him all the way to Costa Rica, particular after Baskin said he would often fly below the radar because he had lost his pilot's licence. Investigators sent to Costa Rica also came up empty-handed, though there were rumours that Don was intending to divorce Carole and move to Costa Rica permanently.

Don's daughter publicly accused Carole of killing him, grinding up his body and feeding it to her tigers. Joe Exotic later echoed the charges.

"It's a perfect scenario to dispose of someone," said Donna Pettis, the oldest of Don's four children. "We were upset that the cops didn't test the DNA on the meat grinder."

This, Carole said, was the "most ludicrous of all the lies."

"My tigers eat meat; they don't eat people. There would be bones and remains of my husband out there. I'm amazed that people would even think such a thing," she said, pointing out that the opening of her meat grinder was just big enough to accommodate a human hand, but not a whole body.

"Meat had to first be cut into one inch cubes… to go through it," she wrote in her blog. "The idea that a human body and skeleton could be put through it is idiotic."

The allegations against her remain unsubstantiated, and police say Carole was never named as a suspect.

"Can you imagine having people think you killed your husband or wife and not being able to prove otherwise?" she asked. "Without a body, there is nothing I can do to clear my name."

However, the water grew muddier when it was discovered that Carole's brother was a deputy sheriff on the Hillsborough County police force and was on duty the night of Lewis' disappearance.

That night, Carole claimed to have gone to the local grocery store at 3 a.m. to buy milk for tiger cubs when her vehicle broke down. Hillsborough County Sheriff, Chad Chronister, said that her brother and another officer corroborated her story. Her brother had been on a call at the time.

"He had asked for one of his other friends, another deputy, to please take her to the home," said Sheriff Chronister. "Another deputy sheriff did pick her up from the Albertson's and give her a ride back to the animal sanctuary."

The case remains open.

"The last thing we did was back in 2011," said Sheriff Chronister. "We asked her to come in and take a polygraph and she declined. And the year before, we took DNA samples from all Don Lewis' children – in case that if a body was ever recovered, it would be in our database. We would be able to track it back that way."

More evidence came out in March 2020 when bestselling author Robert Moor tweeted: "After Don Lewis vanished, but before Carole married her third husband Howard, she dated a guy named Jay Baykal. In 2002, Jay filed a restraining order against Carole, which included some bizarre and suspicious-sounding details regarding Don's disappearance."

Moor shared a link showing the application. Part of it read: "Her prior husband is presumed dead. One day she said to me, when I asked her 'What happens if your husband shows up now?'

Her response was, 'Dead bodies can't talk'." Baykal's statement went on: "Her former husband's daughter told me she could be dangerous and watch my back."

The application also claimed that Carole carried two loaded guns and said that, if bones were ever found on her property, she was "in deep shit". However, as there was no factual evidence of violence or threats, the order was denied. Carole maintained her innocence.

"Don was not easy to live with and like most couples we had our moments," she said. "But I never threatened him and I certainly had nothing to do with his disappearance. When he disappeared, I did everything I could to assist the police. I encouraged them to check out the rumours from Costa Rica, and separately I hired a private investigator."

She went on to say that her husband's behaviour became rather unusual before he vanished and she suspected dementia.

"He started refusing to use the bathroom and defecating outside. He brought in a homeless man to stay in our house," she said. "I rescheduled an appointment for him to see the specialist, Dr. Gold, but he disappeared before the appointment date."

After Don's disappearance, Carole became embroiled in a fierce battle with his children over his sizable estate, estimated at more than $5 million. Carole maintained that the children were entitled only to about $1 million from the properties that belonged to their father before he married her. But the land on Easy Street and all the cats belonged solely to Carole and she won the right to continue running the sanctuary.

"The cats are her life," said Carole's mother, Barbara Stairs, who helped run the real estate side of the business. "She doesn't care what she lives in as long as the cats are taken care of."

With visitors posting stories of their stays at Wildlife on Easy Street, the American Zoological Association, an industry body, refused accreditation in the year 2000. Carole herself grew concerned she was actually encouraging big cat ownership. She tore down the last rows of dog-kennel-style cages and constructed larger enclosures built around shady live oaks, so every cat's feet could touch the earth. She stopped visitors from touching the animals and, in 2003, Wildlife on Easy Street became Big Cat Rescue.

Don Lewis was declared legally dead in 2002. That November she met financial advisor Howard "Howie" Baskin at the inauguration of the newly formed No More Homeless Pets, which aimed to end the euthanasia of healthy dogs and cats in shelters by implementing an aggressive spay and neuter programme. They fell into conversation because he had visited Wildlife on Easy Street.

By the following year Howard had joined Big Cat Rescue as the Chairman of the Advisory Board. In that role, he worked full time with Carole to raise awareness of Big Cat Rescue and its mission, and build a sound financial base for its continued work. They married in November 2004, in a private ceremony on the beach at Florida's Anna Maria Island, where he had first proposed a year earlier. The bride wore white while the groom was dressed as a caveman.

Their individual vows were equally bizarre. Don's included: "You will actively seek ways to keep your relationship, and your partner's life, fresh and interesting, but not so interesting that you drive Howie nuts." Carole's went: "Howie, you promise to close drawers and cabinet doors after removing items, and particularly the closet door to keep your old cat Crystal from peeing on Carole's clothes."

Loyal to a fault, Howard staunchly defended his wife against the accusation that she killed her first husband.

"Anyone who spends an hour with Carole would come away knowing she didn't have any involvement in Don's disappearance," he said.

Their marriage was blissful.

"We have never had an argument. We have never even had a harsh word where the other one had to come back later and say, 'I'm sorry I had to say that.' We make decisions every week. We don't always agree. We talk about it. We listen to each other's reasoning," Howard said. "I honestly believe I am the luckiest man in the world. I could not imagine having a more considerate and caring spouse."

While Howard raised money, Carole taught herself to build websites, creating 911animalabuse.com which she used to call out the people she considered the worst abusers. It told visitors to the site: "Find out who the bad guys really are."

On social media she posted pictures of the big cats she had rescued. Her aim, she said, was to halt the rampant breeding of big cats. The key to this, she realised, was to stop the cub-petting industry, which she estimated was responsible for ninety per cent of the tigers and lions born in America.

In 2009, she was scrolling through photos of various cub-petting operations when she began to notice the same face again and again, at different malls, though operating under different names. It was a scrawny man with a blond mullet and black eyeliner. He was a magician. Sometimes he went by the name Aarron Alex, sometimes Cody Ryan, but most often he called himself Joe Exotic. Other people also brought his name to her attention.

"We were inundated with calls and emails about people who were keeping big cats as pets. There was one name that kept coming up over and over – Joe Exotic," she said. "It wasn't like we targeted him. We didn't. He was the one who was overwhelmingly on the road with his petting cubs, so he attracted a lot of attention. He was holding his circus in the parking lots of malls."

Carole also discovered that the G.W. Zoo was the subject of eight separate legal cases that year and she turned her cross hairs on Joe. She began emailing shopping malls that were hosting these events to voice her outrage and encouraged followers to do the same. She even hired on a part time member of staff to take on the task. She threatened to expose these malls on Big Cat Rescue's YouTube channel, which she said was the second most-viewed non-profit channel in the world at that time. Joe responded by switching names at the first hint of a complaint, using up to twenty company names for his road show "to keep Carole busy".

Nevertheless, via the internet, supporters tracked Joe's whereabouts. At one point, Carole even hired someone to follow his road crew around full time. The key was a program called Capwiz, which was used by organisations to email-blast members of Congress. Her online followers flooded malls with tens of thousands of complaints. Mall managers would call her office to say their system had crashed. Otherwise Carole would phone reporters on local newspapers where Joe was performing and educate them about the abuse.

"It was having some effect and causing a problem for him," Howard Baskin said.

As a result, Joe grew paranoid. He accused crew members of being PETA spies and kept them at the park long after closing time with rambling harangues that might last as much as three hours. Around 2010 he sent John to scope out Big Cat Rescue, visiting the sanctuary himself later. When they flew over the sanctuary in a helicopter, Finlay said Joe talked about dropping grenades on it.

Carole's name was brought up in daily conversations. Joe never stopped talking about the "bitch" who was after his business. He posed with a rifle on Facebook, with the caption "Bring it on, bitch." Her email inbox filled up with rape and death threats. One day she opened her mailbox to find it full of snakes. On another, somebody attached wires to make it seem like the mailbox was a booby trap with a bomb. After a court hearing, Carole was attacked in the parking lot. Joe denied he was behind the incidents, claiming the worst he did was to protest at Big Cat Rescue dressed in a bloody rabbit suit after a rumour circulated that they were feeding the cats with bunnies.

"Carole is a fucking fruit cake," he said.

According to Howard Baskin, later, during mediation, when he mentioned the threats, Joe admitted he'd done it. But he had waited until the two men were alone. "Nothing personal," Joe had said. "What could be more personal?" Howard asked.

With Carole's efforts curtailed, Joe's touring and the abuse at the park continued. Crew would allegedly stroll about tossing live chickens, cats and other animals into big-cat enclosures, or shoot them for fun. Cats, gerbils and rats were fed to snakes and big cats. Even so, many animals went hungry for days on end and some starved to death. When a big cat got sick, Joe turned it into a donation drive, pleading for money online. One employee said she saw staff share a joint with a monkey, and that cubs were "routinely struck with force on the nose, face, eyes, and neck".

One crew member was dared to bite the head off a live snake – which he did. Another said he witnessed Joe run over emus in a four-wheeler so he could sell their bones to the Museum of Osteology in Oklahoma City.

Most of the animals Joe and the crew killed were dumped in a spot toward the back of the park called the "tiger pit". The stench became so bad that Joe's dad said it reminded him of the battlefields of the Korean War. Francie and Shirley still visited most days, though there was nothing to suggest they conspired in the abuse carried out by their son, who was turning into something far more sinister than the fantasist he had been. Many crew members recalled Joe strung out, or acting like he was high on cocaine. Joe allegedly mocked disabled children who visited the park, and joked with one employee that a pocketknife was his "n***er stabber".

"He started to lose grip on who he actually was," said Finlay. "He'd joke about you to your face, or chat shit about you behind your back. He just was an all round fucking asshole."

## THREE: Keeping the Show on the Road

In 2004, Joe Exotic was still getting good press. In July, the Mystical Magic Show turned up at the Frisco Station Mall in Rogers, Arkansas, where the *Benton County Daily Record* said: "Staff members from the G.W. Exotic Animal Park, a non-profit organisation from Wynnewood, Okla., presented a performance." It was the show's first appearance in Arkansas.

According to the paper, the magician Joe Schreibvogel spoke about his strong commitment to saving wild animals and protecting the environment.

"G.W., my brother, always loved animals, especially exotic animals," Schreibvogel said, the *Daily Record* reported. "He was killed by a drunk driver. My family was awarded some money following his death and we wanted it to be used in a way that would honour G.W. That's how we started the animal park in 1997.

"And it's also the reason we emphasise personal responsibility. We try to teach about the dangers of drinking and driving. We also teach that we must stop destroying the rainforest. We emphasise that exotic animals were never intended to be pets. Many of our animals are rescued from owners who bought them as babies, but didn't want them once they grew so large."

Then he raised a laugh when introducing an African lion named Chewbacca, saying: "He's peeing on me!"

From Rogers, the show would be heading to Kansas City, Missouri, and then to New York. The newspaper solicited the "sponsorship of animals, memorials and donations help keep G.W. Exotic Animal Park open and offering help to exotic animals in need", adding: "Overnight campouts, cookouts and educational programs are available at the park."

Later that month, Joe's show turned up in Lawton Oklahoma, as the Mystical Magic of the Endangered. The two-hour performance at Lawton's McMahon Memorial Auditorium, 801 NW Ferris, promised "illusions, magic, music, tigers and nearly fifteen species of endangered animals". Joe Schreibvogel (aka Joe Exotic), the *Lawton Constitution* said, would "introduce the animals and speak on their natural habitats".

The tickets were $10 for adults and $5 for children under ten.

"The show raises funds," the newspaper said, "but also sends a message about drinking and driving and saying no to drugs."

Local businesses were sponsoring the show, so the money raised would go directly to the support of the animals.

"The greatest need this year is the raising of funds for a special operation for Angel, a nine-week-old Barbary lion cub, who was born without a hip. The operation will take place at Oklahoma State University," the newspaper said.

On 23 June 2005, the *Courier-Tribune* in Asheboro, North Carolina, called Joe's show, being put on in the Randolph Mall, "part of an educational program". The newspaper said that Schreibvogel loved this job that kept him on the road soliciting funds 365 days a year.

"The irony is, said Schreibvogel, that he would prefer not to have to be in this business," the newspaper added. "Schreibvogel wishes better laws were in place to prevent people from owning and breeding exotic animals. He knows from experience that no amount of handling will turn an exotic animal into a proper family pet."

However, some residents contacted the Randolph County Public Health Department, USDA and the North Carolina Zoo about "possible salmonella contamination, safety issues and even the very presence of exotic animals in Randolph County".

The county health director, Mimi Cooper, saw the show and determined it was not in violation of local animal, safety or health ordinances. Although Randolph County did have an ordinance regulating the possession of exotic animals, it did not apply in the city limits of Asheboro, she said.

While the road show went on, in 2006 the USDA suspended Joe's park licence for two weeks and fined him $25,000 for a long list of violations. These included failing to provide adequate veterinary care, inadequate record-keeping, not handling animals safely and failing to remove dung from animal enclosures. Specifically the USDA inspector cited the animal park for not caring for an underweight, limping female cougar; failing to remove a metal chain from around a juvenile tiger's neck; failing to remove faeces from a bear cage; failing to protect food supplies from mould and vermin; housing lions in an enclosure with sharp, protruding fencing; failing to keep water receptacles free of algae and mosquito larvae; and failing to build an adequate enclosure, thereby allowing a tiger to escape and attack a camel.

Joe said he had addressed all of the complaints as of 2005 and insisted his park was then in compliance with USDA regulations.

"Those reports don't tell the whole story," he said. "If you keep your veterinary records at the vet's office, they say we failed to provide our records because we couldn't show the inspectors right then.

"This is Oklahoma, if it rains six inches in a day, they say we didn't remove standing water from the cages fast enough. We used to keep our food in a barn, now we've built a $40,000 commissary with stainless steel appliances. We're an open book. We have nothing to hide."

However, Joe had also been fined $25,000 for throwing two inspectors out of the park when they complained about guests petting a baby deer.

"If you look at all those fines, that's how the USDA makes their money," he said. "It's no different than a cop writing speeding tickets. Airlines and shipping companies all pay USDA fines. Getting fined doesn't make you a bad person. It doesn't mean you abuse animals."

Later that year, People for the Ethical Treatment of Animals posted a video showing what they alleged to be the mistreatment of the animals at Joe's zoo and those he used in the road show. PETA's footage showed employees discussing irregular feeding schedules, swatting animals with shovels, and, in one case, striking a tiger with the butt of a rifle.

The organisation also criticized the zoo for allegedly "churning out litters of tigers, lions, bears, and other exotic animals," claiming that "some are deformed, likely because of inbreeding or inadequate nutrition for the mother during pregnancy". Local and federal investigators arrived at the zoo to investigate the allegations, but ultimately in this case no charges were filed.

Joe carped about PETA "spies" who infiltrated the park. He threatened those thinking of hopping the fence that he'd put a "cap in their ass". But the claims that Joe was churning out cub after cub were undeniable.

By then more than one thousand animals were crammed into the little sixteen-acre zoo. For comparison, the Dallas Zoo occupies 106 acres. At Joe's park, there were more than a hundred tigers, along with lions, chimpanzees, leopards, baboons, alligators and smaller reptiles. In 2001 the zoo had reported a total revenue of $117,022. By 2006 that figure had grown to $539,320; the vast majority of the money was from donations. Alongside the turnover of his "non-profit" zoo, Joe expanded his for-profit ventures. In the zoo's gift shop, he sold Joe Exotic-branded skincare products, T-shirts, cotton candy, bullwhips, underwear, wine, and even condoms with his likeness on them. Later, he opened the Safari Bar two miles down the road from the zoo, then a pizza joint named Zooters – previously he had dreamt of calling it Tallywhackers – an all-male-staffed version of Hooters, whose staff all wore hot pants and tight T-shirts.

"It wasn't G.W. Zoo, it was the Joe show," one former employee said. Joe was building a brand.

Sometimes Joe and his staff drove into town in his limousine for a meal at its only Mexican restaurant. But largely the townspeople were relieved their local gay, gun-toting celebrity went back across the Washita River to the insular world of the park.

"The way he just expressed himself, you know, openly, like he was: I think he went against the grain around here," said Mark Lewis, editor of the *Wynnewood Gazette*. "If he was in Las Vegas or something, I think he would've been just another guy on the Strip."

But it wasn't just Joe that made the townspeople wary. The G.W. Park staff was a hodgepodge of homeless people, drug addicts and others down on their luck. Some had arrest warrants outstanding in other states. They lived in trailers at the park, working six days a week for as little as $150, with an extra $50-100 in cash, which Joe called "summer pay".

Joe denied exploiting them because they were powerless. He claimed he was giving them a second chance, saying: "I saw in my life what pushed a lot of people to drugs was being an outcast to society, so being gay I related to that."

The road show got into trouble in San Angelo, Texas, in January 2007, when a lion cub scratched a woman at the Sunset Mall. Joe Exotic said he believed the animal did not mean to injure the woman and was most likely playing when the incident occurred.

"It's just a shame," he said. "Out of the 20,000 people that enjoyed the animals, there was one person that ruined it for everyone."

So it was the customer's fault? The animal was taken into custody by San Angelo's animal control department, but was released after thirty days in quarantine.

In December, Joe was back on the stump in Marion, Illinois. According to the *Marion Republican*: "Joe is trying to educate the public. Big cats don't make good pets. 'They can grow up and hurt somebody,' he said. He said there is no regulation of the ownership of big cats but that people should be aware of the problems of keeping one as a pet."

Joe told that audience that he loved animals and was trying to raise enough money to get his animal park through the winter months.

"I am also trying to get people to respect our environment," he said. "These animals' habitats are being destroyed. They come from India, Russia and Cambodia. People don't know what a rainforest is good for.

"Bonding with a tiger cub helps them to understand the importance of rainforests," he continued. "There are 60,000 unwanted big cats in the United States and there are not enough places to care for them."

In January 2010 Joe issued a press release, picking out an unsung hero in his entourage. This was ex-turbine engineer John

Reinke who, in 1994, fell fifty-five feet while helping a friend with a bungee jump programme. He landed on a metal pole that pierced his colon and stomach. Both his legs were crushed; one of them was amputated, the other rebuilt.

"I pierced my side with a six inch metal stake and I asked my friends to call my wife because I thought that was it," he said. "I broke my hip, my back, shattered both feet and raked my intestines. Needless to say, I was in a coma for eight days after I reached the hospital. My wife Kristi couldn't recognise me when she first saw me. When I finally woke up the doctors told me that I would never walk again."

During his recuperation, Reinke visited the G.W. Exotic Animal Park and fell in love with a grizzly bear named Ozzie. For three years he came to the park every Sunday to visit Ozzie and feed him, then eventually build him houses and swimming pools. In early 2007, he moved in as manager on no pay.

"Nothing slows this man's love down for the animals," said Joe. "He goes and goes, walking, crawling and doing what he has to in order to help care for the animals."

In September 2009, John's reconstructed leg gave out and was amputated. He stayed in the hospital for four days and rested in bed for another six. After learning to walk on what amounted to two metal rods with sneakers on the bottom, he went back to managing the park for no money.

"The world is missing a real hero here," said assistant park manager Ben McAnally. "If anyone deserves to be a hero it is John. So we made him a hero, I have never seen a man work so hard to take care of so many things for nothing but love."

According to the press release: "After putting in a fourteen-hour day at the park you would think that a person would be tired and needing to get away from animals long enough to get some sleep. What does John do? He goes home to a crowded house and crawls into bed with a crippled African lion named Bonedigger. Weighing in at 115 pounds John shares his bed with Bonedigger and any other animal needing night attention."

Joe said: "*Animal Planet* (the TV show) and the rest of the world is missing the story of their lives – just to see this crippled man love a crippled lion."

The press release then solicited donations "to save the park for John and the animals". The zoo was heavily dependent on funds raised by the road show, which was facing mounting criticism from Carole Baskin and her supporters. So Joe simply co-opted the name of her organisation and called his road show Big Cat Rescue Entertainment. Few were fooled, though some of Carole's associates began emailing her about a mall petting act in which Big Cat Rescue was seemingly involved. When Big Cat Rescue Entertainment was booked to perform at Mounds Mall in Anderson, Indiana, PETA complained to the owner. A spokesperson for PETA told the *Herald Bulletin*: "Joe Shreibvogel is one of the, if not the top, exploiter of animals in the country. He breeds exotic animals when there's already a horrible surplus, he tears them from their mothers when they are days old, carts them around the country to make money off them and then dumps many of them when they're no longer useful to him. Animals are not ours to use for entertainment."

Carole and Howard Baskin decided that they could not have Big Cat Rescue's name tarnished this way. They sued Joe for trademark infringement. But Joe would not back down. He countersued for libel and slander, demanding $15 million in damages.

PETA told the *Herald Bulletin* that they had sent an undercover investigator into the G.W. Zoo and published a full report of the findings, including allegations ranging from starvation of animals to improper handling. Specific charges included two lion cubs forced to interact with the public until their paws bled, employees using scared goats and chickens as bait to move big cats into cages, and employees striking animals with rakes and shovels. In one instance, two healthy adult tigers were killed so their teeth could be given away as gifts. Their carcasses were dumped in a garbage pit, the report states. The thousand animals in the park sometimes went without food for days while employees intentionally falsified USDA feeding records.

The investigator said they saw animals starved for nearly a week as food supplies ran low. While pregnant lions and tigers were fed, the others were left to starve. On 28 February 2006, the investigator's log recorded: "Today was the third day that the cats (who are not pregnant) had not been fed. The bears were not fed either today."

PETA's undercover investigator "found dead, dying, and injured animals; extremely crowded conditions; a serious lack of basic necessities such as food, water and veterinary care; shamefully inadequate cages; and untrained and insufficient staff who were intentionally cruel to numerous animals.

"Animals were routinely hit, punched, kicked, sprayed with cold water, and struck with rakes and shovels. And they were blasted with fire extinguishers to break up frequent fights."

Other allegations included tiger cubs being punched, dragged, and hit with whips. Horses Joe took in were shot in the head to be given to the tigers as food.

The allegations continued: "G.W. transferred a tiger named Blondy to the Hillcrest Zoo, a roadside zoo in Clovis, New Mexico that has been repeatedly cited for a multitude of violations of the Animal Welfare Act, including failing to provide sufficient food to three zebras who all died within a two-day period."

PETA urged animal lovers to steer clear of the Mounds Mall tiger exhibit, saying: "If you care about animals, do not patronise this show and call the mall and ask them to cancel the show. We have sent them all the info we have about Joe and we've asked them to cancel the show."

Joe told the newspaper that PETA was lying about his operation and insisted that his ranch is a sanctuary for unwanted animals, and that he only puts tiger cubs on exhibition to help pay for the rescue operation. Furthermore, the PETA allegations were causing him and his staff to have safety concerns.

"We get three or four death threats a day," he said.

He acknowledged he was breeding tiger and lion cubs for his road show, but only as a means of putting backyard breeders out of business and ensuring that he could afford to look after the 1,400 animals on his ranch. He said he donated tiger and lion cubs to zoos around the world once they were too old to be exhibited in public.

"For anybody who's been out of the country and seen the condition of most zoos, sending an animal there is a despicable act," PETA responded.

Joe said that he would gladly release his animals into the wild instead of selling them, but to do so would be illegal.

"Half the animals I have here could live in the wild," he said. "They could be released in the wild, but the government won't allow it."

He said he didn't host his own tiger and lion shows anymore because of the negative attention by PETA, and that he was appearing as a magician, not an animal broker. The show went ahead, but the public taste was beginning to wane. A letter in *The Hawk Eye* in Burlington, Iowa, condemned Joe for "P.T. Barnum-style sideshow hucksterism".

"The magic show and the 'anti-bullying and anti-drunk driving' talk that accompanies the exhibit is gimmickry designed to put a good face on a cruel act," it went on. "Breeding big cats and confining them to travelling sideshows is not new. It has always been and continues to be done solely for profit, not compassion for the animals. Only man, it seems, in pursuit of a buck has the capacity to defy God's will in such a way."

Nevertheless, in May 2011, OUT TV Pittsburgh and GLTV added Oklahoma's Joe Exotic to their weekly online live video talk show *Talk It Out*.

"As an already public figure who has toured the United States, Canada, and Mexico performing magic in front of nearly 2 million people per year and owning one of the largest privately owned exotic animal facilities in the country, [Joe has] accepted the offer to be on the talk show every Wednesday at noon eastern standard time," they announced.

David Stanton, producer and co-owner of OUT TV Pittsburgh, Pennsylvania, offered Joe a regular spot. The company also owned the forty-year-old paper *OUT* which was founded to support the LGBT community in the Pittsburgh metro area. Their TV station had been broadcasting for three years and said it now aimed to reach a more mainstream audience.

Stanton said he was an animal lover and also had a lifelong dream of becoming a veterinarian.

"Maybe this is one of my callings – to have a show that involves animals and helps educate the public about what really needs to happen to help the animals and keep them from becoming extinct and abused all at the same time," he said.

"Things will be very fun and exciting," said Joe. "There will be different animals on the show, real facts about the truth of what's going on with exotic animals in the United States and the animal's native countries, and guests via call-in, chat, and live in-studio. We want people to ask real questions so they can learn the truth about the lives of exotic animals today. The most important thing we need to make happen is that we have fun, laugh and educate all at the same time. We will have some of the most fascinating animal ambassadors as guests on this show."

As always, Joe was ready to defend his business.

"There is nothing wrong with professional pet owners and private breeders of exotic animals," he was quoted saying in OUT TV's press release. The zoos simply cannot keep a big enough gene pool to keep a healthy species alive without the private sector. "And I would be the first to fight to take away an animal from an irresponsible owner."

Joe said his primary purpose is to correct misconceptions about exotic animal ownership and stewardship while providing educational entertainment. He also saw a parallel between the hatred some people express toward homosexuals and the way that exotic animal owners were treated. He had been on the receiving end in both cases, he said.

"I'm openly gay and the biggest thing about exotic animals right now and gay people is that the hate crime is the same," he said. "The animal rights people have you targeted so bad if you own an exotic animal that you have to literally hide.

"My facility here in Oklahoma, due to the animal rights people, we get hate mail, we get death threats. And it's no different from being gay. You're hated. I have a speaker coming in from Ohio in a couple weeks to do the show just to talk about how legislation needs to be changed, to make [aggression] against exotic animal owners a hate crime."

His show *Get OUT and Wild* premiered on 1 June 2011. Three weeks later he condemned PETA and other detractors who tried to disrupt his podcast.

"Those kind of people don't want live debate because they know the answers and don't want to risk debating it with me live because they're not going to win," he said. "We have a very strategic, logical plan as to what it's going to take to save our environment and our animals.

"We'll be the first ones to step up and say that if you're abusing an animal, we'll do whatever we can to take your animal away from you. But, still, as an American citizen, you have the right to own whatever animal you want as long as you take care of it."

Joe had big plans for his show. He invested in video technology and built a studio in the park. The weekly shows would be open to park visitors and, during good weather, he intended to take production outdoors. He also scheduled zoology experts as guests.

"The show is about teaching people about animals, about how to save the environment, about animal rights," he said. "It's about how to treat animals with respect... I'm trying to teach people that chimpanzees aren't pets. It's an open, controversial show."

But that summer there was a heatwave and a drought.

"We had no business when the temperatures were over a hundred for sixty-something days," he said. "We had only one big cat that passed away during that heat."

Visitors stayed away and Joe turned to collecting scrap metal to fund his zoo.

"We hauled $45,000 worth of scrap iron," Joe said. "It's a way that people can help because it doesn't cost them anything and we clean up their yard by hauling the junk off – farmers dump all kinds of crap like refrigerators in creek bottoms on the back of their properties – while we collect money to build more cages. So it's a win-win situation for the planet."

In October 2011, Joe Exotic got more media exposure when he appeared on *Louis Theroux: America's Most Dangerous Pets* on BBC TV. The response was not uncritical. Under the headline "Free the animals, cage the keepers", *The Times* said: "Theroux met a character straight out of *Napoleon Dynamite* – Joe Exotic who, dressed like a cop, with Peter Stringfellow hair, a goatee beard and wearing guy-liner, owns one of the largest collections of big cats in the world… When Theroux suggested that perhaps the animals, bred in captivity, would be better off in the wild, Exotic contested that they couldn't miss something they'd never known. 'If you were born in a wheelchair,' Exotic said, 'are you sure you're gonna be happier walkin' instead of riding?'"

Theroux noted the paradox that rescue park operators like Joe create as they bring in exotic animals that should not be kept as pets and then breed some of them to sell in order to generate revenue to continue operations.

Joe plainly relished appearing on TV, but complained that media work paid little or nothing and so used it primarily to promote the park. Nevertheless he welcomed the publicity and said that he was in negotiations with producers to make three movies and further develop online television programming with OutOnline.com.

However, raising his profile also invited greater scrutiny. Vernon Weir, director of the American Sanctuary Association, said they had Joe's operation in their sights.

"He's been on our radar for at least ten years," he said. "They do absolutely nothing that we would approve of. We require that our sanctuary members do not breed, sell or trade animals or take animals off-site to use them for any commercial purpose or exhibit. And they do all those things. There's nothing that I could say of a positive nature."

Weir also said a reputable rescue operation or zoo would make greater efforts to provide shaded areas and water-misting systems to protect animals from Oklahoma's weather. Tigers were naturally suited for cooler, northern climes and one had died in the recent heatwave.

That September, the USDA, who check up on registered parks regularly, found an underweight baboon and a New Guinea singing dog that also weighed too little and had a coat in poor condition. Joe said the baboon was subsequently found to have cancer and had to be put down.

Joe complained his detractors judged him unfairly because they failed to appreciate the context of his work. The animals he rescued were already in dire straits. Moving them to the park was a big improvement in their lives.

"The cats are all provided with big horse tubs to play in the water and cool off," he said. "This particular cat that died had that available. But the problem is that when you rescue animals like we do, you don't know the condition of their heart muscles or whether they've been inbred. So when Oklahoma State University did the necropsy on this cat, they found his heart was just blubber."

He struck back a critics, saying: "The thing that kills me about the animal rights people is that they'll come into my place and take pictures of a three-legged bear. But, hell, we rescued him with three legs. We can't put the leg back on, but we can make him comfortable instead of euthanising him."

Carole Baskin was picked out for particular vitriol. On Christmas Day in 2011, Joe left a comment beneath an article about the zoo by a local news station in Oklahoma: "Dear Carole Baskin," he began, "You should watch my show this Tuesday as it is going to be about your back yard zoo, why you have not found your husbands body… The next time you step foot in my business, you better run and hide real far and fast, and this is a promise to you for Christmas. You want to take this BS to the next level, lets play. See if your up to it… You don't know just how crazy I can be."

Joe regularly taunted Carole on his internet TV channel that broadcast from his TV studio at the zoo.

"For Carole and all of her friends that are watching out there, if you think for one minute I was nuts before, I am the most dangerous exotic animal owner on this planet right now," Joe said in 2012. "And before you bring me down, it is my belief that you will stop breathing. Got that?"

In videos posted to his YouTube channel Joe would read out extracts from Carole's diary, insinuating that she had killed her first husband. He would sign off saying: "Carole, I ain't got nothing better to do than fuck with you."

Undeterred by criticism, Joe bought another 120 acres in Ardmore for the rescue of domestic farm animals such as horses and goats. He also said he was happy to take on a ten-year-old Siberian-Bengal-mix tiger called Tony from the Tiger Truck Stop in Grosse Tête, Louisiana, if the owner was forced to give him up by a court action taken by Animal Legal Defense Fund based in California. While the case went to the Louisiana Supreme Court, Joe stepped in to build Tony a pool to cool off in. He raised $3,800 from the viewers of his daily internet show *Exotic Animal TV Starring Joe Exotic* and turned up with a construction crew of five to build it. Joe's involvement was also recorded in the documentary *How To Not Kill A Tiger* by local filmmaker, Ted Baldwin.

"There is no animal sanctuary in America that has this nice of a cage," he said. As for animal rights activists: "If they cared so much for Tony, why didn't they build him a pool?"

Lynn Dool, a truck driver from Ontario, Canada, who dropped by to see Tony said: "He seems domesticated. He's been here for twelve years and there haven't been any problems. I say let him live here."

Meanwhile the USDA were investigating G. W. Exotic Animal Park again after learning that twenty-three tiger cubs died there in 2010. Joe defended his park against this and the numerous Animal Welfare Act violations he'd been cited for, saying they could "be chalked up to growing pains he experienced while learning how to run an animal sanctuary on the fly". By then the park had been open for more than ten years.

When it came to the twenty-three dead tiger cubs, Joe said they died after they were fed an allegedly rotten, powder-based formula known as KMR that he purchased from PetAg, an animal nutrition company based in Illinois. He said the formula spoiled while in transit. When mixed with water and fed to the cubs, the powder separated from the water in the cubs' stomachs and accumulated enough bacteria to kill the cubs four hours after they swallowed it.

"I spent $10,000 to try and save those babies," he said. "I reported what happened to the FDA myself. I went on TV to warn people about KMR. It was bad formula."

PetAg president, Darlene Frudakis, disputed Joe's claims.

"The Food and Drug Administration has always found our products to be fully compliant and safe to use as directed," she said. "PetAg and our dry milk replacement powders have been victimised by misinformation."

FDA spokeswoman Stephanie Yao said the agency inspected the KMR from PetAg in 2010 after receiving complaints, but was "not able to detect any adulteration in the product."

The most damning report came in 2012 from the Humane Society of the United States who had an undercover investigator working at the park for four months over the summer and autumn of the previous year. The report claimed animals were kept in "barren conditions" and "bred to provide infant animals for public photo shoots and 'play time' sessions and were often cared for by workers who have little-to-no experience handling large carnivores or primates".

Tiger cubs were also "punched, dragged, and hit with whips" while "visitors, including children, were bitten, scratched and knocked down by tiger cubs, some of whom were too mature to be used for public handling or photo shoots".

The report said: "One tiger named Sarge was used in a photo shoot at G.W. despite being nearly a year old and capable of inflicting severe injuries to the public. The owner of G.W. told park staff that allowing Sarge to interact freely with patrons was 'very illegal' even though photo sessions conducted that same day had allowed such interaction.

"G.W.'s park manager told staff that if patrons ask the age of a tiger, '…just say they're, they're just a couple months old. You're not lying, you're not telling the truth… couple of months old. That's all they need to know. Ah, don't tell 'em it's sixteen-weeks-old and that cat over there we're going to play with later is eighteen-weeks-old, the one over there is a month older…'."

During their time at Exotic's park, the undercover investigator reported that five endangered tigers died, and he alleged that two sick tigers were never seen by a vet and were killed and buried.

"A worker confirmed G.W.'s method of tiger euthanasia was gunshot and described it as 'pretty gruesome'," they reported.

Another cub was said to have suffered a head injury in Exotic's house while the body of a tiger named Hobbes "was picked up by a worker from a 'bone museum' in Oklahoma City who commented that it would be a shame to let the tiger's skin go to waste".

The investigator also said newly born tiger cubs were removed from their mothers to be hand-reared while unwanted animals were offloaded to other facilities. One of the most disturbing accounts was the death of a horse that was allegedly shot five times before its body was fed to some of the park's big cats.

The report quoted an unnamed member of staff at the park who was said to have told HSUS' undercover investigator: "…and Scott takes the horse and we put it by the dumpster… and Davie goes — 'POW!' Hits the motherfucker right here... blood start gushing out of his nose... three fingers [width] under his eyes... the nose... horse ran crazy... he start gushing blood everywhere on Davie, on the fucking cars parked over there... the dumpster was covered in blood... 'shoot again Davie, shoot again!'. 'POW!' Again. Fucking horse wouldn't die... 'POW!' Third time, still no, man. Fuck, the horse was kicking, the fucking blood squirting everywhere. Fourth time. 'POW!' Fuck no! The fifth one, he finally fucking shot it... God damn!"

Other allegations include a sick serval that went without veterinary care for weeks. It was later put down. It was noted that tigers and lions were bred to create ligers, one of Joe's "controversial species not found in the wild". Conservationists said ligers can have genetic defects and therefore their breeding was unethical and solely for greed. Toddlers and children were allowed into enclosures with adult wolves. Bears were left without water in temperatures above 100°F. Then there was the park manager who said that claims the park would need to close because it couldn't pay its water bill during a heatwave were an "an advertising ploy... to get people to generate money".

# FOUR: Exotic at Law

In May 2012, Joe appeared on *CBS This Morning*, after Ohio lawmakers began drawing up a bill restricting private ownership of exotic pets. This was following an incident where a Vietnam veteran, Terry Thompson, in Zanesville, Ohio, had released fifty-six wild animals before shooting himself in the head. Forty-eight of his animals were eventually killed by authorities concerned over public safety, while two were thought to have been eaten by the other animals. The animals confirmed to be dead were eighteen tigers, six black bears, two grizzly bears, two wolves, one macaque monkey, one baboon, three mountain lions, nine male lions, and eight lionesses. Three leopards, a small bear, and two monkeys were left caged inside Thompson's home in Zanesville. These animals were tranquillised and sent to the Columbus Zoo. One of the surviving leopards was subsequently injured in an accident at the zoo and was put down.

The case had kicked off a fierce debate between the owners of exotic animals and animal rights activists, the show said, and Joe was introduced as "arguably the loudest, most defiant voice on the front lines of the big cat debate". He said he was standing up for the US Constitution and the right "to be able to own whatever I want to own, as long as it's legal". CBS News Chief Investigative Correspondent Armen Keteyian then asked Joe about the cross-breed ligers and tiligers he was selling for $5,000 each.

"Do you have a background in this?" he asked.

"I grew up a farm kid," said Joe. "That's pretty much my background."

Joe was then confronted by Wayne Pacelle, president and CEO of the Humane Society of the United States with video from their undercover investigator's report. Footage showed Joe giving instructions on animal handling, saying: "If they don't to walk, pop them in the ass and make them walk."

This was described as "alarming and abusive behaviour". The Humane Society also had undercover video showing a boy who was suddenly attacked while interacting with a young tiger.

"Any person with any whit of common sense knows that large, predatory animals are going to lash out at people," said Pacelle. "That's why sensible organisations say you've got to keep people and dangerous wild animals separate."

Shown the video, Joe claimed that the incident with the boy had been set up by the Humane Society.

"You're saying the Humane Society would put a little boy in harm's way?" Joe was asked.

"Oh, hell yeah, in a heartbeat," said Joe. "Am I saying Wayne Pacelle would stoop low enough to put a little kid at risk? Yes, to get his agenda, so he could continue to make money."

The Humane Society's undercover operative also said that at least six visitors had been scratched or bitten while he worked there.

The president of the Humane Society called Joe's park "A ticking time bomb and potentially ten times worse than Zanesville."

"It is a ticking time bomb if somebody thinks they're going to walk in here and take my animals away. It's going to be a small Waco," said Joe. "I have poured my entire life into what I do – to care for animals. Nobody is going to walk in here and freely shut me down and take my rights away from me as long as I'm not breaking the law."

Interviewer, Armen Keteyian then gave his assessment of Joe, saying: "He's on the extreme end, obviously. He believes in the right to hold these animals, have these animals, both privately and for the viewing public. As far as regulation is concerned, Schreibvogel says he's in favour of the right regulation. What that right regulation may be, he didn't say. Just to give you an idea, just for tigers. There are twenty-eight states that ban any kind of private ownership. There are seventeen where you have to have some sort of registration or a permit. But then there are eight in which it's just – it's basically open season."

Co-presenter Erica Hill said it was surprising that, after the Zanesville incident, the regulations were so inconsistent.

Keteyian pointed out that Oklahoma was in tornado alley: "If something did happen, there are eight hundred animals; and a hundred seventy of these big cats. And you start to do the calculations…"

He conceded that Joe did have control of the situation.

"When we were there, there were at least a half dozen to a dozen workers there. There are barriers," he said. "There's a lot of security there. But these are large animals. I was this close to a 900 pound lion. And I got to tell you something, when it stood up on its hind legs, it was thirteen feet tall. So that catches your attention."

However, moves were afoot in the US Congress to make national legislation which would see a tightening on these laws nationwide. Big Cat Rescue was one of a handful of animal welfare organisations that helped craft the Big Cat Public Safety Act, which would ban the possession and breeding of large cats as pets and prohibit licenced exhibitors from running cub encounters. The bill was introduced in Congress in 2012, but soon stalled in committee despite bipartisan support.

Carole Baskin championed the bill, saying such a law would make the conservation arena safer for animals and humans, as bad actors would no longer be able to duck federal oversight. Checking up on roadside zoos such as Joe's should not be left to animal rights activists.

"This shouldn't happen," Baskin said. "I shouldn't be out there taking the brunt of this alone, because the USDA knows that these people are breaking the law."

In August 2012, Joe's road show turned up at the Monroe County Fair in Tomah, Wisconsin, where six adult tigers, two babies and two baby leopards were exhibited alongside the regular fare of horses, goats and other farm animals. Writing in the *Tomah Journal*, correspondent Nicole Rusch noted that Joe's show appeared under twenty different names – "due to all of the negative publicity he has received, one might conclude that he operates his business under so many names in an effort to confuse the public and those hiring him for appearances and fairs."

She noted that Joe travelled around the country, stopping at fairs and malls so that people could spend several minutes with the cubs and have their picture taken.

"It is all done under the pretence of educating people about tigers, discouraging them from owning exotic animals as pets, and to save the species," Rusch said. "After observing the display at the fair this past weekend for over an hour and on two separate occasions, I witnessed minimal efforts to educate anyone about anything."

The fact sheets given out claimed that a percentage of the money raised would go towards conservation. She asked what percentage specifically. "He would not answer that question," she said.

She asked where the cubs' mothers were. Joe said that they were taken from their mothers within the first eight to ten days so that they could bond with humans instead. But Nicole had been doing her research.

"The USDA prohibits public interaction with tiger cubs before the age of eight weeks because their immune system has not yet developed enough, and beyond the age of twelve weeks because after that age they can be too dangerous," she wrote. "That leaves just four weeks when they can interact with the public and have their picture taken."

She noted that mother tigers are fiercely protective of their young. Typically, in the wild, baby tigers stay with their mother until they were about two years old. But the baby tigers at the Monroe County Fair were taken from their mothers just as their eyes were first opening so they could be driven all over the country for four weeks of photo opportunities.

Joe insisted that taking an infant tiger away from its mother was the same as a parent sending their child to day care.

"Seeing as how that baby tiger and mother will never again be reunited, I'm not sure how he can even begin to compare the two," she wrote. "It's certainly not as if he's returning the babies back to their mothers at the end of each day."

She then asked what happened to the tigers when they reached twelve weeks and were too old for the public to safely interact with and was told that some went back to Oklahoma to live in a cage for the rest of their lives. Some were sold to small zoos, while others were sold or given away to individuals who thought it might be fun to own a tiger as a pet.

"These tigers are being born to be exploited for four weeks," Rusch wrote, "then to live a life in captivity in questionable surroundings."

Joe assured her that this would ensure the species' survival.

"I would disagree," said Rusch. "The six tigers who travel the country in cages barely bigger than they are would disagree as well. Training a tiger to perform circus tricks is about as far from a natural life as you can get… It's that type of attitude that allows the abuse and exploitation of animals and can eventually lead to the extinction of a species."

She pointed out that the extinction of tigers in the wild was caused by the destruction of their habitat. Keeping them in captivity in the US was doing nothing to help conservation. While Rusch conceded that carting baby tigers around the country was not against the law, she asked, was it ethical?

"Just because something is legal, that doesn't mean it's necessarily the right thing to do," she said. "I think that if Joe Schreibvogel really cared about educating the public about tigers and saving them from extinction, he would be going about it in a much different way."

She called for the law to be changed to protect tigers and other animals from being exploited. She urged readers to boycott such exhibitions at fairs, circuses and similar events where animals were being exploited for entertainment purposes. They should join her in asking members of the Monroe County Fair Board to not bring tigers or any other exotic animals to the fair ever again.

Not all the publicity was bad. Back in Oklahoma, Joe was seen to be doing his bit by joining the search for a missing kangaroo, a family pet that had escaped. Meanwhile a new battle with Carole Baskin flared. On 12 February 2013, in federal court Joe was ordered to pay nearly $1 million for trademark infringement. The suit involved Big Cat Rescue Entertainment's use of logos and images that were very similar to those created and owned by Big Cat Rescue. Joe's attorney's dropped his $15 million countersuit, but Joe said he would not pay a dime. So she went after the 235-acre plot the family still owned in Kansas.

Joe was blasé. He boasted that the high profile he'd attained since becoming an outspoken critic of those seeking to prevent private individuals owning exotic animals had opened "all kinds of things up for me".

"I'm going Hollywood," he said. "They made me a star."

In an interview with *The Oklahoman*, Joe said the court ruling in favour of Carole Baskin's Big Cat Rescue was more "dirty politics" than a fair legal battle. He claimed that the judge didn't give his legal team enough time to proceed at trial.

"Obviously, it's dirty pool," Joe said. "I let her get her judgment, file bankruptcy, and the hell with it."

He said the G.W. Exotic Memorial Animal Foundation, which owned the park's real estate, would file for bankruptcy, but the park itself would remain open and nothing would change as far as the public was concerned.

"The park is under a new corporation," Joe said. "But they're my animals... I'm still licenced to exhibit."

The licence to exhibit was in his name, not that of the corporation.

In the lawsuit, Carole Baskin's lawyers had complained that Joe used a logo and other artistic elements that were "confusingly similar" to those trademarked by Big Cat Rescue. Joe admitted that he and his colleagues did model a logo for Big Cat Rescue Entertainment after the Florida sanctuary's design. But he said he didn't realise he was infringing on the organisation's intellectual property.

"We thought we were in the clear," he said. "We thought they only owned 'Big Cat Rescue' with a cat jumping over it."

The judge had also found that Joe – doing business as Entertainment Group Inc. and G.W. Exotic Memorial Animal

Foundation – had also used photographs belonging to Big Cat Rescue.

Baskin's lawyers then accused Joe and his associates of launching a "counter-campaign of disinformation, misinformation and disparagement" aimed at damaging Big Cat Rescue's credibility. They said that this was part of a bigger fight. One of Big Cat Rescue's missions was to end unnecessary breeding of exotic animals, including tigers, lions, bears and other large beasts.

Frank Jakes, an attorney representing Big Cat Rescue, said: "My client… also has a mission of trying to prevent abuse… that comes from unfettered breeding of exotic animals. Private ownership is an issue as well, because of the abuse that comes with that."

Big Cat Rescue would speak out against those who "breed cats incessantly, as Mr. Schreibvogel does". Jakes also condemned the exploitation of cubs in Joe's road shows.

"He makes money by having people pet them and take pictures with them," he said. "My client feels that's an abusive practice."

Jakes noted Schreibvogel didn't take kindly to criticism from the sanctuary's leadership, most notably its founder, Carole Baskin.

"So, he decided he would get back at us, basically, by copying our name and posting all these terrible things about us on the Internet," Jakes said. "That's basically the story."

And the battle between Big Cat Rescue and Joe Exotic was set to continue.

"If the other party doesn't voluntarily pay the judgment, you have to go and try and take it from them," said Jakes. "I suspect that's the next step."

Joe was happy to play the underdog. He said that Baskin and her "multimillion dollar" organisation targeted him because he stood up to them. In the realm if exotic animals, he said, she was known as a "master marketeer".

"I do what I do – the magic shows, the TV shows – I do it for the animals," Joe said and he accused Carole of using the trademark suit to drain him dry financially.

"It didn't work," he said. "They can sue 'til the cows come home, but they have no control over my licence. Only the federal government can take my licence, and only if I violate their laws."

In the meantime, Joe Exotic said he had a new career as a model. After posting provocative photos of himself on the "Joe Exotic" Facebook page, he claimed that magazines, including *Playgirl*, were showing a strong interest in him.

"It's funny. I mean, with all the negative energy they focused on me, they made me famous," he said.

To avoid giving $1 million to Carole Baskin, Joe sold G.W. Exotic Animal Park to John Finlay and an animal rescuer in Michigan he identified as Tracy Schultz. The business was renamed the G.W. Interactive Zoological Park. In his federal court filings for bankruptcy protection, Joe listed assets of $127,739. Roughly half of that was in the form of vehicles used to run the animal park. He listed forty-three tigers and five black bears as his personal property. The records said the carnivores were worth an "unknown" sum of money. Joe also owed more than $30,000 to attorneys who worked on the trademark infringement case. Still trying to raise money, he posted his $1,300 water bill on Facebook and asked for the public to help pay it.

In an affidavit signed by Schreibvogel and filed in federal court, he stated he became unemployed on 26 February 2013 and no longer had a monthly income.

"I'm solely concentrating on making my own TV show," he said. "I'll still rescue animals, but as far as having anything to do with the business of running a zoo anymore, I'm done with it."

He had other fish to fry.

"I'm going to Hollywood," he said. "Let the animal rights people have this shit. I'm doing a lot of travelling back and forth for filming and I've got some other things in the works right now."

Despite the lure of the silver screen, Joe stayed on in Wynnewood. In mid-May 2013, *Joe Exotic TV* posted a video on YouTube showing a small dachshund named Milo playing with the disabled, five-hundred-pound lion, Bonedigger. The two animals were said to be inseparable. Bonedigger had been born with a metabolic bone disease that had left him mildly crippled. Brought to the zoo when he was just four weeks old, Bonedigger had been hand-reared by John Reinke along with Siberian-Bengal-mix tiger Tony.

"They used to live with me in the house. I raised them both with bottled formula and raw meat until they grew too big for the house," said Reinke. "Bonedigger's like a dog and when he hasn't seen me for ages he gets all excited and runs up to me. Tony is perfectly healthy, but is a bit too playful. When Bonedigger senses that I am losing control of the play, he snarls at Tony and you can tell he is being protective and telling him to stop. Bringing up Bonedigger and Tony helped me recover [from the accident], especially my relationship with Bonedigger."

He also hand-reared two other tiger cubs called Tippy and Orlando.

"They keep me busy and they need to be entertained every day," he said. "Tippy likes to play tug of war with my prosthetic legs, which is good, because I guess that would hurt otherwise."

Reinke said he witnessed the bond develop between Bonedigger and his canine friend. When Milo and two other five-year-old dachshunds, Bullet and Angel, sensed that the lion was disabled they sought to comfort and protect him. Now

Bonedigger and his pack of dogs cuddled, feasted on raw meat and played in the grounds together.

"This friendship between an eleven-pound wiener dog and a five-hundred-pound lion is the only one of its kind in the world ever seen," said Reinke. "Milo does his best to copy Bonedigger when the lion tries puffing to communicate with other lions in the park."

Now masquerading as an "animal expert", Joe Exotic said he experimented introducing the dogs to the lonely feline so that he would have some friends. Eventually the pack of five-year-olds became inseparable, he said. His justification was simple. Although many people condemned keeping animals caged in a zoo setting it was thanks to his zoo that Bonedigger had a chance at life. With his disability, he may not have ever survived in the wild. He would certainly have been shunned by other lions for being a weakling. At least in the zoo, he had food, shelter and the best friends that life could provide.

The video got some 40,000 views. A second video of canine-feline playmates received well over 134,000 views. However, *Joe Exotic TV* pumped out a series of more sinister videos, including one showing three male tigers attacking a female.

With the future of the park uncertain, the United States Zoological Association teamed up with Joe Exotic and the G.W. Interactive Zoo in a bid to stop thirty-one exotic animals being killed unnecessarily. The animals that were under threat of being killed included nine tigers, six bears, eight wolves, three bobcats, a lemur, a mountain lion, an African lion and two lynx.

A press release from the USZA said: "Changes in some state laws have resulted in the private ownership of these animals, which was previously allowed, being banned. However, while the laws in certain states have been changed by the government, no resources or measures have been put into place to get the animals rehomed elsewhere or moved to other states.

"This appeal by the United States Zoological Association is aimed at raising awareness of the issue and helping to raise funds in order to get the endangered animals moved to the G.W. Zoo in Wynnewood, Oklahoma. This is the second biggest rescue in the history of the association, and will involve the rescue of these animals from across three different states."

A representative from the United States Zoological Association added: "This is an urgent appeal and we urge the public to get behind us to help us save the lives of these animals. Over thirty exotic animals could be destroyed unnecessarily because of changes to state laws, and this appeal is aimed at stopping this and ensuring that the animals find a safe, new home at the G.W. Zoo in Wynnewood."

The USZA billed itself as "an organisation that provides support to commercial zoos, breeders, and private owners of exotic animals. It also aims to educate people and protect animals". In the battle lines of the Tiger Wars, it stood firmly beside Joe.

Despite the troubles with the park, Joe still occasionally went out on the road. In August 2013, the *Quad-City Times*, published in the Davenport-Bettendorf-Moline and Rock Island conglomerate on the Iowa-Illinois border, reported on the appearance of Joe Exotic's road show at the Mississippi Valley Fair.

"These bleachers are always filled to capacity," said the fair's director, Bob Fox, when he visited Joe Exotic's cages where fair-goers were putting down cash to spend a few minutes in a cage with nine-week-old Bengal tiger cubs.

"They're such cute little things. It's hard to believe they grow up to be man-eaters," Fox said.

But Joe's appearances were becoming rarer.

"This is the only fair I still do because Bob has been so good to me over the years," Joe Exotic told the *Quad-City Times*. He said he was then splitting his time between Hollywood as host of the *Exotic Animal* TV show and the animal sanctuary and zoo. His conservation work there was essential. With an estimated 3,200 tigers remaining in the wild, he said: "Experts say in ten years they will be gone, extinct in the wild. Our only hope is captive breeding to keep them on our planet."

He again said it was his goal to educate people about the destruction of the rainforests and the impact of that on big cats and other animals threatened by extinction. And Joe was not the only exhibitor of exotic animals on the road. Another animal show at the fair featured alligators.

"No one got a better view than ten-year-old Courtney Lankford of Davenport, who was pulled from the crowd to help in the act," the *Quad-City Times* said. "Brought up to touch the creature, the men tried to scare her by telling her that she might not leave the stage with all of her limbs intact."

"I got to hold a baby alligator and sit on the big one," the fifth grader told the newspaper after her stage debut. "It was bumpy on the top and smooth on the sides. It was cool."

There was another good news story when G.W. Interactive Zoological Park took in a kangaroo named Irwin that Christine Carr had been forced by the authorities to give up in Broken Arrow, Oklahoma. She called Irwin her "therapy kangaroo". Indeed, her therapist had certified Irwin as a therapy pet under the Americans with Disabilities Act. Three-year-old Irwin slept in a bed, wore boy's clothes and ate Twizzlers. He had been nursed back to health after being partially paralysed when he had run into a fence a few years earlier.

Nevertheless the city officials in Broken Arrow feared that Irwin could pose a threat to the public's safety. A healthy, male great red kangaroo was a powerful creature. They could grow up to seven feet tall, weigh more than two hundred pounds, and leap twenty-five feet in a single bound. However, veterinarians said Irwin would probably not grow larger than fifty pounds because of his injury and because he had been neutered.

The city council eventually voted to create an exotic animal ordinance exemption that allowed Carr to keep Irwin within city limits under certain conditions. The permit required exotic animal owners to, among other things, have a $50,000 liability insurance policy for any injuries inflicted by the animal, certification that the animal had adequate housing, and had met all federal and state guidelines for licensing. An anonymous donor paid for Carr's insurance policy. But growing frustration with city officials caused Carr to move herself and Irwin, at first to her parents' home in McAlester. Then Joe came to the rescue.

"We called her up and offered her a place to stay and Irwin a zoo to hang out with a bunch of other animals, and they've been here ever since," he said.

Christine moved into the zoo's staff house.

"Just me and him [Irwin] together, it's almost like he was feeding off my depression," said Carr. "He likes people, he likes to be around people and here, there is something always going on."

Irwin lived in a wooden pen, where he sat in a comfy chair and played with his new sister, Larsen, a baby Siberian tiger. However, he couldn't play with the park's other kangaroo, Pluto, who lived near a pond. Joe was scared Irwin could lose his balance and fall into the water, but he was hoping to build a new kangaroo enclosure in the future.

Irwin's move to Joe's park brought a backlash from animal rights activists.

"Everybody has an opinion, and everybody has a right to an opinion," Joe said. "If they would have euthanised him three years ago, he wouldn't be walking around, hopping now, so not everyone knows what they are talking about."

With the trademark battle with Carole Baskin still going on, Joe was now billed as the entertainment director at the zoo. Otherwise it was business as usual.

"One of the best tours we have right now is the Endangered Animal Adventure Tour. It is a two-hour tour that is up close and personal and is unlike any other zoo experience in the world," Joe told the *Bethany Tribune*. "There are no fences between you and the animals and people will get to interact with baby tigers, alligators, raccoons, skunks – the whole nine yards. How can you educate people about saving all these animals in the wild when they haven't ever seen or met the animal."

Joe said the park offered guests the chance to not only learn about the habits and characteristics of some of the most exotic animals in the world, but also to interact and fall in love with them.

"We have an awesome kids program that I teach called 'Joe's Exotic Zoo School' too," he said. "We get the kids together and bring out our baby animals and teach them about the different animals, how their mom takes care of them and all sorts of stuff – you can never be too young to learn to love an animal."

He told the paper that they had recently been rescuing animals from private zoos and sanctuaries that had been driven out of business. To continue doing that, G.W. Zoo relied heavily on donations to feed and care for the animals and keep their doors open to the public.

And he urged people to come to the park even in the winter time.

"A lot of people think that because it is chilly out or because it is winter that it is a bad time to go to the zoo, but really, it is one of the best especially if you like big cats and bears," he explained. A lot of the species of cats and bears the zoo housed were native to cold, tundra areas which had brutal winters. The animals were perfectly adapted for it. He said their big cats were ten times more active when it's cold outside and people should enjoy the rare excitement of seeing a grown tiger playing in the snow.

# FIVE: Dangerous Animals

In October 2013, news broke that Kelci "Saff" Saffery, a staff member at G.W. Zoo, had been mauled by a tiger. Or rather the news didn't break. Joe managed to keep his name out of the media and denied that he had been mauled. Joe said that, if anything had gone wrong, Saff was "at fault" because he had broken the park's strict rules against introducing any body part into a wild animal enclosure – despite the fact that *Joe Exotic TV* regularly posted videos on YouTube showing Joe cavorting with tigers in their pens.

Saff was an army veteran who had toured Iraq and Afghanistan and identified as a man for many years, though Joe and others involved referred to her as female. Saff put his arm through a four-inch hole in the fence of an enclosure belonging to a four-hundred-pound tiger. The sleeve of his puffy goose-down jacket had then caught on the wire when he tried to withdraw it.

"She pulled her own arm out. The tiger didn't maul her," said Joe. "The tiger was in his cage, and she violated his space by sticking her arm into his space."

However, the Garvin County Sheriff's Office confirmed that a "woman" had been mauled by an adult tiger and was airlifted to OU Medical Center in Oklahoma City after being tended by a co-worker. Joe said the fourteen-year-old mixed-breed tiger concerned would not be put down because "it was not the tiger's fault". However, it would be quarantined for ten days.

Joe maintained that there was no way of avoiding such an incident except for handcuffing his employees' hands behind their backs.

"I can't babysit them," he said.

A post on the park's Facebook page said the "woman" was out of surgery and that her arm had been saved, while omitting to mention her name.

"She has a long road of repairs ahead of her but this is a miracle and thanks for the prayers everyone," said an update that evening. "During the entire event, she was awake and saying it was her fault."

Joe told the press: "This was an employee error of violating the safety protocols of placing any part of the body inside a cage."

In an interview on CNN, he said: "My heart goes out to her that one of my tigers did this. She assured me even in the helicopter that she was going to come back to work."

The animal park was closed shortly after the incident, but opened again a few hours later. Rather than face two years of reconstructive surgery, Saff elected to have his arm amputated and went back to work at the zoo.

In the *Tampa Bay Examiner*, Carole Baskin asked: "What on earth constitutes a mauling if not, as Schreibvogel described on television, a person's arm having the flesh stripped from the bone up to the elbow, by a tiger pulling a person through the fence?"

Joe's press release had stated: "Park medics were on the scene within two minutes and gave emergency medical attention to the staff member."

"Really?" said Carole. "Who at the G.W. Zoo has even been to college, much less is qualified to give 'emergency medical attention' or be called a 'park medic'?" In a story that circulated that day, Joe Schreibvogel was quoted as saying that he was the one who provided the emergency procedures, including a tourniquet.

Carole cited his siblings saying that he used to dress up like a doctor when he owned a pet store in Texas. He had videos online of him pretending to be a vet. Then she took a swing at "his latest bizarre impersonation" which was that of a country singer, "where he apparently lip syncs and pretends to play the guitar. Anyone who has ever heard his whiney, nasal voice will know immediately that the person singing on the recording can't possibly be Joe Schreibvogel... Pretending to be someone you are not and misrepresenting things has recently cost Joseph Schreibvogel more than a million dollars."

As far as Carole was concerned, Saff's mauling was an accident waiting to happen. She pointed out: "Until the tragedy struck, the opening page of the G.W. Zoo website displayed a video of Joe 'Exotic' Schreibvogel hugging a full grown tiger, who appeared to be restrained merely by a leash, at the zoo. There are many, many photos online of the "park manager" John Reinke, a double amputee, in the cage with a full grown lion and sometimes a full grown lion and tiger at the same time... How could this impressionable young woman resist being just like her boss and co-workers by sneaking in a little scratch behind the tiger's ears?"

She blamed "not only a lack of training", but the entire culture at the park as "one of treating tigers like house pets". The park was "known for capitalising on the homeless and those who have been otherwise rejected by society or their families".

"These kind of people make the perfect victims," said Carole. "They have nowhere else to go and are loyal to those who put a roof over their heads and food in their stomachs. Add to this that they are often allowed to bottle-feed baby lions, tigers and ligers, and they feel 'special' for the first time in their lives."

Joe had been quoted in the media saying that this was the first time there had been an incident at the G.W. Zoo, but Carole provided a link where you could see a video of a child being knocked down and bitten by a tiger in 2011. The footage had been shot during the undercover investigation by the Humane Society. The tiger was said to be twenty-four months old, when the regulations were that only big cats up to twelve months could interact with humans.

But Carole said that the media was missing the main story, which was how Joe and others like him continue to breed lions and tigers to be used as photo and petting props. It was the *real* animal protection groups, including Big Cat Rescue, the Humane Society of the United States, the International Fund for Animal Welfare, World Wildlife Fund, Born Free, the Ian Somerhalder Foundation, the Global Federation of Animal Sanctuaries and the Animal Legal Defense Fund that were all working together to end the trade in big cats to be owned as pets, used as ego props or for their parts. Measures were being put before Congress, the USDA and the U.S. Fish and Wildlife Service, she said.

On CNN, Joe retorted: "I don't worry about what the Humane Society or PETA has to say about anything because, A, they're not here, and, B, they know nothing about our facility and, C, I really would not comment on an organisation that killed eighty-seven per cent of the animals that they got their hands on last year while we work 24/7 to give up everything in our lives to keep these animals alive."

After Zanesville, Ohio eventually passed some of the country's toughest exotic-animal ownership laws. Joe was determined to prevent this happening in Oklahoma, so he upped his publicity campaign. He posted Craigslist ads for production staff to film reality shows at the park. He hoped to promote himself as the next Steve Irwin, Australia's "crocodile hunter" who had died in 2006 while filming on the Great Barrier Reef.

However, most film staff left soon after they arrived, unable to package the abuse they witnessed into a family-friendly product. Rick Kirkham, a former *Inside Edition* journalist whose crack-cocaine addiction was the subject of a 2006 documentary called *TV Junkie*, lasted eleven months. He witnessed the worst of his employer's cultish behaviour.

Joe shot at walls, and near employees. His staff ate the meat Joe pooled from Oklahoma Walmarts. If staff did anything wrong, Joe cut off their food. Joe controlled when crew members slept, when they got up, and forbade relations between them.

"We worked with animals that kill people," Joe said. "There was no room for grab-ass or kissing."

"They could not leave the park," Rick said. "They were totally in a trance-like state."

The trailers were dumps, and some employees slept on insect-covered floors. One time, Joe caught two crew members cavorting in a trailer. He frogmarched the young woman to the park gate and said: "Good luck, bitch."

Rick saw Joe shoot one tiger during his year at the park. Another day, an old lady brought a horse to the park and told Joe she couldn't look after it any more. Joe hugged her and said he'd care for the creature. When she left, Joe told Rick to turn his camera on. Then he whipped out his gun and shot the horse in the head while it was still standing in its trailer. "What the fuck?" Rick cried.

"I'm not a charity," Joe replied. He fed the horse to the lions. Rick also claimed that Joe shot at him.

"If he had to pull his gun and shoot at you, he'd do it," he said. "He shot at me three times. Sometimes we'd be sitting in a TV studio, and somebody would say something he didn't like, and he'd take his gun out and shoot it right through the wall of the TV studio, saying, 'You want to fuck with me?'"

Joe often griped to Rick about Carole: how she was mad and would never get his money. He fretted she'd get the park when Shirley died, and tried putting his share of its ownership in the names of others. It seemed like he was stalling for time. But the biggest revelation Rick had was that Joe was scared to death of lions and tigers.

"In the shots that you see in there, where he's in with the two tigers, the white one and the other one – the white one is blind and the other one is on tranquilisers," said Kirkham. "It's idiotic to think how he's become famous as 'The Tiger King' when he's so terrified of big cats."

Keeper Erik Cowie confirmed this.

"Joe would often brag about being in a cage with sixteen tigers, but in reality it was more like two or three of them," he said. "I would take the mean ones out of the cage, the cats who didn't like him."

He was better with the babies though.

"For one reason or another, a cub would become unruly so Joe would take the baby cub out of view of the people at the zoo and pop the cub in the nose and bring it back out," Cowie said.

This made his job more difficult.

"I then had to deal with a baby cub who had just been popped in the nose and then make sure it wouldn't act up and bite some older women or child," he said.

In his career as an ersatz country singer, Joe turned on Carole. The video of one of his songs, *Here Kitty Kitty*, featured a model feeding meat to tigers from a mannequin's head – supposedly a reference to Carole's deceased husband – while Joe, wearing shades, a pastor's collar and black hat like a spaghetti western preacher mimed the lines:

> *So if you're ever down in Tampa on a big-cat refuge,*
> *Don't pick a fight with your wife,*
> *'Cause it's a big forty acres and if you're not careful,*
> *You'll be gone in the blink of an eye.*

The recording of the albums was farmed out to songwriter Vince Johnson and singer Danny Clinton, though Joe continued to insist that it was him singing. The couple had no idea that Joe was going to pretend that he was singing on the album, but were forbearing.

"We all get what's coming to us in the end, be it good or bad. Joe, all in all, was likable," Johnson told *Vanity Fair*. "Most people just bore the hell out of me. They have the personality of a lobster. He's a seedy shyster, but he's got personality."

Baskin was less forgiving.

"Schreibvogel may not be a vet, nor a doctor, nor a country and western singer, but he is a magician and thus well versed in the art of deception," she said. "Is anyone looking past the smoke and mirrors?"

Joe responded to her criticism with a threat. On his show one night in February 2014, Joe brought out a blow-up doll with a blonde wig, apparently a crude rendering of Baskin.

"You wanna know why Carole Baskin better never, ever, ever see me face to face ever, ever, ever again?" Joe asked, before suddenly raising a pistol to the doll's head and pulling the trigger. There was a loud bang, and the doll keeled over.

"That is how sick and tired of this shit I am," Joe said. "Have a great night, ladies and gentlemen, and I will see you tomorrow night."

Carole said that this was the first time she genuinely believed "that he would pay somebody. You could see him trying to whip people into a frenzy to kill me."

In 2015 he wrote on his YouTube page that he was "going to Florida to commit suicide in eight days". In a later comment, he wrote "a murder suicide".

While Kelci Saffery did return to work at G.W. Zoo after issuing a public statement accepting blame for not following proper procedures while feeding the animal, the park was fined $5,000 by the Occupational Safety and Health Administration.

"Everybody said I should have fired her for messing up, but who better to teach my employees to keep their damn hands out of the cages," Joe said.

Indeed Saff was falling apart. He was arrested at least eight times according to the Garvin County Oklahoma Sheriff's Department, for driving under the influence, carrying weapons, obtaining goods by false pretences or with a bad cheque, and failing to appear to warrants. In one mugshot, Saff was seen wearing his zoo uniform, complete with his radio.

The animals themselves were not the only danger. In December 2014, PETA reported that Joe had been diagnosed with tuberculosis and brucellosis, and wrote to the Oklahoma State Veterinarian Dr. Rod Hall and the USDA to ask authorities to quarantine the facility and take measures to evaluate employees and animals for exposure. Both diseases were dangerous and transmissible to animals and humans, so posed a risk to the animals on display as well as visitors to the park.

"It is possible Joe Schreibvogel contracted one or both of these diseases from wild deer carcasses that he fed to carnivores at his deplorable roadside zoo," said PETA Foundation Deputy General Counsel, Delcianna Winders. "By putting those around him at risk for the sake of a few dollars, Schreibvogel has shown once again that he cares as little about his employees and visitors as he does about the animals he imprisons, and PETA is warning everyone to stay far away from his facility."

Joe said that his doctors had cleared him of the diseases, but NBC found a post on his Facebook page that stated otherwise.

The following month PETA filed fresh complaints with the USDA and the Occupational Safety and Health Administration after a whistleblower reported seeing animals being left to suffer from untreated injuries and untrained employees being forced into direct contact with dangerous animals.

"This isn't the first time that this seedy menagerie has been accused of leaving animals to suffer from illness and injury and of endangering humans," said Winders. "PETA is calling on the authorities to hold Schreibvogel and the G.W. Zoo accountable for every animal-welfare and employee-safety violation they may find at his facility."

In a sworn affidavit, the whistle-blower reported being ordered to handle a skunk with no protective gloves, even after the animal became agitated and bit the whistle-blower, who then required a trip to the emergency room. Another staff member apparently reported to the whistle-blower that they had been attacked by a monkey two days earlier, while Joe himself apparently reported having had his "ass handed to him by a tiger". Employees with no training were apparently expected to enter enclosures with no barriers between themselves and a hyena, an exotic cat and other animals.

Other informants followed. One said that, among other apparently wounded or sick animals, they had seen a yellow python whose spine was allegedly crushed after staff tried to mate her with a boa constrictor. Another reported seeing a juvenile big cat bite two members of the public.

The death threats Joe received turned more serious. When a fire burnt down Joe's video production studio and killed one crocodile and seven alligators – that Joe said had belonged to Michael Jackson – Joe suspected arson.

"After receiving death threats by email and again this week on a Facebook post, someone made good on setting an arson fire at the zoo, burning down Joe Exotic's recording studio and indoor alligator facility, killing eight animals," Joe's press statement said. "Zoo officials are concerned what could be next, either from animal rights activists or people that believe the lies put out online in order to get others to carry out their mission of destroying the zoo. Officials stated it was amazing that the fire did not spread through the park killing more animals with as much accelerant that was used to start the fire."

"The fire was out when we got there," said Garvin County Sheriff Larry Rhodes. "It occurred sometime overnight and burned itself out on its own."

The large building, thirty feet by sixty, was badly damaged.

"It didn't burn to the ground, but it was completely gutted," Rhodes added. He confirmed that it appeared the fire had been deliberately set.

"We determined there was an odour of gasoline around the fire," he said. "This is being investigated as arson as well as a burglary. We did determine some items were missing from inside the building."

Joe said that the crocodiles had been retrieved from Neverland after Jackson had died.

"When they closed down Neverland Ranch and auctioned off his property, they asked us to come get all the reptiles and alligators and other stuff," said Joe. "We also helped them relocate and move some giraffes he had on the property." The animals were housed in the building Brian had lived in at the depth of his depression.

One crocodile, a female that Joe claimed was "between thirty-five and forty years old", survived the blaze by escaping her enclosure when its doors blew off. The others were "boiled alive in a towering inferno," he said. He believed that the rogue animal-rights activists responsible for setting the fire also stole a large number of electronic storage devices used for recording his TV show.

"All they took were the external hard drives and all the cameras," he said. "They left all the computers and all the other equipment. Whoever it is has all my footage... 60,000 hours of footage. Everything since 1999, the day we opened, is gone."

Expensive computers and other costly production equipment were left to burn.

"This was personal," said Joe. "They targeted the studio to shut me up. They wanted to get me off the air... or else they would've targeted something else."

He called the perpetrators "animal terrorists" and said they were trying to destroy his life's work as chronicled by *Joe Exotic TV*.

"It's just a show to help fight for our rights, as Americans, to own animals and they didn't like that," he said. "Obviously, I hit a nerve."

The night of the fire, Joe had been away from the park. He had had a row with Rick Kirkham who'd told Joe he nedeed to calm down when on camera. Joe told him to fuck off. They rowed frequently. Six months earlier, in December 2014, Rick threatened to release footage of animal abuse. He told Joe: "I'm the guy that has video that could put your ass in jail and you know it, so don't fuck with me."

That night, Joe had changed the locks on the studio and announced he'd leave town for three days. Seeing the back of him, Rick and the crew threw an impromptu party at the trailer. The next morning around 7 a.m., Rick recalled, one of the park managers kicked in the door of his trailer.

"Grab your camera," the intruder yelled.

"Camera?" Rick replied. "The cameras are all in the studio."

"There is no studio! The studio burned down overnight."

News of the fire, brought Joe back to the park.

"He blamed me. He blamed anybody and everybody but himself," said Rick. "But the bottom line is two days before the studio fire, he and I got into an argument over the fact that I had a contract with him to make the reality show. He was so upset. He made an immediate departure, said, 'I'm gone from the park for a couple of days'."

Sheriff Rhodes believed that the arson had been used in an attempt to cover up the burglary. The state fire marshal had ruled out electrical or weather-related causes for the fire.

"He ruled out lightning, from the storms we had out here last week," Sheriff Rhodes said.

The FBI "have been poking around, too," said the sheriff. With the Animal Enterprise Terrorism Act of 2006, it had become a federal crime to damage or interfere with roadside zoos like Joe's.

"By no means are we close to any conclusion in this investigation," Sheriff Rhodes said. "But we do have a clear criminal act in this case... whereas, in the past, we haven't always had that."

He said that the zoo had been targeted over the last two years, since a dead chinchilla was left at the entrance in August 2013. Sheriff Rhodes said the man who left the chinchilla near the zoo was from out of state and "there wasn't enough there to actually prove he caused the animal to die, so there were no charges filed".

Since the summer of 2013, Rhodes said there had been a lot of occurrences at the zoo. Joe was often targeted, the sheriff said. "It's an ongoing pattern at the zoo. Joe is very passionate about his exhibition of animals, particularly the big cats, and he's on one extreme of that spectrum. And then you have animal rights groups, extremists who are on the other side of that spectrum."

Joe also complained that the fire was just the latest in a long series of incidents and run-ins with individuals and groups that he described as "terrorists, plain and simple".

"I think you're going to be surprised when they put a close to this… as far as who is going to tie this together," Joe told *The Oklahoman*. "We have a lot of information. We have video footage and all of that."

He said that the fire was a personal attack perpetrated by someone trying to "make a statement" and get him off the air.

"They might have shut me up for just a little while, but let me tell you they have awoken a monster," he said. "Now, Joe Exotic is pissed off."

The property was not insured and repairs would cost $250,000. To raise the money, Joe launched a GoFundMe crowdfunding campaign. The goal was $150,000 and $125,000 would go towards repairs. The remaining $25,000 was offered as a reward for information leading to the arrest of the perpetrator.

"This was not random. Someone targeted our zoo," said Joe announcing the appeal. "We need your help to right this wrong. For the baby 'gators who died in the fire. For the memorabilia turned to ashes. To make the zoo whole again. We really appreciate any amount people care to donate."

For a $30 pledge, supporters would receive a handmade Broken Heart Alligator necklace. The crocs had been in the Steve Irwin Compound, named in honour of the late Australian crocodile hunter.

"Aside from the strife we feel for this loss, we want to heal our monument built to a great man," Joe said. "We need to heal our park after this attack."

Meanwhile Joe was becoming increasingly paranoid that animal rights groups were sending spies to the zoo. He wouldn't allow guests to bring cameras into the park. Sometimes employees would be told to check a person's belt buckle area to make sure there wasn't a hidden camera in it. Joe repeatedly posted social media photos and videos of himself firing weapons and toying with explosives, warning animal rights activists: "Don't fuck with me."

Having lost his first chance of becoming a TV reality star with Rick Kirkham, in August 2015 Joe decided the show must go on and returned to the Mississippi Valley Fair. This time USDA inspectors were on hand. They cited him for leaving a nineteen-day-old golden tabby tiger exposed to the elements.

According to the report, Joe had housed the cub in an open-air playpen without any form of heating or cooling system.

"Animals this young… are not able to adequately thermoregulate and exposures to temperatures which may be comfortable for adults may still be detrimental to the health of young cubs," the report said.

Later Joe moved the animal to his climate-controlled RV and he said he planned to file a discrimination lawsuit against the USDA.

"You've got tigers, ligers, elephants, alligators and even monkeys on top of dogs here, and Joe is the only one who got inspected," he said. "They didn't take his temperature to know whether or not I was properly regulating it. They're not event veterinarians and they tried to tell me how to raise my tiger."

It was the fifth year running he had been at the fair and he was still allowing fairgoers to interact with his eight-week-old cubs.

"How many times can you say 'I took a selfie with a tiger,'?" said one visitor. "It was cool just to be able to do something you can't do anywhere else."

Joe continued to claim that his team had educated thousands of people about tiger conservation. Nevertheless, in response to the USDA report, PETA wrote to the organisers asking them to bar Joe from future fairs.

"Again and again, and now once more at the Mississippi Valley Fair, Joe Schreibvogel has demonstrated a complete indifference toward the health and safety of tiger cubs," said Brittany Peet, deputy director of captive animal law enforcement for PETA.

Fair director Bob Fox responded: "I know Joe and his animals are well taken care of. I'm a big animal lover so if I thought they were mistreating animals, they wouldn't be here."

## SIX: A Political Animal

In November 2015, Joe Exotic announced that he was going to run for president of the United States the following year. He mailed his statement of candidacy to the Federal Election Commission under the name Joseph Maldonado. The change of surname spoke volumes about Joe's complex personal life.

Nineteen-year-old, six-foot-four Travis Maldonado arrived at Joe's zoo in December 2013. Back home in Southern California, Travis had a roll-call of girlfriends and a good job at American Tire that he'd gotten after ditching high school at eighteen. But he was bored and experimented with drugs. Soon he was struggling with addiction to crystal meth. One of Joe's employees suggested he take Maldonado on in the hope that working around animals would help him recover. Travis and his father Danny, a twenty-three-year veteran of the US Marines with a snow-white handlebar moustache, saw moving to Oklahoma as a chance for Travis to clean up and work on something fun.

Travis loved bikes and thought nothing of cycling the 1,200 miles to his new home on the $4,000 racing bike his father had bought him. Nor was Travis a down-and-out, as Joe would later insist. The day he left, Danny handed him $1,000 to get him to Wynnewood.

"He thought he was having the chance of a lifetime," Sherry Peck, Danny's girlfriend, said. "He didn't know he was walking into hell."

Joe took a liking to Maldonado straight away and employed him to film Joe's upcoming web show. He also joined Joe and John Finlay on their weekends at motels, where other men joined them. Less than a month after Travis arrived, he, Joe Exotic and John Finlay went through a marriage of sorts in a three-way ceremony in a dance hall across the street from the zoo.

The big day itself was nine months before the first legal gay wedding would be held in Oklahoma. It was another extravaganza that Joe hoped would project him to the media world. In a video posted to the *Joe Exotic TV* YouTube channel, Joe invited a clothing store clerk to drop by. "It's for a TV show," he told her with a shrug.

The ceremony was zoo-themed. The orange cake had black tiger stripes. It was decorated with miniature chocolate cowboy boots and crocodiles made out of butterscotch. Some of the bridesmaids were dressed as monkeys. The ring bearer was a Celebes crested macaque. The three men wore matching pink, button-down shirts and black pants. A candle near the altar was lit in memory of Joe's brother, Garold. Joe stood in the middle, wearing a black, wide-brimmed hat. Neither Finlay nor Maldonado claimed they were gay, but Joe boasted about seducing straight guys because there were not too many gay guys at the park.

Joe choreographed the wedding. Travis' father Danny wasn't invited. Joe didn't want his girlfriend Sherry Peck there either. Only Travis' older sisters, Ashley and Danielle, were asked to attend.

"Joe said no and what Joe said, went," Danny said. Asked why Joe kept him away, Danny said: "Control."

After the contrived ceremony, Travis seemed happy. Joe treated him like a big kid. He bought Travis a four-wheeler, gave him cash and let him roam the park. Travis liked to shoot guns into the ground. He smoked a lot of pot. He could be mean, throwing live chickens into the cat cages. He also hit cubs. One staff member described him as "particularly sadistic". Others liked him. "Travis was a blast, man," said former crew member Dianna Mazak. "He was loud and crazy and didn't care."

However, the threesome did not work out and Joe's relationship with John began to fall apart. John said that Joe had become manipulative and controlling. The park dominated their lives and they rarely left it for anything not work-related. Joe had also become obsessed with his Internet TV show as episodes started gleaning more views. He relied on increasingly wild stunts to drum up interest. John had seen enough and was ready to leave. It was a messy break-up.

John's steroid and meth addiction worsened. He overdosed and almost died. He often woke up in the middle of the night "ready for a fight," Joe said. On 18 August 2014, John attacked Joe in the back parking lot. He was arrested and charged with assault and battery. John eventually got the park receptionist pregnant, which hastened his departure.

In 2015, the Supreme Court legalised gay marriage across the states. Joe Exotic then legally wed Travis Maldonado and took his new husband's name.

NBC caught up with Joe and Travis at Will Rogers World Airport on 22 November 2015. They were flying to Columbus, Ohio to hold a presidential press conference. Joe also had tickets for Donald Trump's rally there.

"What's my chances of winning?" he said. "Who knows, you know? Pretty slim. But I'm going to give them a run for their money."

Clearly, for Joe, his battles over animal rights would be an issue. He addressed his run-ins with the USDA and activists in the forty-seventh video he said he had put out since deciding to run for president.

"You know all you people that are friends with Carole and the animal rights people and the people who don't like me. Ya'll go play somewhere else because right now we don't even have time to respond to your bullshit," he said in the video, posted on his Facebook page. He claimed to have 17 million viewers on YouTube and said more than 38,000 worldwide had watched his show the previous night on *Joe Exotic TV*.

While he did not have millions of dollars like Donald Trump or Hillary Clinton, he said he had people in every state committed to running campaign offices.

"It's going to be a grassroots organisation, grassroots campaign for the small people for a change," said Joe. He said running for office was not a publicity stunt and that he was serious about the campaign. It didn't bother him if he didn't look or act like a regular candidate.

"It shouldn't be about my sexual preference. It shouldn't be about the way I look. It shouldn't be about anything else," Joe said. "I'm not going to wear a suit. I'm not cutting my hair because I'm not going to be fake."

Plainly his hair was important to him. In a campaign video that showed him strolling past lounging lions, he said: "First thing is, I am not cutting my hair. I am not changing the way I dress. I refuse to wear a suit. I am gay. I've had two boyfriends most of my life. I currently got legally married – thank god it's finally legal in America. I've had some kinky sex. I have tried drugs through my younger years of my life. I am broke as shit."

He went on to say that he ran one of "the nicest facilities for exotic animals in this country" before adding, "I have a judgment against me from some bitch down in Florida."

Proclaiming himself a "redneck" he said he would not deny anything he had done in the past. Although he had never held public office, he said he had always been involved in politics and had once been a police chief. The issues that were important to him were healthcare and the rights of veterans, but he had several websites under construction so that people could comment and let him know what they want to see being done. As a result, his list of concerns quickly expanded to include social security, healthcare, gun rights and medicare.

Joe hired Josh Dial, a gun-store clerk in the Oklahoma Walmart in Pauls Valley, as his campaign manager. Only thirty-one, Dial had been arrested five times for the possession of drugs and driving under the influence.

According to Dial, at that time, Joe was so politically naïve that he didn't know the difference between Republicans, Democrats and Libertarians.

"My job was to make him appealing to the Libertarian crowd, even though he wasn't a Libertarian," Josh said. "I really just tried to drill as much as I could in him."

At his press conference in Ohio, Joe said he was running as an independent candidate to give a voice to ordinary citizens.

"The small people of this country never get a voice," he said. "They're never heard."

Speaking of himself in the third person, he said: "Maldonado has more interest in the people of this country that have never had a voice before. It seems all the other candidates have nothing to do with the farmer, the rancher, the person that works forty hours a week and has more of their rights taken away daily by the very people that have taken an oath to look out for them. It's time to kick the lobbyist and the animal rights along with the special interest groups out of the politicians pockets."

He claimed to be able to interact with young people while also gaining the respect of the older crowd. Joe said: "How can you save a generation that you have nothing to do with? Politicians are about the rich and the powerful, they never get out and beat the sidewalks and really get to know people and hear their issues. It's time we give Americans their voice back."

Carole Baskin picked her moment. In February 2016, lawyers for Big Cat Rescue filed a suit against Joe's mother Shirley in a court in Oklahoma, accusing her of helping him conceal the G.W. Zoo's assets from its many creditors through a series of fraudulent schemes. The lawsuit said that Shirley Schreibvogel had helped her son transfer cash and assets into her name to avoid paying the trademark infringement judgement then standing at $1,028,000. It also alleged that she allowed assets to be financed in her name rather than the zoo's to avoid creditors and that an outdoor storage facility on her property in Pauls Valley was used for zoo business.

"Shirley Schreibvogel does not pay for, or make the bulk of the payments on financing for, these assets with her own funds," the lawsuit said. "Rather, Garold Wayne Zoo transfers cash to Shirley Schreibvogel so that she can physically purchase, or make payments on financing for, these assets."

In addition, the lawsuit stated that zoo funds were "regularly" transferred to Shirley Schreibvogel, "but never deposited into Garold Wayne Zoo's bank accounts".

Rather that persecuting an old woman, Heather Hintz, an Oklahoma City attorney representing Big Cat Rescue Corp, said her client was "simply attempting to collect on a debt".

Big Cat Rescue may have been barking up the wrong tree. With John Finlay out of the way, Joe transferred ownership of the zoo to Jeff Lowe, another big name in the big cat world, to prevent Carole Baskin getting her hands on it. However, Lowe had a somewhat chequered past. He had twelve tigers himself and had tried to start a zoo in his hometown of Beaufort, South Carolina, which was closed by city officials.

In 2006, his USDA exhibitor's licence was suspended and he was ordered to pay a $25,000 fine to settle violations for failing to provide clean water, structurally sound facilities and train employees. Then, in 2007, he was sued by musician Prince for allegedly selling clothes with his trademarked symbol on them. According to Lowe's website, he had worked with Prince, but Dale Atkins, one of Prince's legal team, said: "The thing about him working with Prince... I'm not gonna call him a liar but, based on any information I have, he never worked for Prince – unless you call getting sued working for him."

The following year, Lowe pleaded guilty to federal mail-fraud charges in the USA for posing as an employee of the Citizens Opposed to Domestic Abuse charity in order to obtain $1 million worth of merchandise that he later resold. In 2015 he exhibited his big cats in his discount clothing store, Beaufort Liquidation. Although he had a licence from the USDA to display two tigers and one lion, he came under the scrutiny of Beaufort County Council after they received a hundred letters of concern from local residents and interest groups. He was cited by Beaufort County for zoning ordinance violations. If he lost, he said he would close his flea market and turn it into an animal sanctuary that was closed to the public.

"I'm going to fill this place. Absolutely fill it with animals," Lowe said. "They think they're going to discourage me because I can't show them to people, but that's not what this is about.

This is about housing animals and giving them lives that are safe and secure."

In the end, he was found not guilty. Even so, he upped sticks and moved to Oklahoma to team up with Joe, moving into G.W. Zoo while having a house built.

Joe had first met Lowe around June 2015, when Lowe stopped by the G.W. Zoo to buy a baby tiliger cub. Lowe was no stranger to big cats. With his operation in South Carolina, he had twelve big cats to house. Big cats ran in his blood. His grandfather had founded a circus and worked with Ringling Brothers.

What impressed Joe was that Lowe pulled up in a Hummer towing a trailer that had once been owned by stunt rider Evel Knievel. Apparently Lowe had managed Evel's son Robbie, who followed in his father's footsteps and later called Lowe a "fraud", "fake" and a "loser".

Lowe was short and stocky, with doughy eyes. He always wore a biker jacket and do-rag, under which locks of grey hair tumbled out like instant noodles. He accessorised his Ferrari sports car with a Ferrari-branded baseball cap. His girlfriend, Lauren, who became his second wife, was slim and glamorous with silken red hair.

Some might have sniffed out trouble. Joe smelled success. He needed cash, what with Carole owed the $1 million from her lawsuit.

"He saw the Ferraris and the Porsches and all the exotic vehicles," Lowe said. "And I think he saw me as his meal ticket."

Lowe paid $7,500 cash for the tiliger and told Joe that he planned to open a sanctuary in Colorado. Lowe flew Joe and Travis out to his 12,000-square-foot home there in September. The trip was their honeymoon. They went skydiving and hung around the pool. Joe was having health problems, and he had become increasingly worried about what would happen to the zoo if he died or could no longer manage it. According to Joe, Lowe offered to put the zoo in his name, to ensure it never went to Baskin.

Lowe saw his houseguest as a chance to start anew. He told Joe to dissolve the G.W. Park's LLC (Limited Liability Company), open another in Lowe's name, and continue running tours and shows as its entertainment director. Joe was short of food and hadn't paid utilities: Lowe would keep the park alive. According to Lauren, he sweetened the deal with an additional $100,000.

Later Lowe complained that Joe had conned him into investing in his zoo by claiming he was HIV positive and only had a few years left to live.

"He presented me these pictures of himself on his phone with his face all swelled up and his lips all purple. Joe told me, at that time, he was HIV positive," Lowe said. "Joe told us he had a $5 million life insurance policy and he was going to put us down as a fifty per cent beneficiary so we would have money to take care of the animals, with his husband Travis getting the other fifty per cent."

Just days after Joe flew back to Oklahoma, he was overloading Lowe's phone with pictures of his life insurance policies as proof he wasn't lying.

Lowe said: "He basically begged us to come out there to help him save it."

Later Lowe discovered that most of the policies had been cancelled for non-payment or Joe had already cashed them out.

"Joe not only told us he was HIV positive on several occasions, but told several other people. He used it to his advantage so he could scam something out of them. If it wasn't HIV, it was cancer," said Lowe.

In reality, Lowe discovered that Joe did have an autoimmune disease called CVID – common variable immune deficiency. It's not transmitted sexually like HIV, but mimics the genetic code of HIV. CVID impairs the immune system, making sufferers highly susceptible to infection. Whenever Joe had to go to the hospital or to the doctors for treatment for his CVID, he said it was either cancer, HIV or something else, Lowe said. "I mean he used that as a crutch whenever times were tough and he'd get out of line, he'd say, 'I've got this cancer, I have this autoimmune deficiency you know, and I can't pay the bills'."

At the time, Joe had been moving toward a settlement that would have ended Carole Baskin's continuing litigation to collect the $1 million judgment. After a ten-hour-long mediation hearing with the Baskins in downtown Oklahoma City, the parties reached an agreement – Joe would pay modest monthly payments toward the $1 million judgment. He would keep the zoo, but could no longer offer cub-petting and would stop breeding big cats. Baskin's lawyers sent a draft of the agreement to Joe's attorneys, thinking their protracted legal epic was nearly over.

Days went by, but they got no response from Joe or his attorneys. The mediator set up a conference call with Joe and his legal team on 12 November 2015 to see what was holding things up. An unfamiliar voice came over the line. It said: "There is no deal. We're not doing this deal."

Someone asked who was speaking.

"Jeff Lowe," the voice said.

Not only was there no deal, but Lowe immediately made things worse in Carole Baskin's eyes. After he moved in, he opened a storefront petting zoo called Neon Jungle in a mall in Oklahoma City, which offered two-person play sessions for $25 with tiger, black bear cubs, a lemur and a wolf pup. Customers were allowed to take their own photographs with the animals during the play sessions. Stuffed toy tigers and other exotic animal-related merchandise. A month later he and Lauren wed at the MGM Grand in Las Vegas. Jeff wore a black do-rag.

Within a few months, the relationship between Joe and Jeff had soured. Both men had strong personalities. Tensions grew as they shared the same living space and jointly ran the zoo. Meanwhile, Baskin's continued attempts to collect on the $1 million judgment only agitated Joe more.

Then Joe's presidential campaign took an unusual turn. Casey Harris's seven-year-old daughter had been taken to Joe's zoo by her grandmother during the child's spring break when they were stopped by Joe, who gave them a speech.

"He comes out to give his little spiel, and he used a little off-colour language," said the child's grandmother. The topic was Joe's presidential run, but she said the speech took a suggestive turn.

"He says that we need some of these buttons, and starts pitching them up in the crowd, to all ages of the children," she said. "A friend of mine, her granddaughter picks one up off the ground, and it's a condom."

And it wasn't just any condom. It was a "Tiger King" condom, complete with Joe's picture on it and directions for use on the back.

"They wanted to know 'Why can't we have it?'" the child's grandmother said. "All we could think of was, 'It's for little boys.'"

The Harris family said they would probably never go back to the G.W. Zoo. For the family, the zoo was a place to learn about animals – not the birds and the bees.

"We'll talk to her when it's time, but that's just not the place and time," Casey Harris said.

Joe told Newschannel 4 the condom tossing had been part of his zoo presentations for years. It was used as an icebreaker between him and the crowd, which included people of all ages. He said he didn't plan to stop the presentation any time soon.

Which made it all the more disappointing when he discovered that, as an independent, he would not be allowed to join the debate with the major parties.

"It is so unfair," he said. "I can't challenge them for an open debate and call their bluffs. I am not allowed to debate as I am an independent, the rule says, but seems to me that I am actually not allowed to make them look like fools in front of the TV cameras and the whole nation. I am being deprived, as is the whole population of [the] United States of America, from having real solutions to the problems and challenges being faced by our great country.

"I appeal to the residents of the United States of America to ask their government and the media if they are being fair to independent presidential candidates like myself by depriving us of a chance to debate with the candidates of the Republican and Democratic parties."

Joe was garnering a lot of support on social media platforms though.

"I would like to request each one of my supporters and every proud American, to please bombard all election officials, state and national authorities and the TV, print and online media with emails, calls, faxes, messages on social platforms like Facebook and Twitter, and whatever else you think can work, and ask them for a debate with Joe Exotic, as I can offer out-of-the-box solutions for the problems and challenges that our great country faces today," he said. "I wouldn't be surprised to find that this archaic rule was enacted by someone in the past to avoid an independent candidate like me from firing some bigwig and blow them out of the water! Aren't they all hanging on to this rule even today because they are afraid of being exposed in front of the nation? I bet they are!"

Joe had no alternative but to go out on the stump. Stopping in Abilene on 30 April, he told supporters that he was running for president as an independent so he could be "the voice of the working class people who built this country".

"It is time the people have their own rights to be free to do what you want on your own property," he told the crowd at the CK Restaurant in North Abilene. "It is time the elderly get the social security they deserve, our vets get the healthcare they need and kids get to eat at school. Bottom line: It's time we take our voice back."

By then he had offices in nineteen states and was busy getting his name on the ballot. He was already registered in Arkansas, Colorado and Louisiana, and nine signatures short of getting his name on the ballot in Oklahoma. He was then petitioning for the 100,000 signatures required to get his name on the ballot in Texas.

"I have until August 1 to get my name on the ballot in most states, so I am spending a lot of time on the road, telling people about who I am, what I stand for, and why they should support me," he said.

Outlining his policies, Joe said he was a strong supporter of the right to bear arms, was a pro-choice candidate, hated Obamacare, was against all animal rights and animal laws, was against welfare for people able to work, and was against big business tax breaks.

"There are nearly 1.5 million non-profit organisations in the United States," he said. "If we got rid of every non-profit – except for the life-saving hospitals – and closed the tax loophole for the rest, making them pay a flat eight per cent tax rate per year, I could have the country out of debt in three years."

Of course, some of these non-profit organisations were run by animal welfare activists.

Troy Bonar, a Libertarian running for the District 19 US Congressional seat, attended the hustings to see what Joe was all about.

"Most of the time, when someone enters a political race as an independent, they're either extremist or have crazy ideas," Bonar said. "I was curious to learn more about what he stands for. What I learned is that he aligns pretty closely with the libertarian school of thought."

Again, Joe complained about the rule that excluded independent candidates from the debates.

"That rule – established fifteen years ago – needs to be abolished," he said. "Excluding independents, or any other third party candidate, is unfair and harmful to our democracy."

Joe was adamant: "If Donald Trump or Hillary Clinton won't give me the time of day after emails, certified letters and the making of 244 videos posted to Facebook and YouTube, you can guarantee that they really don't give a crap about you or your problems – facing how you pay your bills, get healthcare or anything about social security being paid back. And we don't even want to discuss how this country is going to get out of debt. But I have solutions to most of these problems and they won't even acknowledge that I am running in this election."

Joe said he was going to make politicians listen to the people of [the USA] for a change, not just make promises that they never kept. But he was realistic about his electoral prospects.

"You will probably never see me win," he told the audience. "It's a rigged system, but I will have a voice, and we will have an impact on whoever gets elected."

By August, Joe said he had his name on the ballot in thirty-one states, though in most of these he only seems to have submitted the paperwork to register as a write-in. Not all write-ins count. It was said that he was the first non-millionaire independent to get that far in the presidential election process – and all on a budget of $10,000. He was even praised for coming up with an innovative healthcare and immigration policy. Knowing that the US could not afford to throw ten million immigrants out of the country, effectively decimating the workforce, he proposed fining illegal immigrants and using the money for citizen's healthcare by reforming Medicare and stopping the wealthy insurance companies paying CEOs $66 million a year while ordinary people struggled to pay for medical attention.

"It is time someone from the real, working world stood up for the people for a change instead of some rich politician or billionaire that has made money off the people for years," Joe said. "Term limits must be made for all politicians, frivolous lawsuits must be stopped, and the rights of the people need to be given back to the people instead of Congress."

Joe did most of his electioneering online, releasing 272 political videos in the first ten months of his campaign. He had a live internet show five nights a week and claimed to have spent more time answering people's questions than anyone else in the race.

"There are so many issues that face this country that are not getting any attention from the front runners," he said. "At some point someone has to stop and listen to what is really going on out here in the real world. There are more than enough jobs out here for people to take. The problem is this country hands out so much free stuff no one wants to work anymore. Have you driven through a fast food restaurant and got your order right? And they want to raise their pay to $15 per hour which means by the time the employer matches taxes they are now paying close to $20 per hour. What do the Democrats want to do? Shut down more businesses? The problem is the politicians that are in office and have been for thirty years never step foot out here in the real, working world, so they have no clue."

Joe said that another problem that never got addressed was domestic terrorism in the United States. By that he meant animal rights activists.

"When the FBI and Congress has had hearings that the animal rights groups are this nation's top terrorist problem and they are still non-profit in this country, we seem to have a bit of a problem," said Joe.

There was also a certain self-interest in his call for an end to "frivolous lawsuits", saying that litigants were using the federal court system to stalk, harass and bankrupt people for an agenda. Social Security was another huge issue for him.

"If a person wants a savings account they should set one up and be responsible for their own retirement savings," he said. "The government should have nothing to do with it. They basically stole $2.7 trillion from Social Security on bad investments with money that did not belong to them. If it was anyone else they would be in jail for theft or embezzlement."

Joe had a cunning plan to get people out to vote in the election on 8 November. Since in a lot of states he was a write-in, and knowing people had busy lives, he had ordered red, white and blue silicone wristbands with "Vote Joseph Maldonado" on them. There would be a mass mail-out of them in the last thirty days in the hope that people would wear them into the voting booth, so they would know who to vote for and how to spell his name.

Joe was thrown out of a Trump fundraiser in Norman, Oklahoma, in September. Then he was even excluded from the "Presidential Debate for the People" for third party candidates at the University of Colorado in Boulder for being too obscure. However, comedian John Oliver gave him a minute on an edition of *Last Week Tonight* dedicated to election outsiders. Showing a clip from his outré campaign video, Oliver said: "Wow! Just wow!"

Joe's name appeared as a joke candidate in some local papers and university rags. So it's not surprising that he was not elected president of the United States. It would be trite to say that he was beaten by a man with an even more astonishing hairdo.

During the election, Joe's campaign committee – Joe Exotic for the People of America – had raised more than $15,000, according to federal election filings. Donald Trump spent $350 million, including $66 million of his own money. Hardly a fair fight. Nevertheless, after nursing his wounds, Joe became a Donald Trump fan.

# SEVEN: Outlaws

By 2017, Oklahoma was one of the few states that had almost no laws governing the private ownership of exotic animals and roadside attractions. However, private zoos were subject to federal law. At least two of them – Tiger Safari in Tuttle and G.W. Exotic Animal Park in Wynnewood – were under investigation by the USDA. Safari's Sanctuary in Broken Arrow had already had its USDA licence revoked after inspectors found a series of shortcomings in animal care, but the facility could still operate as a private animal sanctuary and operate a touring animal show with little state and federal oversight. The Arbuckle Wilderness Park, a drive-thru zoo in Davis, was the subject of an ongoing complaint under the federal Animal Welfare Act filed by the USDA.

Joe said he and other zookeepers in the state had unfairly come under fire from federal regulators and animal welfare groups. A banner proclaiming People for the Ethical Treatment of Animals to be "domestic terrorists" was hung on the front of one of his tiger cages. The zoo also sold anti-Humane Society DVDs in its gift shop.

"The whole game is to shut down public contact and interaction with animals," Joe said of the tactics of animal welfare groups. "If I can put a tiger in your lap and get you to love it, you are going to care more about where it comes from than you ever would before."

*The Oklahoman* pointed out that, while there was virtually no state laws to regulate the ownership of exotic animals in Oklahoma, the Oklahoma Department of Wildlife Conservation did inspect some zoos. But it only had authority over animals that were native to the state, said Bill Hale, the department's chief of law enforcement. While the department enforced a ban on exotic venomous snakes in the state, animals such lions, tigers and elephants fell outside of the agency's jurisdiction.

The Humane Society of the United States ranked Oklahoma as one of the five worst states for the regulation of exotic animals and repeatedly called on the state to pass more stringent laws regulating ownership.

"Oklahoma is really lagging behind the rest of the country in addressing this issue," said Lisa Wathne, the organisation's manager of captive wildlife protection. "Certainly it would make sense for the state of Oklahoma to prohibit the possession of dangerous wild animals altogether."

However, the USDA had the attractions in their sights. Arbuckle Wilderness Park in Davis had been a well-known day trip destination for Oklahoma families. For decades, families had been able to drive their cars through the park and feed the exotic animals from paper cups for an admission fee. However, the USDA claimed in inspection reports that Arbuckle Wilderness was not licenced to exhibit animals in the drive-thru portion of the park and lacked a proper perimeter fence to keep the animals secure. In October 2015, it filed a formal complaint for multiple alleged violations of the Animal Welfare Act.

The owner, David Teuma, said the park had always been licenced, but a series of changes in ownership at the park had caused a misunderstanding with the USDA. At first, Teuma said he had only been an investor in the park, but took over its management after some of its property and animals were seized by the federal government following the failure of the First National Bank of Davis in 2011. The Federal Deposit Insurance Corporation and USDA controlled the park for two years after the bank failure.

"We had to re-buy everything to save the animals and our park," Teuma said.

His former business partner, Vic Garrett, who had previously operated Arbuckle Wilderness, was indicted on federal bank charges of fraud and conspiracy in connection with the Davis bank failure, but was later acquitted.

According to the complaint, USDA inspectors had found a number of sick, dying and dead animals at Arbuckle Wilderness over the past few years. The park also failed to provide adequate veterinary care, the USDA said. Teuma denied this and showed *The Oklahoman* copies of receipts for payment for ongoing veterinary care. Animal care specialists from Oklahoma State University also paid regular visits to Arbuckle Wilderness to monitor the health of the animals, Teuma said.

"Our park is forty years old," he added. "We inherited some animals that are twenty years old and we can't keep animals alive for a hundred years. We take good care of them. I extend their lives as much as I can."

In February 2015, a USDA inspector reported that a male rhinoceros called Tank was noticeably thin and lethargic. However, on a visit to the park, *The Oklahoman* saw no animals that appeared to be sick or malnourished. Tank the rhinoceros appeared healthy, although he had no companions in his outdoor enclosure, which was about the size of a large suburban house. There was also an attached barn where Tank slept.

A USDA inspector also observed an "extremely thin" juvenile male llama that was "nonresponsive and barely conscious". It was recommended that the staff obtain veterinary care immediately, but the llama died before the veterinarian arrived.

Three months later, a malnourished female oryx, a large type of African antelope, with multiple parasites was found dead at Arbuckle Wilderness. Park staff had not noticed that the oryx was pregnant before it died, the complaint said. It also claimed that many animal shelters were faulty or in need of repair and that some animals lacked adequate access to clean drinking water.

The USDA also had an ongoing investigation into Tiger Safari Inc., a zoological park in Tuttle that offers visitors encounters with tiger and cougar cubs. Inspection records show Tiger Safari was cited in January 2015 for repeatedly failing to provide adequate veterinary care to its exotic cats. A male tiger named Rajah was found to have an unusual mass on his tail that had not been treated six months after it was first observed by inspectors.

During the same inspection, a male white tiger named O-jaus was found "to be in thin body condition and had a very unusual posture and gait," according to UDSA documents.

"His backbone area appeared hunched," the inspector wrote.

Previously, in May 2014, the USDA had issued a warning to Tiger Safari for violating animal care standards. That June the owner, Bill Meadows, assured *The Oklahoman* that the problems at the park had been corrected.

"We have growing pains," Meadows said. "All of the animals are well taken care of and we have one of the cleanest parks in the state."

The Humane Society then conducted an undercover investigation and found that tiger cubs at Tiger Safari were exploited for profit. They were separated from their mothers at an early age and subjected to endless photo and petting sessions with paying customers. After the investigation, a complaint was filed with the Oklahoma Department of Wildlife Conservation that claimed two tiger cubs, named Maximus and Sarabi, were treated with particular cruelty by Meadows. According to the complaint they were subjected to "striking, choking, slapping, dragging, pushing and being lifted and dragged by one or two legs and/or the tail, being tossed at patrons and being physically subdued". But the department had no authority to do anything about it. Within two years, Maximus and Sarabi were dead.

"They lived very miserable lives as cubs and once they were too big, they were both relegated to cages – both died very young," Lisa Wathne said.

It was also pointed out that Tiger Safari displayed the logo of the Feline Conservation Federation on its website and claimed to be accredited by the organisation. However, the accreditation had expired in 2009 and had not been renewed.

*The Oklahoman* reported that there had been at least two cases in the past ten years where workers at Oklahoma roadside zoos had been attacked by big cats during feedings. After being fined $5,000 in 2014 over the incident where Kelci Saffery lost an arm, G.W. Zoo was fined again in November 2016 by the Occupational Safety and Health Administration, this time $10,974, for failing to provide adequate protective barriers in place to protect employees from big cats. Joe contested the citations and threatened to sue the OSHA over the fines.

But Joe wasn't the only culprit. In 2008, a volunteer worker, thirty-two-year-old Peter Getz, died after being attacked by a liger named Rocky during a feeding session at Safari's Sanctuary in Broken Arrow. The incident received national media attention.

According to an OSHA report on the accident, Getz broke with zoo protocol to open the animal's cage and feed it a deer carcass. He reached down to pet the animal on its head during the feeding, provoking the attack, according to the report. The Sanctuary continued operating as a zoo for several years, but the USDA eventually revoked its licence in 2012 after a series of animal care problems.

Even though the facility was closed to the public, owner Lori Ensign-Scroggins went on accepting volunteers to work there. Safari's Sanctuary had only lost its USDA licence as an animal exhibitor, but Ensign-Scroggins still operated Zoo 2 You, a travelling animal exhibit available for parties and corporate events that featured exotic birds, snakes, lizards and a baby donkey.

"Everybody is under investigation with the USDA," she said. "They put people out of business."

Zoo 2 You also offered children backyard swimming sessions with small alligators. In 2014, photographs appeared showing the crocs had their mouths taped shut. This attracted a good deal of media attention, but no action could be taken as the federal Animal Welfare Act does not regulate reptiles, amphibians or most farm animals.

The most recent USDA inspection reports on file for the G.W. Exotic Animal Park showed only a few minor violations and Joe insisted that he had nothing to hide.

"Their goal is to build a case against you and let it get up to eighty or ninety violations and then they're going to take me to court, which I'm going to enjoy," he said. "I have one of the nicest private zoos in the country and I got written up for a dead mouse on my sidewalk."

However, in December 2016, Tanya Espinosa, a spokeswoman for the USDA's Animal and Plant Inspection Service, confirmed Joe was under investigation, but said she could not say more because the matter was ongoing. Nevertheless the Humane Society had filed formal complaints, claiming the park's breeding programme "resulted in the need to offload animals who had outlived their usefulness to G.W."

Lisa Wathne said: "This is one of the largest tiger breeders in the country and it's pumping out tiger cubs for use in public photo sessions or handling sessions. It's fun for people and they hold a cub for a minute, but what they don't realise is that in order to have that kind of experience, they are contributing to a lot of suffering for the animals."

Joe also drew criticism for producing several combinations of exotic cats through mixed breeding – tigons (offspring of a male tiger and a female lion), ligers, tiligers and liligers. He boasted that he was one of the world's leading experts on creating hybrid cats.

"I have one of the best bloodlines in the country," he said. He claimed that breeding hybrids strengthened the genetics of big cats and that he "donates" many cubs to other zoos when they got too big for public play sessions. However, Susan Bass, spokeswoman for Big Cat Rescue, said there was no way to really know what happened to cubs from G.W. Exotic Animal Park's extensive breeding programme.

"That's kind of a million dollar question – no government agency tracks these cats or what happens to them," Bass said. "These breeders are more than happy to sell them cheaply or even give them away."

In May 2017, a coalition of US conservation groups launched an attempt to outlaw the breeding of what the *Guardian* newspaper called "frankencats". They filed a petition with the USDA calling for an end to the "inhumane" interbreeding of large felines. The practice, they said, contravened federal animal welfare laws because of the increased probability of resulting health problems such as cancer, clef palates, arthritis and depression.

Research had shown that cross-breeding heightened the risk of various ailments. Tigons can experience dwarfism while gigantism was known to occur in ligers. Hercules, a liger who resides at the Myrtle Beach Safari wildlife reserve in South Carolina, was named the world's largest living cat in 2014, weighing 922 pounds.

There were other problems with white tigers which were prone to becoming cross-eyed and suffered from other maladies as a result of inbreeding. White tigers were virtually extinct in India and almost all of the white tigers in the US could be traced back to a single individual. They had become popular as pets for various celebrities, such as former basketball player Shaquille O'Neal, who kept two white tigers on a Florida farm. Former heavyweight boxing world champion Mike Tyson had three big cats which, he revealed in press coverage in 2020, he feared may have originated from Joe Exotic. Magicians, Siegfried and Roy, made white tigers famous as part of their act and funded the breeding of the animals. In 2015, two white tiger cubs called Justice and Liberty, died from kidney failure while being raised by the magicians' non-profit organisation.

However, most cross-bred large cats in the US were kept in private zoos like Joe's for the amusement of passing tourists. These roadside zoos had blossomed since the 1950s. By 2017 there were roughly 2,800 exhibitors licenced by USDA across the country, less than ten per cent were accredited by the Association of Zoos and Aquariums, which has strict requirements for enriched housing, social groupings and conservation plans.

"These disreputable zoos breed tigers with lions to provide a novelty for tourists in order to make money," said Carney Anne Nasser, a campaigner at PETA, one of eight animal welfare groups behind the USDA petition. "This kind of breeding virtually guarantees health problems. There's no conservation purpose to it and it should be banned. There is a big cat crisis in the US."

The Association of Zoos and Aquariums, which accredits zoos, advised against intentional inbreeding as it was "clearly linked with various abnormal, debilitating and, at times, lethal external and internal conditions and characteristics". The AZA also expressed its concern that zoo visitors were often very interested in seeing the offspring of this sort of breeding, which perpetuates the practice.

"Even among today's frequently well informed and educated zoo visitors, the interest in seeing white tigers, white lions, white alligators or king cheetahs continues, often in preference over the 'normal' looking individuals of the same species," the AZA policy position paper states. "Of greater concern, in some cases, there exists the misconception that these unusual colour morphs, or other phenotypic aberrations, may represent a separate endangered species in need of conservation."

However, the USDA did not regulate the actual breeding of animals. Its remit was confined to veterinary care and the handling of animals. The conservation groups behind the petition wanted the agency to broaden its definition of animal welfare to include the breeding programmes that produced animals at risk of defects and illness.

This did not discourage Joe. On 11 September 2017, Joe announced the birth of the first litter of male liligers – three quarters lion, one quarter tiger – in the world. The first known liliger, a female, was born at Russia's Novosibirsk Zoo in 2012 and Joe announced the births of three female liligers at his zoo the following year. He said the hybrids he bred at his zoo were aimed at creating more durable breeds that could survive climate change and other threats to the lion and tiger species, but experts called his methods into question.

Craig Packer, director of the Lion Research Center at the University of Minnesota, said hybrid animals do not factor into conservation efforts, as they do not occur in nature. In terms of conservation, Packer told *National Geographic*, "it's so far away from anything, it's kind of pointless to even say it's irrelevant." It was time for Joe to get back into politics.

Undeterred by the failure of his bid for the White House, Joe decided to run for governor of Oklahoma in 2018 on a platform that supported abortion, the LGBTQ community, and unfettered gun ownership. His campaign signs read "Joe F★★king Exotic" and he campaigned on the internet using the hashtag #FixThisShit. Again, part of his promotional package were condoms decorated with photos of him in a suggestive pose.

And Joe hired Josh Dial as his campaign manager again. He moved into one of the park's trailers. In June 2017 he and Josh, who was also gay, visited the OKC Pride parade in Joe's limo. Joe jumped on the car roof and waved to the crowd. They erupted.

"That was probably the only time I thought, 'Wow, this guy could actually do something,'" Josh said.

As one of three candidates for the Libertarian Party, Joe supported the blanket legalisation of marijuana. Profiling the candidates, *Tulsa World* described Joe as "the colourful entertainment director of the Greater Wynnewood Exotic Animal Park".

"His profanity-laced YouTube videos may be a turn-off to some but endear him to others as a straight shooter as he tries to reach voters with a message that will appeal to working people struggling to get by," the newspaper went on. "He is gay and has been married to Travis Maldonado for three years. He is pro-choice, supports LGBT rights and is against the reform of gun laws. His numerous appearances in the news probably give him a bit more name recognition than the other two Libertarian candidates."

Detailing his TV output during the campaign, the University of Tulsa's student newspaper *The Collegian* said: "One video, posted in August 2017, is labelled 'Joe Exposes PETA as Terrorist.' Another channel, *Joe Gone Wild TV*, includes such videos as 'Joe Exotic kicked out of Donald Trump Fundraiser 1' and 'PETA spy caught in the Zoo,' in which Joe and employees follow and berate a man they believe to have recorded video for PETA. 'Nat Geo screws Joe Exotic' and 'Monkey Love,' in which he records a monkey seemingly masturbating, are some included on a third channel. 'This is what happens when your in a cage and get borde [sic],' Joe writes in the description."

He reported raising $3,012. Most of the total was a $2,635 in kind donation from the G.W. Exotic Animal Park for the "purchase of T-shirts to be given away". This lagged somewhat behind the Republicans' candidate, Todd Lamb – the incumbent lieutenant governor, who had raised more than $2 million.

Meanwhile Joe was involved in a battle over nineteen tigers that had come from a troubled Florida zoo called Wild Things in Dade City. PETA wanted them sent to a 720-acre wildlife sanctuary in Colorado but Joe said the tigers legally belonged to him and that he had built new cages for them.

"The tigers are here to stay," he said. "They are comfortable and they are home."

Brittany Peet, deputy director of captive animal law enforcement for PETA, said the organisation was "gravely concerned about the safety" of the Florida tigers at the G.W. Exotic Animal Park.

"It has a long history of federal Animal Welfare Act violations which proves that it's unable or unwilling to meet animals' needs, and PETA will not stop working to relocate these complex big cats to a reputable sanctuary," Peet said.

The problem began when PETA filed a lawsuit against Wild Things, claiming that the zoo violated the federal Endangered Species Act by separating tiger cubs from their mothers for paid photo sessions with customers. It also allegedly allowed customers to swim in a pool with tiger cubs, charging $200 in exchange for half an hour.

Law enforcement officers accompanied PETA at the instruction of a federal judge after owner Kathy Stearns prevented the group from entering her facility for a court-mandated inspection.

Stearns and about twenty Wild Things supporters wearing shirts reading "PETA kills" were forced to move aside. They then followed PETA experts during the two-hour inspection, "making abusive remarks" and doing "everything they could, kind of physically getting in our way," said PETA legal counsel Jenni James. Stearns' husband, Kenneth, and son, Randy, were armed, "touching their holsters and posturing, following us every step of the way," James said.

The inspection team, which comprised an animal behaviourist, a videographer, a private investigator and two PETA lawyers, collected evidence from the enclosures and the nursery to show the living conditions of the animals.

"The lives those tigers lived in those enclosures were of deprivation and torture," James said. "Those enclosures denied the tigers everything they need, everything that would be natural for them. Many were concrete… virtually barren. None of the enclosures were large enough for tigers to get adequate exercise."

The tigers left Florida the same day a federal judge issued an injunction ordering the zoo not to remove any of the animals. They were transported from Florida to Oklahoma in a metal livestock trailer in the heat of a southern July. The 1,200-mile drive took two days. On the way, a female tiger gave birth to three cubs inside the trailer that were either stillborn or died shortly after being born.

Joe posted a video of the big cats' arrival on Facebook. It showed the animals being tranquilised and dragged out of the trailer by their feet and tails. The video included footage of the dead cubs found in the trailer. Joe blamed PETA for their deaths.

"I want to show you what [expletive] PETA is responsible for," Travis Maldonado said in the video. "Look at these dead babies."

Speaking from an enclosure while a staff member off camera threw dead chickens for the tiger to eat at his feet, Joe compared PETA to ISIS and said that the Florida tigers would be better off in his zoo.

"Who the hell is PETA to me?" he said. "They are domestic terrorists."

Joe railed about PETA's legal efforts to inspect private zoos.

"They are no government agency so why is our federal court system granting them permission to go in and inspect private zoos?" he said. "That would be like letting ISIS go in and inspect the Pentagon."

PETA paid big cat expert, Jay Pratte, to view the videos, who said in court papers that the Florida tigers were treated in a careless, dangerous manner. He testified that the videos show the tigers were transported in an uninsulated trailer with no climate control and with areas of it reaching more than 100°F. The cats had no water and arrived severely dehydrated.

The tiger cubs could have died after being smothered or crushed to death inside the cramped cattle trailer during the drive to Oklahoma. Stressed from the transport, it was also likely the mother tiger devoured at least some of the cubs, Pratte wrote in an affidavit.

Deborah Warrick, founder of the St. Augustine Wild Reserve in Florida, had also offered to take some of the tigers. She also provided an affidavit saying: "The nineteen in the larger cow trailer were foaming at the mouth, urinating on each other."

"All Joe did was receive them," said Joe. "Joe didn't load them or nothing."

The animals were visibly stressed and severely dehydrated when they arrived in Oklahoma, Pratte said. Acting on Joe's instructions, inexperienced zoo staff shot the tigers with sedatives without regard for proper dosage or sterilisation. They were shot through the slats of the trailer "completely from the hip", with no regard for the gender or weight of the animals. One worker shouted: "This is gonna be a drug party!" according to the court record.

Dragging the tranquilised animals out of the trailer by their feet and tails, put the cats "at a high risk of injury through muscle, ligament, tendon bruising strains or tears," Pratte said.

"The unloading process is literally being handled like a rodeo," he continued. "People with firearms manhandling large carnivores... The cacophonous sideshow is highly stressful to the animals."

Pratte said the stress of transportation, noise and heat, and the proximity of a male in the confinement of the trailer pushed the female tiger to give birth. The cubs may have died from the mother being too stressed to clear the amniotic sacs, from heat or dehydration, or by being crushed. "The tiger cubs died as a direct result of the inhumane transport decisions," Pratte insisted.

The alternative had been to send them to the Wild Animal Sanctuary in Colorado. The owner, Pat Craig, said his facility housed tigers in natural terrain with dens, lakes and climbing structures that allowed for species-typical behaviour. But Joe said he would "euthanise them before they go to Pat Craig".

After that remark, a federal court ordered G.W. Exotic Animal Park not to move the tigers. PETA asked that Joe and Jeff Lowe be held in contempt of court for interfering in a lawsuit concerning the tigers by removing them from the Florida zoo on the day an injunction was issued prohibiting the removal of the animals.

"PETA stands ready to help the scofflaws at G.W. Zoo cure their contempt of court by transferring these tigers to a reputable sanctuary where they'd be able to roam, explore, run, climb and live like the wild animals they are," said Delcianna Winders, now vice president for the PETA Foundation, in a statement.

PETA's legal counsel, Jenni James, said: "Right now those tigers are in as much danger as they've ever been, and this lawsuit was brought to protect those tigers."

Commenting on the story in the *Tampa Bay Times*, Carole Baskin said: "People are just dumbfounded about the stories the cats have and wonder how is this even legal in America."

Her Big Cat Rescue, she said, was a true sanctuary with eighty animals on sixty-seven acres. Her cats were never allowed to breed, they lived in stimulating environments and were fed a species-appropriate diet of raw meat. The smallest tiger enclosure measured 1,800 square feet, and the animals get rotated into a 2.5-acre "vacation area" of grass and climbing structures every two weeks.

"The only way we'll save the tiger in the wild is by ending the private possession of them because it creates that legal smokescreen to hide the illegal activity that's causing the tiger to go extinct in the wild," Baskin said. "With three thousand in the wild, we don't have time to screw around. We have to stop this now."

PETA said that the G.W. Exotic Animal Park should not keep the tigers because of its poor history of animal care. It released a statement condemning Joe's zoo for an incident in May where staff shot and killed a female tiger that was roaming free inside the park after escaping a cage. The zoo was closed at the time of the incident and there were no visitors inside the park.

"Ramshackle enclosures and dangerous wild animals could easily be a deadly combination," Brittany Peet said in a statement. "G.W. Zoo's history of showing a flagrant disregard for the safety of both big cats and employees is exactly why PETA urges everyone to stay away from roadside zoos like this one."

Garvin County Sheriff, Larry Rhodes, said although the animal did not escape the zoo's perimeter fence, he believed he should have been notified of the incident. The sheriff's department has no record of any calls about an escaped animal from the zoo and Rhodes was unaware of the incident.

"As sheriff, I am interested in knowing what these guidelines are in these type of situations," Rhodes said. "It has been years since I have received or been asked to approve any protocols."

The tiger had escaped from an exercise enclosure during the evening feeding at the zoo and was near the zoo's perimeter fence when it was shot, according to a USDA report on the incident. The report noted that the staff followed emergency protocols for the tiger escape and immediately notified the USDA of the incident.

Joe said zoo staff were forced to kill the tiger because it was getting dark and they didn't want to risk the animal escaping over the zoo's eight-foot perimeter fence.

"We have nothing to be ashamed of," he said. "It was 9.30 at night and we couldn't chase a tiger in the dark. Any zoo in America would have done the same."

Lowe's response was that he was not worried about PETA's latest legal manoeuvres.

"I'm not concerned with PETA, I'm not a dog or a cat," he said.

What did concern him was whether the zoo would ever make money. With the bad publicity surrounding the park, Walmart had stopped providing the free food ostensibly for the animals. Feeding the inmates – both human and animal – was now costing a fortune.

"There really isn't much left here besides cats for people to look at," he texted Joe. "The place just eats money."

The park's reputation was damaged further when the police arrested Safari Bar staff for dealing meth. Meanwhile

Lowe planned a potentially lucrative sideline – a "Jungle Bus" mobile cub-petting zoo in Las Vegas. This went wrong when, in November 2017, cops raided the Lowes' Las Vegas property and impounded a tiger, a liliger and a lemur, which vets said were ill. They cited Lowe for doing business and handling animals without a licence.

"Who cares?" Lowe said. "I got caught with exotic animals in a city that bans exotics. It's a municipal court ticket just like jaywalking."

Back in the political arena, the newly formed Libertarian Party had to decide who was eligible to vote in their primary – all independent voters or only the four thousand who had registered as Libertarians. Joe said that, by letting independents in the door, they might then decide to register, boosting party numbers.

"In order to grow this party, you're going to have to invite some people in and educate them in the standards and beliefs of the Libertarian Party," said Joe. "Fighting for one small, little group right now of 3,900 people, and just shutting the door on that idea, is not common sense for me at all."

The primary campaign kicked off at the Grove Community Center in northeast Oklahoma. Again Joe's platform included the legalisation of marijuana as well as a variety of issues concerning the state's finances. He said marijuana could bring in revenue for the state. Local authorities should be able to sell off confiscated weed and keep the proceeds. He also championed legislation that would protect Oklahomans' individual rights, such as keeping exotic animals.

# EIGHT: A Death in the Family

Around 12.30 p.m. on 6 October 2017, the police received a 911 call from the G.W. Exotic Animal Park saying that someone had shot themselves in the head in the office. The victim turned out to be Joe's husband, twenty-three-year-old Travis Maldonado. He had a fatal gunshot wound to the head and was declared dead at the scene. A .45-calibre handgun was recovered at the scene and security footage was being reviewed. When Joe heard the news, he was devastated.

It had been a clear, sunny day and Josh and Travis had been sitting in the office. Travis was toying with a .45 Ruger pistol that Joe had bought him. According to Josh, he said: "Hey, did you know a Ruger won't fire without a clip."

He racked its slide, put the barrel to his temple and pulled the trigger. The gun fired. The magazine was out, but a bullet had been left in the chamber. It went straight through Travis' brain and into the wall the other side of him. For a few seconds, Josh thought it was a prank.

"It looked like Hollywood shit, blood spurting out from everywhere," he said.

But it was all too real. Travis' head fell back, his Adam's apple bobbing up and down. Erik Cowie, a military veteran, was on hand. He took the gun from Travis' hand and wrapped a white shirt around his head to stem the bleeding. Travis died minutes later. Josh went into shock.

"I don't think I'll ever be the same person," he said.

Joe had been in Pauls Valley. When he returned, he howled. It was twenty years to the day since Garold's car accident.

The police conceded that employees routinely carried firearms during their park duties, but they did not know if Maldonado was licenced to carry the firearm either in an armed security capacity or as an open carry licence – or was authorised by the USDA. The park was open at the time, but visitors were not in the immediate vicinity.

The sheriff's office said: "While the cause of death is believed to be a fatal gunshot wound to the head, the manner of death remains to be determined."

Joe held a press conference at the zoo the following day. Standing in front of a backdrop covered in *Joe Exotic TV* logos, he wore a pink, button-down shirt like the one he wore on the day they were married. He said he was inconsolable and explained that the shooting was an accident, not suicide.

Weeping, Joe said: "The witnesses – the staff who were in the office when he shot himself – said that he thought that the gun wouldn't go off without the clip on it. He was so good with his guns, he got his guns every day. He made me smile every day of my life for four years. One careless mistake snuffed him out from the rest of us."

According to Joe, Maldonado had been joking around with the staff in the zoo's gift shop. He was showing off his Ruger pistol. In an effort to prove something he thought he had read on the internet, he believed that if he pulled the trigger it would not fire. He was wrong. Maldonado died before the first responders arrived.

Joe posted on Facebook that Travis' death was a "terrible accident". In the video, Joe was seen wearing the same hot pink shirt, blue jeans and he was carrying a sidearm. He also wore a knee brace and carried a cane as he walked to address an audience at the animal park.

"My husband accidently got shot and killed yesterday," he told them. "He would be so mad at me if I didn't do his show and teach you what you paid to come here and see. So I'm going to try real hard to do this."

Joe also complained that he was so broke from being "falsely sued" by animal rights activists that he asked the audience for donations towards his husband's funeral. He then told Oklahoma City TV station, KOCO 5 News, that his husband made a careless mistake that had ended his life.

Sheriff Rhodes said witnesses reported Maldonado put the loaded firearm to his head and pulled the trigger. Travis had known there was a bullet in the chamber, but believed the weapon would not fire with the magazine removed. He then squeezed the trigger, Rhodes said. At the time, Maldonado had a small amount of marijuana on him and had a pipe in his pants pocket. Joe was not present at the time.

Late one night, not long after Maldonado's death, John Finlay got a phone call from Joe. Finlay, the estranged third member of Joe's three-way union, had by now come back into Joe's orbit and was manager of the Safari Bar. He couldn't understand what Joe was saying, but he could hear that Joe was crying uncontrollably. Finlay drove over to Joe's house. He searched the living room, the kitchen, and two bedrooms but found no sign of Joe. Finlay finally discovered Joe sitting in the converted garage. He was sobbing, and he held a cell phone in one hand and a gun in the other. He'd blasted a hole in a television beside him.

Danny Maldonado only found out about his son's death from Facebook. Joe asked the family to stay away from the funeral and cremated Travis' body four days later, before Danny arrived in Oklahoma.

Joe then claimed that he was being discriminated against when the funeral home in Pauls Valley was denied an escort by the Garvin County Sheriff's Department to the G.W. Exotic Animal Park. Instead he appealed to local bikers on their Harley-Davidsons to escort the funeral procession.

Joe wore the faux pastor's outfit from his *Here Kitty Kitty* video, complete with hat and wraparound shades. He stood at a lectern, flanked by friends, family and former lovers.

"I met Travis when he was basically homeless and had a backpack on his back," said Joe, which was somewhat at odds with the truth. He exalted their relationship, ending: "If we can pull one thing off with this horrible tragedy, it is to continue to bypass the hate and the judgment that we cast upon each other no matter what we do."

Travis' father Danny was furious when he heard about this.

"He's not an ordained priest," he said. "He's such a fake. It's all BS – everything. It's all for publicity… the whole thing's a circus."

Joe gave the Maldonado family Travis' ashes in a container bought at Walmart. During his military service Danny had often seen ashes. They were grey. The ashes Joe gave him were white.

"I did not believe what he gave me was my son's remains," Danny said.

But Joe was adamant.

"Danny needs to let his son rest in peace," he said. Danny said he had his doubts that his son's death was accidental and aimed to have the ashes tested.

Travis' death did not deter Joe from politics. Three weeks later he was with the Libertarian Party's "Liberty Tour" when it arrived as the Claremore Community Center in Rogers County. By 2 November, candidates had raised more than $10 million. Republican candidate, Lieutenant Governor Lamb, had raised $2,720,112. Joe was up to $6,593 – but that was more than four times what the other Libertarian candidates had put together. They moved on to University of Central Oklahoma on 6 November. A staff writer from the *Antlers American* asked Joe how he hoped to win voters with his pro-gay, pro-choice and pro-gun stances. Was he on his way to become Oklahoma's first openly gay governor? At a Libertarian gubernatorial debate in Oklahoma City, Joe cussed and disparaged the ethnicity of audience members. "It was going off the rails," one observer said.

Travis' suicide didn't inhibit Joe's personal life either. Just two months later, on 11 December, he married Dillon Passage, and changed his surname to Maldonado-Passage, though he filed in the gubernatorial race as Joe Exotic. Travis' mother was a witness at the private ceremony on a mountain at Turner Falls. A public wedding would follow on 3 March 2018. The theme would be "A Love Story" and the colours would be sky blue and buckskin to represent Oklahoma and non-discrimination.

Twenty-two-year-old Dillon was from Austin, Texas, and had been sleeping on his cousin's airbed. According to Joe: "He just texted me out of the blue. It took me a day-and-a-half to talk him into dinner and he never left. He enjoys smoking weed, playing video games and interacting with the animals at the zoo. Basically, he's your typical twenty-two-year-old."

Joe said that Dillon "holds no jealousy" about the love he continued to have for his late husband Travis and would support him during his gubernatorial campaign. Joe said he believed that Travis had sent Dillon to the park to keep him from committing suicide. The two applied for a marriage licence in Pauls Valley fifty-nine days after Travis' death.

"I could not ask for a more amazing person to land in my life," Joe said.

On Norman's Christmas parade, Joe was seen waving from the top of a limousine. Addressing the crowd, he told voters: "If I want to open a savings account, I'll open a damn savings account when I'm sixty-five years old."

Soon after, Joe was injured in a traffic accident. He had been driving his pick-up down a country road when he failed to stop at a stop sign and was struck by on oncoming truck. The other driver was not hurt, but Joe suffered a broken shoulder blade, a fractured right femur and two fractured vertebrae in the crash. He was taken by ambulance to OU Medical Center. Dillon posted on Joe's personal Facebook page: "We appreciate all of your concerns and prayers. Joe is doing fine, he's pretty banged up but we will make it through this. Joe says thank you to everyone and that he is still very much alive."

Another GoFundMe page was set up to help with the medical bills.

In memory of his husband, Joe had created the Travis Maldonado Foundation whose aim, its website said, was to provide "no-cost resources for those struggling with meth addiction and gun safety education". Donations would go to the United States Zoological Association. When Joe was up and about again, the Foundation partnered with Discount Guns in Pauls Valley to host free gun safety classes. The first would be held in Zooters restaurant next to the G.W. Zoo. A certified firearms instructor would teach gun owners how to use their weapons properly.

Back on the campaign trail, the issue of the day that all the gubernatorial candidates had to speak out on was the fact that the teachers were on strike. Joe said: "I am all in favour of what the teachers are marching for. I have spent two days out there with them. It is not all about a raise; they want respect in the classroom from students and their parents, school supplies and a raise…"

Then Joe seized the opportunity to take a swing at high taxation. "… However, the gas tax, cigarette tax just took money right back out of their same pockets. Not to mention, schools pay that same gas tax driving buses. I spent one hour and thirty-one minutes on hold yesterday with the Oklahoma Tax Commission to see if any of the school bus tax on gas gets repaid and no one knew that answer… None of them make sense when all we have to do is hold departments accountable for the lost or misspent money. And a lot of this could have been solved by working our districts a bit better, by not having so many superintendents. Garvin [County] has eight getting paid over three-quarters of a million dollars for only 5,400 students. This could be fixed with smart business."

He said, as governor, he would not have signed the bill imposing additional tax on cigarettes and cigars, gasoline and diesel fuel, hotels and other businesses to give teachers a pay rise. He said that education must be rebuilt from the ground up.

"Schools are being used as babysitters by mothers on welfare and food stamps. They are not teaching their children how to graduate and be ready for college. We have go to start at the bottom and work our way back up," he insisted.

Asked what he thought of Donald Trump, he said: "He's not a bad man. If they would leave him alone, he might get something done."

Joe also said that the state would go broke from incarcerating nonviolent offenders. He had plans to give current drug offenders an opportunity to do a work programme instead of prison time. Decriminalisation of marijuana was on the top of his agenda.

"Prohibition didn't work for alcohol, and it is not working with marijuana," he said. Oklahoma should get into the market before it crashed when other states legalised weed.

At a gubernatorial forum, held at the Oklahoma Press Association's convention at the Citizen Potawatomi Nation's

Grand Casino Hotel and Resort in Shawnee, Joe handed out rolling paper with his name and picture on it.

"I'm your wild card," he told the audience. The rest of his answers were peppered with profanities.

"About the abortion thing – it is your body," he went on to say. Joe said he wanted to give a voice back to the people who make up this state – "if you own your own property and pay taxes on it the government should not have a right to tell you what you can do on that property." The Oklahoma City *Journal Record* said: "Speaking plainly and sometimes profanely, Joe Exotic enlivened the forum."

However, in the Libertarian Party primary, Joe came third behind the other two candidates, with just 19 per cent of the 3,549 votes. Explaining the result, one political commentator said: "His existence as an Oklahoman is more like a roadside attraction. Like, he's the world's largest peanut, or whatever. I think people kind of view him as that. He's the goofy part of Oklahoma. That's what he represents: how silly we can be sometimes."

With the campaign over, Josh Dial disappeared and went off the radar until 2017 when he was arrested for felony assault and battery with a Japanese katana samurai sword. He pled no contest to an amended misdemeanour of carrying an unlawful weapon. Later he attended a university in Oklahoma and a GoFundMe account was opened up to pay for his mental health care after his experiences with Joe Exotic and the zoo.

# NINE: Murder for Hire

On 5 September 2018, Joe was indicted by a federal grand jury on two counts of hiring a person to commit murder. Two days later he was arrested by US Marshals in Gulf Breeze, Florida. The charges were the result of an investigation by the U.S. Fish and Wildlife Service Office of Law Enforcement and the FBI.

The indictment accused Joseph Maldonado-Passage, aged fifty-five and formerly of Wynnewood, of hiring a person in November 2017 to murder "Jane Doe" in Florida. According to the indictment, Maldonado-Passage, who also went by the name "Joe Exotic", gave a person $3,000 to travel from Oklahoma to South Carolina, then to Florida to carry out the murder. Joe allegedly agreed to pay him thousands more after the deed was done. The indictment also alleged Joe had someone travel to Dallas to get fake identification for use in the plot and mailed the intended assassin's cell phone to Nevada to conceal his involvement. According to the indictment, the person travelled from Oklahoma to South Carolina on 26 November 2017.

The second count alleges that, beginning in July 2016, Joe Exotic repeatedly asked a different person to find a hitman to murder "Jane Doe" in exchange for money. The second person put Joe Exotic in contact with an undercover FBI agent who posed as a hitman. He met the undercover agent on 8 December

2017 to discuss details of the murder. The plan was discussed over the phone several times.

If found guilty, Joe would face imprisonment for ten years on each count. He would also be subject to up to three years of supervised released and a fine of up to $250,000 per count. He made his initial appearance before a judge in the Pensacola Division of the Northern District of Florida, followed by further proceedings in the Western District of Oklahoma.

Although Joe had often joked about killing Carole Baskin, in 2016 her pursuit of him over the $1 million damages had begun to agitate him. Around that time, a former Dallas strip club owner named James Garretson started spending time at the zoo. The rotund Garretson – who Joe referred to as "a giant Chucky Doll" – had decided he wanted to open an exotic animal-themed bed-and-breakfast along the lines of Wildlife on Easy Street in Ringling, Oklahoma, and he bought several tigers from Joe.

"Everyone knew him as the person to buy and sell animals," Garretson said. "He would breed anything he could get his hands on."

As he was from the sleazy underside of Dallas and perhaps because he was often accompanied by people with a lot of tattoos, Joe assumed that Garretson had underworld connections and asked him if he knew any hitmen. Indeed Garretson did have a criminal record. He had pleaded guilty to felonious assault some years earlier for pointing a firearm at his father-in-law during a domestic dispute with his then wife. He was given a deferred sentence of four years in prison, fifty hours of community service and a $2,500 fine.

Joe told Garretson that he wanted to have Carole Baskin killed and would pay $10,000 for the job. Garretson told Joe that he'd look around, but didn't follow through.

In February 2017, Joe took on a new employee at the zoo named Ashley Webster. She overheard Joe and Jeff Lowe talking about Carole Baskin. Joe then turned to Webster and asked if she would travel to Florida and put a bullet in Baskin's head for a few thousand dollars. Webster laughed it off, but she believed Joe was serious. Two weeks later, she quit her job, called Carole and left a voicemail warning her of Joe's threats.

"I just wanted to apologise to you because I have believed the bullshit that Joe Exotic has said," Webster told Baskin. "I am currently here at his place right now, and I'm leaving… He was actually talking about paying someone to kill you. He tried to get me to do it. I'm not going to fucking do that… He was offering, like, a couple of thousand dollars. I feel like your life is in danger."

Carole forwarded the voicemail to her attorney. He contacted Special Agent Matthew Bryant with the U.S. Fish and Wildlife Service which was already investigating Joe and the zoo for possible wildlife crimes. Murder for hire was not the sort of crime Bryant was usually involved with so, after listening to the voicemail, he contacted FBI agent Andrew Fairbow and federal prosecutors.

Garretson stopped by Joe's office in late August where Lowe pulled up Baskin's property in Tampa on Google Earth.

"He started showing me easy ways to kill her," Garretson said. Lowe pointed out bike paths Baskin used and the location of the gift shop at her sanctuary. He also had images of her house, which was isolated at the edge of an inlet. Jeff said simply "burn her shit to the ground".

Joe then came in with a thick manila folder which he said contained detailed information on Baskin. It was unclear to Garretson whether they were seriously considering murdering Baskin. Joe may have been, but Lowe was playing a double game.

Later that month, he suggested that Garretson call Baskin and ask her if she wanted to buy the zoo. If she bought it, he would give Garretson a $100,000 commission. To sweeten the deal, Lowe told Garretson he should let Baskin know that all of Joe's files and computers would be included in the sale. Clearly he was offering Joe up to Baskin on a silver platter.

Garretson did not hear back from Carole Baskin, but he did get a call from Matthew Bryant. They set up a meeting in September where Bryant asked Garretson to do some undercover work for him. By this time Garretson had turned against Joe, believing that he was mistreating the animals.

"He was doing some evil things down there with the animals," he later told the *Daily Beast*.

Bryant showed him how to use a wire and how to bug a telephone. The plan was for Garretson to put Joe in touch with a hitman who was actually an undercover FBI agent.

On 29 September 2017, Garretson was wearing a wire when he met Joe outside his office and turned the conversation to Carole Baskin.

"When is she ever gonna fucking stop?" Garretson asked.

"She won't until somebody shoots her," Joe replied. "Her day is coming, man."

But Joe was already a mess. After Travis Maldonado died, Joe began to lose his drive running the zoo. Clearly his deal with Lowe had not worked out. He was unsettled and would often walk through the zoo in the early morning, gazing up into the clouds in the forlorn hope of seeing Maldonado's face. He became disillusioned with the whole project. The rows of cages filled with pacing tigers were hardly what his brother Garold dreamt of.

"I have all these animals on display, suffering, so I can suck donations out of people," Joe said.

The zoo also had its problems. In October, they were expecting a shipment of big cats from a circus that was paying to have them boarded there over the off-season. But there was no room. One evening, Joe asked Erik Cowie, a long-time employee of the zoo, to lead newer members of staff away from the tiger cages. Joe then picked five aging tigers – Samson, Delilah, Lauren, Trinity and Cuddles – and shot them in the head, one after another.

"Jesus," he said, "if I knew it was this easy, I'd just blast them all."

He later told KOCO 5 News: "I put five tigers to sleep because they were in pain. They had toenails coming out of their ankles. They had no teeth. They had exposed root canals."

But according to Cowie, the animals were perfectly fit and healthy. "I treat every one of them like they're my kids," he had said in an online promotional video for the zoo.

One of the new employees was maintenance man, Allen Glover, who had been hired by Lowe. A sixth grade dropout with a long record of felony convictions starting from age seventeen, he had had a teardrop tattooed under his eye while serving time in Louisiana. In prison this has several meanings, one of which was that the wearer had killed someone. It gave Joe an idea.

According to Glover, he had just finished work one night at eleven and was on his way back to his trailer when he bumped into Joe on the front porch of the gift shop. Joe asked Glover to kill Baskin, offering him $5,000 up front for the job. Glover agreed. Joe suggested he shoot her with a crossbow or a sniper's rifle while she was taking a walk along one of the trails around her home. Joe said he'd get Glover some hunting camouflage. Glover then suggested cutting Baskin's head off with a knife. Joe liked the idea, Glover said.

Garretson got wind of this and called Lowe, who said: "He's serious, but I don't think he's capable without fucking it up.

He's reckless. He's careless... This whole fucking crew is like a clown assassin."

He also called Joe, who was confident.

"As long as we don't get caught red-handed, we got this," Joe said. "But if they bust him red-handed, me and Jeff got our story down to where we fired him and he just went off the deep end."

One day in mid-November, Joe handed Glover an envelope. It contained $3,000, not the $5,000 they had agreed. Glover did not complain. He was leaving the zoo anyway and accepted it as severance pay. He hated Joe, who he described as "an asshole".

"Treat his employees like dirt," Glover said. "He would downgrade me to the point where it was coming close to blows, that's how bad it got... he's just – he's really a cruel, cruel person."

Filmmaker Eric Goode concurred: "Joe committed some really serious crimes and Joe was not only cruel and inhumane to his animals, he was cruel to the people around him," he said.

"You bet I was cruel," Joe said. "I am an asshole to work for. Peoples' lives depend on me making them follow rules. They let out the chimps, tigers, leopards, wolves – you name it – and guess who's ass was always in trouble when they did... Who the hell do you think is paid to do a job? The staff. Why was I written up? Because the staff won't do their job. But I am supposed to be nice? Go fuck yourself."

As far as Garretson knew, the plan was for Glover to take a bus to Tampa on 25 November. Bryant and the feds were going to stake out the bus stations. Once Glover was on board, they were going to arrest him and Joe. But Glover had hurt this back. There was no way he was going to take a long journey across country on a bus. Instead he went to Will Rogers Airport in Oklahoma City and took a plane to Savannah, then crossed the border into South Carolina.

Now they had lost Glover, Bryant and Fairbow called Carole Baskin to warned her. Told that she was in imminent danger, Carole took precautions. She had security cameras installed around her property and blinds put up in her house so that a sniper could not see her inside. She stopped riding her bike to work and avoided the mailbox in case it was rigged with explosives.

She also began carrying a gun, keeping it beside her bed at night. One night, she was terrified when she heard the screen on her back porch rattling. It turned out to be the neighbour's dog.

In the street she watched out for vans, in case someone tried to kidnap her. If someone had parked next to her when she came out of the grocery store, she would go back inside until the other car drove off. This was difficult because people knew Carole in Tampa and often strangers stopped her in the street or supermarket. One time she was filling up at a gas station when a man approached her. Recalling the incident, she remembers that she had wondered: "Do I need to grab the gas and spray this guy?"

Weeks went by. All the time Baskin was entirely safe as Glover had no intention of killing her. He just wanted to rip Joe off. He never even made it to Tampa. Once in South Carolina, he figured that he ought to warn Carole that Joe was deadly serious about having her killed, so he hired a car and drove down to Florida. But along the way he stopped off and blew the money on a beach party. Then he drove back to South Carolina without contacting Carole Baskin. Glover said when Joe found out he hadn't carried out the job, he called him, yelling and screaming, and demanding his money back.

With Glover off the radar, Garretson introduced Joe to the fake hitman who used the name "Mark Williams". He came to the zoo on 8 December. Joe offered him $5,000 upfront and another $5,000 when the job was done. But he said he could not raise the money straight away. It was low season and three days later he was getting married to Dillon Passage. Over the next few months, Garretson had several more conversations with Joe all of which he recorded, but still no money was forthcoming.

Lowe had been away in Las Vegas. When he returned, he and Joe had another row. Their relationship was now at an all-time low. The park's finances were in tatters, but Joe had still siphoned park funds for his gubernatorial race, forging cheques and spending cash on gifts for Dillon, including a Ford Mustang. Lowe also said Joe was using the money he had embezzled from both the zoo and his parents to pay male prostitutes he contacted on Craigslist.

Lowe said there were several times he would get up early and find a young man wandering around the parking lot after Joe had just kicked him out of his house after having sex. On one occasion Lowe said one of them told him: "I'm not leaving until I get my money, Joe promised me $400." Lowe later produced emails that showed that Joe was spending money on prostitutes regularly.

"Joe was embezzling money from the zoo in order to pay all of these men to come have sex with him. He was only making $150 a week at the time. He was using the zoo as his own personal piggy bank," Lowe said.

Lowe and Joe exchanged bitter text messages. Then there was a shouting match in the park's office.

"You commit more crimes than any of us combined, but you never get in trouble because you pass the buck on to someone else," Lowe told Joe, adding that Dillon was a "cheerleading faggot".

"He's not even a man like you. He's a sissy boy," Lowe said.

In an effort to get his own back, Joe opened a dialogue with Brittany Peet from PETA, hoping to bring down Lowe and others. Joe told her Travis' death had changed his perspective.

"He felt he was wasting his life," Peet said. "He also felt that a lot of the people in the exotic animal business that he had defended over the years had thrown him under the bus."

Joe had stopped talking to Garretson too, believing that he and Lowe were spiking his medication and putting perfume on his boots so that the lions would attack him. Then he heard that there has been some sort of altercation between Lowe and Dillon in the parking lot. For Joe, this was the last straw.

Lowe then wrote Joe out of the park's ownership. He renamed the zoo the "Greater Wynnewood Exotic Animal Park", keeping the "G.W. Exotic Park" signs along I-35. Joe now wanted out. He had spoken about fleeing to Belize with several people at the zoo. That June he sold some tiger cubs, then packed a camel and some dogs in a trailer. With Dillon, he drove seventy miles to Yukon, Oklahoma, where he paid $2,000 to rent a six-acre property. After Joe left the park, Lowe let the employees trash Joe's bungalow.

"They hated him, they wanted to celebrate him never coming back," Lowe said.

In Yukon Joe did not have the carnival of the zoo to protect him. He was a misfit – a gay cowboy in the buckle of the Bible Belt. He and Dillon rarely left home. The couple texted love notes from different rooms so they would never be apart. Locals shunned them. They didn't chat across the fence.

"The other neighbours were upset there was a camel," one resident said.

Threats from Lowe continued.

"Fuck with me and I will bulldoze your house off the property," he texted Dillon.

Over the summer, Joe sold most of his guns, except for his AR-15 assault rifle. That one "is for Carole," he said. He also made fake Instagram posts, making it appear that he was in Mexico or Belize.

He planned to find a job, but potential employers recognised him immediately. Everyone wanted to take selfies with Joe Exotic, but nobody wanted to employ him. The move to Yukon was not working out as Joe had intended. Dillon said he fancied living near a beach, so one night in August they upped sticks again and moved to Florida. Joe posted a photo to Instagram with the hashtag #Belize. They were actually in Gulf Breeze, Florida, where Joe washed dishes at a pirate-themed restaurant.

By then, the feds were looking for him. They contacted his niece, Chealsi Putnam. She said that Joe started out as a "good guy and genuinely cared for the animals", but towards the end he only saw them as a money-making tool and she claimed he had become abusive toward them. According to Chealsi, he froze dead tiger cubs in order to sell them to taxidermists and had videos of people performing sex acts with animals at the zoo.

A former park security employee told Lowe that Joe and John Finlay would dress up in lingerie and in the middle of the night bring goats, sheep or llamas to their house and have sex with them.

"You would hear horrible things coming from inside that house," Lowe said the employee had told him.

After Joe left, Lowe said he found boxes of dildos, leather whips, chains and bondage devices. There were hooks in the ceiling where Joe would affix a chair and film men having sex while swinging. In filing cabinets, Lowe said he found "penis pumps in several different sizes, condoms, lube you name it". There were also stuffed animals that were used as sex toys.

He also found pictures and videos of Finlay having sex acts performed on him by other men. Finlay appeared bored in the videos, fixing a motorcycle helmet in his hands, smoking a cigarette and flipping through magazines, while Joe called out to him: "What do you think, John? You don't like it today?"

"Joe is one creepy guy," Lowe said.

Chealsi said that Joe was an evil, conniving person who tried to take advantage of anyone who crossed his path. She had worked on and off at the zoo, cleaning the animal cages, running the cash register and bookkeeping, from 1999 to 2017.

"Our relationship was up and down, mainly because I wouldn't put up with his bullshit," she said: "I've personally witnessed Joe spray a tiger with a fire extinguisher, not out of a safety or for a life-saving reason, but because the tiger didn't react the way Joe had wanted it to."

Joe sold countless baby tigers illegally, according to Chealsi.

"He would either take cash under the table for the sale of the tiger, or if someone sent a cheque, it would be made out to another person or if the money was wired to a store, it would be in another person's name," she said. "Joe always attempted to distance himself from any illegal activity, but he had no problem involving his employees in it."

She said that when a tiger cub died, Joe would freeze it. He said he was involved in research with Texas A&M University, but Chealsi said he sold them to private individuals to get stuffed.

"Over the years there must have been at least ten tiger cubs that he froze," she said. "I have no idea what happened to them, they would just disappear." However, once she recalls that he asked her to take a dead tiger cub up to a taxidermist in Oklahoma City to get it stuffed. She refused. Joe also sold baby monkeys.

"A few years ago, at the zoo we had a monkey who just had a baby, Joe wanted to take the baby monkey away from its mother so he could sell it," she told the *Daily Mail*. "The mother monkey naturally wouldn't let Joe take the baby away from her, so he decided to 'dart' the mother monkey. He was going to shoot a tranquiliser dart into the mother monkey so he could take the newborn baby away from her. Joe shot one dart into the monkey, but after a few minutes the tranquiliser hadn't worked, so he shot another dart into the mother, and another.

"He shot a total of five darts into the mother until she dozed off so he could pry the baby monkey away from its arms. I was disgusted by his actions, he's lucky the mother monkey didn't die."

Everything about Joe's operation was about turning a buck. Expired meat donated by local stores to feed the animals was used in his pizza restaurant. Some of the pet food donated by the local Dollar General store was fed to his circus bear. The rest, he sold on to other people for profit.

"There wasn't much Joe wouldn't do for a dollar," Chealsi said. Although she had not seen them, she said that she had heard about the videos of people performing sex acts on some of the animals at the zoo.

"I didn't want to see them, I just heard about them," she said.

She also said that Joe liked to film his partners having sex with other men, sometimes participating himself. And he had "piercing parties" at the zoo, where employees would come and get drunk and then get piercings. Joe often bragged about having his own Prince Albert piercing the size of a padlock.

Chealsi also told the newspaper about her cousin – Joe's son, Brandon.

"Joe was in and out of Brandon's life when he was growing up. At one point, just a few years ago, Brandon and his then wife both worked at the zoo with Joe," Putnam said. "Joe would go around telling everyone this was his son, he made no secret about it."

She claimed things soured between the father and son when Joe allegedly wanted Brandon's wife to do some fraudulent activities with the zoo's books and chequing account. This caused an argument between Joe and Brandon. Eventually, Brandon, who then had three kids of his own, packed up with his family and returned to Texas.

Chealsi said she had seen Joe repeatedly conning her grandparents, who had raised her.

"My grandparents were Joe's personal slush fund," she said, explaining that Joe's parents had a lot of money on Shirley's side of the family, from owning land in Kansas and leasing out farm equipment. She said her grandmother would receive monthly rental cheques and the only time Joe would stop by their house was to pick up the cheques.

"He would deposit some of the checks in their bank accounts and the others he would tell his parents that he cashed and would pay them back later, which he never did," she said.

He never visited his father, who suffers from dementia and long-term PTSD, in a local VA hospital. While he was in prison, he never once called or wrote to his mother.

"I don't think he ever really cared for them, he saw them as pawns in his game," Chealsi said. "Most of the bills, policies and loans for the zoo where in his parents' name."

Like almost everyone in his life, Joe eventually fell out with Lowe. The initial dispute was over some missing money, but that was not the whole of the story, according to Chealsi.

"Joe had been planning on leaving the zoo for some time, unbeknownst to almost everyone," Chealsi said. "He started to sell everything he could get his hands on in early May 2018. He knew the feds were onto him and he wanted to get out. He told my grandmother on more than one occasion that he was being set up and some people were out to get him and frame him. So, in the middle of the night, Joe and Dillon packed up the rest of their belongings and moved to … At the time the only people who knew Joe's whereabouts were his parents, Shirley and Francie."

When Joe left Yukon, Oklahoma in July 2018, Shirley thought he had fled to Texas or Alabama, but no one knew exactly where Joe was hiding out. In September, the FBI contacted Chealsi to ask for her help in locating Joe. They had a warrant for his arrest. She knew her grandmother was still in contact with Joe because he would call her on her house phone from Dillon's number.

One day, her grandmother's cell phone rang. Chealsi said she didn't even know that her grandmother had a cell phone. She discovered that Joe had bought his mother a burner phone that no one knew about so he could communicate with her. A few days later Chealsi managed to get her hands on her grandmother's cell phone and retrieved Joe's number, which she gave to the FBI.

On 5 September, Joe called his mother from his cell phone. Again, Chealsi happened to be with her. She snuck away and called the FBI to tell them that Joe was talking to his mother at that very moment. The FBI was then able to ping Joe's cell number and find his exact location. Two days later Joe was arrested in Florida.

It was the sunny morning of 7 September 2018, eighty-one days after Joe had left the zoo. He had left their rented apartment to drive to a local hospital to apply for a third job. He always fancied himself as a doctor, if not a vet. It was a warm day, but there was still dew on the grass when he parked near the hospital and stepped down from his blue Ford F-150, résumé in hand. Suddenly, four unmarked cars skidded to a stop around him. Before he could react he was surrounded by plain-clothes law enforcement officers. They pointed their handguns at him and shouted: "Get on the ground! Get on the ground!"

He dropped and felt a knee in his back. They frisked him, cuffed him and took him to the federal courthouse for an arraignment hearing. He was accused of attempting to hire two hitmen to kill Carole Baskin. Joe was then held in Santa Rosa County jail without bond.

# TEN: A Big Sigh of Relief

When her attorney told her that Joe Exotic was in custody, Carole Baskin said she breathed "a big sigh of relief".

"Every day is a gift, but this one feels like a new lease on life," she said. "He's been threatening me for many, many years. So, there's no doubt in anybody's mind who knows him he intended to kill me."

She confirmed that she was the "Jane Doe" mentioned in the indictment. The crusade continued.

"I think it's important for people to know that he's not just one crazy, bad apple," Baskin said. "This is an industry that is rife with this kind of personality. The type of people who would rip cubs away from their moms and then use them as pay-to-play props. Those people don't have any kind of sense, feeling or compassion for animals or for people."

Howard Baskin said that they had previously been notified of the federal investigation and had taken "precautions". Carole said on Facebook Live: "Because Big Cat Rescue has been a leader in working to stop what we view as abuse of big cats and we have been very effective in our work, I have received multiple death threats over the years, including, at one point, a number of snakes placed in my mailbox." She told the *Tampa Bay Times* that someone had mailed her cornstarch during the anthrax scare of 2001 and her mailbox had been stuffed with spiders as well as snakes.

"I quit opening the mail box," Carole said. "They now bring it to the front door."

She admitted that Joe was not the only one who had been targeting her.

"A number of people in that industry of breeding the tigers and using the cubs have been threatening me for years, since the nineties," said Carole. "It's just the first time any one of them has gotten caught."

Clearly Joe was the prime suspect in this case.

"He's been saying, openly for years, that he wanted me dead," she said. "There have been a number of people who have come to us over the years saying that he tried to hire them to kill me. We, of course, always try to get them to talk to law enforcement."

Naturally, she used the publicity surrounding his arrest to continue her onslaught on Joe. It wasn't just about the $1 million lawsuit.

"I think that's part of it, but I think the bigger issue is that we are the most outspoken sanctuary against the abuse of tigers and their cubs being used as pay-to-play props and he was, in our opinion, one of the worst perpetrators of that industry," Carole said. "So as we became more effective in raising awareness about all of the cruelty involved in that, that's inherent, I think he retaliated by trying to bully me into being quiet."

Big Cat Rescue posted: "Maldonado-Passage had made threats online over a period of years including a video of him shooting in the head a blow-up doll dressed to look like Carole and an image hanging her in effigy."

Joe was in the county jail, but for Carole the war was not over. Big Cat Rescue was then home to sixty cats, but a decade earlier there had been double that number. She wished there were none.

"That is my goal. My goal is to never have to rescue another cat," she said. "To have every single one of these cages empty so that we can plough them under because we have better laws so that these animals don't end up abused their whole lives before being rescued by a sanctuary like us."

News reports were rather dismissive of Joe, calling him a "minor internet celebrity... known for his blond mullet and expletive-laden rants on YouTube". The digital media carrying the story signed off footage with: "WARNING: The following video contains explicit language."

It seemed he had no friends. On the G.W. Zoo's Facebook page that day, a post read: "THIS IS A WONDERFUL DAY FOR THE ZOO!! The animals are rejoicing and so are the owners and the staff!!! Thank you to the feds for taking down Joe Exotic!! IT WAS TIME!!"

By then, Jeff Lowe was no longer part of the operation. In an email filed on 23 August as part of the ongoing litigation, he said he was ending his involvement with the park.

"Joe's animals will remain on the park site until the federal authorities have him incarcerated, then whomever is in control of the zoo... will inherit the animals that I identify as his, upon his conviction," Lowe wrote. "When I threw Joe off my park a couple months ago, he took everything that wasn't nailed down."

Talking to the TV news, he said: "The feds have asked us not to say much." But he did say that he had been in contact with the authorities since October 2017, adding that he was not one of the "individuals" mentioned in the indictment.

His wife Lauren told another news channel: "We did contact authorities, not your local police. We actually contacted the feds."

The Park released a statement saying: "The Greater Wynnewood Exotic Animal Park would first like to thank the

Federal agents involved in this investigation. Because of them, our animals woke up today in a safer place. This has been an exhaustive process for all involved, but we could not be more pleased with the outcome. Now everyone's focus can go back to providing our animals with the love and care they deserve.

"Never again will this narcissistic man negatively impact this zoo or its inhabitants. We hope his incarceration begins a healing process in this industry. We may have philosophical differences with Joe's alleged victim, but we hope our assistance in his arrest provides the Baskin family some level of comfort and hope for the future. We wish we could tell you that this ends the fiasco that was 'Joe Exotic'. Unfortunately, this is the tip of a very large iceberg. The important thing to know, is the animals here are finally safe and back in the loving care and supervision of the park owners."

On 26 September Jeff Lowe announced that the Greater Wynnewood Exotic Animal Park would be closed, so he could open another zoo sixty miles away near the WinStar Casino at Thackerville. Joe's former home would be demolished.

"We think it's best to let this zoo die with Joe's conviction and not make the next generation of animals live here and forever suffer as a result of his outrageous behaviour and reputation," he posted on Facebook. "There is SO MUCH MORE to be revealed about Joe and his crimes against animals and we don't want to be associated with him any longer."

All of the animals would be transferred to the new zoo which would expand its range of animals to include elephants, rhinoceroses and giraffes.

"The new property is amazing, and so much of it is already in place that we could realistically be open by spring or sooner if the weather cooperates," he said. "Trust me, this new zoo will be much nicer than this zoo, and it will be in a geographical location that can support an operation like this without relying so much on cub breeding."

Clearly he was pretty confident that Joe would be convicted, though he had yet to stand trial. The following day, Joe appeared in federal court wearing jail-issued orange scrubs, socks and sandals, with shackles on his ankles. He was represented by court-appointed attorney, Bill Earley.

Joe pleaded not guilty, putting the blame squarely on Jeff Lowe. He claimed he had been framed in the first instance and was not serious in the second. He had never had any intention of trying to kill Carole Baskin and he was just "playing along". While Joe admitted to making the threats on social media against Baskin, Earley suggested they were scripted remarks designed to attract online viewers and possibly visitors to the zoo.

"He's a showman," said Earley. "There's nothing more to it than that."

US Magistrate Judge Bernard Jones disagreed the videos were "just skits", saying that, "the words were on the verge of becoming reality". He ruled that there were no conditions that would reasonably assure the safety of the community if the defendant were released.

"If I don't get bond, I'm going to go live with Travis," Joe told a friend.

During the detention hearing, Lisa Sparks, who had met Joe during his gubernatorial campaign, said he could live with her while awaiting trial. Earley argued that it would be unfair to keep Joe locked up until trial given the real possibility of an acquittal.

A prosecutor countered that the case was not a "he said, she said" deal.

"There are recordings of Mr. Maldonado talking about murdering Miss Baskin," Assistant US Attorney Amanda Green said. "That's powerful evidence."

The judge also expressed his concerns about Joe's mental state. Bail was denied as there were fears that he might commit suicide if released. Joe would remain in custody until his trial, then set for November.

The trial was delayed because, on 7 November, Joe faced fresh charges. A federal grand jury accused him of killing five tigers in October 2017, and selling and offering to sell animals in violation of the Endangered Species Act.

According to a new indictment, Joe was expecting the "arrival of certain big cats that were to be boarded for a fee at the exotic animal park" in or around October 2017, and needed to empty cages to house them. The indictment said Joe "knowingly and unlawfully took the lives of the following endangered species of wildlife, by shooting and killing them" to make room for the animals and listed five counts – one for each tiger – thus violating the Endangered Species Act.

The prosecution alleged: "In October 2017, defendant killed five healthy adult tigers because they were not breeding, because his exotic animal park was at capacity for large predators and because he anticipated the arrival of other big cats that would be a source of income in boarding fees."

Another count under the same violation said Joe also "knowingly and unlawfully offered for sale in interstate commerce endangered species of wildlife, namely two tiger cubs" in or on 30 October 2017. Three other counts alleged that he did the same with a male tiger cub sent to Brown Zoo, Illinois in 2016, an eight-week-old tiger female sent to Indiana in 2018 and a six-week-old tiger female, also in 2018.

The indictment listed nine more counts that alleged he violated the Lacey Act's clause on the "False Labelling of Wildlife", saying he "knowingly made and submitted and caused to be made and submitted a false record, account and label for, and a false identification of the following wildlife with a market value great than $350, that was transported and that was intended to be transported in interstate commerce".

Further he "specifically designated and caused to be designated on delivery forms and Certificates of Veterinary Inspection (CVI) that the wildlife was being donated to the recipient or transported for exhibition only, when he knew the wildlife was being sold interstate commerce". This concerned the transportation of twelve different tigers and lions to zoos in Illinois, California, Indiana, Wisconsin and Missouri, and was a violation of federal law.

The last count alleged Joe violated the same Act with a ten-week-old lemur and created a delivery form showing that he was donating the lemur to Ringling Animal Care in Ringling, Oklahoma, when he knew the lemur had been sold and transported in interstate commerce. There were nineteen counts in all. If convicted of a violation of the Endangered Species Act, he could be sentenced on each count to one year in prison, a fine of $100,000, and one year of supervised release. Each Lacey Act violation could carry a prison term of five years, a fine of $250,000, and three years of supervised release.

What's more, the wildlife charges were related to the other felonies. The prosecution alleged that Joe planned to sell big cat cubs in order to pay for the murder. According to court documents, a witness reportedly admitted to picking up a big cat cub and putting it in a vehicle, and saw "the driver of the vehicle give an envelope of cash to Mr. Maldonado-Passage to pay for the cub". The next day, the witness said Joe gave him the same envelope. The cash inside was to pay for the murder.

"The government does not allege that the sale of the big cat described in paragraph 22 and in Individual 1's testimony is one of the sales of the tigers and lions charged against Mr. Maldonado-Passage in counts eight to twenty," the court document stated.

"Indeed, the government currently has no evidence that this sale was illegal. However, this sale is fully consistent with Mr. Maldonado-Passage's business model of breeding and selling big cat cubs and thereby deriving a significant source of his income in cash. The cash from this particular transaction gave him the ability to fund the hit on C.B."

The prosecution said they also had recordings of Joe negotiating the hiring of a hitman who was, in fact, an undercover FBI agent.

"What's somethin' like that run?" the defendant asked.

"Mmm, usually about ten," the agent responded.

"Really?" said the defendant.

"Yep," the agent said.

The discussion then turned to a down payment.

"Hey man, if you're serious about it, you let me know," the agent said.

"We'll get game with the money," the defendant answered.

"So, I'd need… What do you think you could get up front?" the agent asked.

"Oh, we can get five easy."

"You can get five?"

"Yeah."

"That's perfect, man. That'd be perfect," the agent said.

The agent instructed Joe to get the first payment together along with two cell phones, and told him "that's the last time we're gonna meet until after". The agent also told Joe to take his time getting the other half of the money together.

"I'll just sell a bunch of tigers," Joe said.

The prosecution also alleged that, a month before the meeting, Joe had paid $3,000 to a zoo worker to kill Carole Baskin.

"The reason the defendant delayed using the second hitman is that he was waiting for the first hitman to perform the act he was hired to do," prosecution said. The prosecutors also believed that Joe had sold another big cat cub for cash to make the $3,000 payment to the first hitman.

Joe now faced the whole panoply of law enforcement. The wildlife charges were brought by Robert J. Troester of the US Attorney's Office for the Western District of Oklahoma. He said: "The investigation of murder for hire and wildlife allegations has required close coordination among law enforcement. We will work hard to protect people as well as wildlife and deter these sorts of crimes."

Acting Assistant Director of Law Enforcement for the U.S. Fish and Wildlife Service Edward Grace added: "The U.S. Fish and Wildlife Service is committed to combating illegal wildlife trafficking and protecting our wildlife resources for the benefit of future generations. We thank our partners at the FBI, U.S. Marshals Service, Oklahoma Department of Wildlife Conservation and the Department of Justice for their help in this case. Together we will continue to investigate and prosecute those who engage in unlawful wildlife trafficking for monetary gain."

While Oklahoma City FBI Special Agent-in-Charge Kathryn Peterson said: "The FBI appreciates our law enforcement partners and the combined efforts which thwarted this murder for hire plot and uncovered these serious wildlife crimes."

The trial was rescheduled for 8 January in federal court in Oklahoma City.

PETA were delighted at the new charges. Brittany Peet said: "This indictment demonstrates respect for every animal who suffered and died at the hands of this shameless, feckless profiteer and serves as a warning to animal exhibitors that no one is above the law. PETA is actively working to ensure that the gavel hits the table for every other 'Joe Exotic' who still treats animals as expendable, disposable commodities."

On 21 December the defence filed a petition to postpone the trial again to give them more time to prepare. It was put back to 12 March 2019. It then had to be moved to a bigger courtroom because of the number of journalists who have come from across the country to cover the case. They included writers for *New York* magazine and *Texas Monthly*, and producers for *Dateline*, the long-running NBC news magazine programme.

"Rumoured to be present was a representative of Netflix, the online TV network whose original programming includes a number of true crime shows," said *The Oklahoman*. "Oklahoma City TV reporters did regular live shots from outside the Oklahoma City federal courthouse. Sketch artists created detailed drawings of the scene inside the courtroom. A documentary crew conducted an interview while jurors deliberated."

However, Joe's day in court did not make the Netflix documentary.

# ELEVEN: Joe's Day in Court

On the first day of the trial, Joe arrived at the federal courthouse in downtown Oklahoma City wearing a grey suit with a tie and dress shoes. This was a shock to those who had never seen him without a flashy button-down shirt and a baseball cap or a fringed jacket. But true to his campaign pledges he still had his blond mullet.

After the jury was selected the charges were read to him. He stood accused of attempted murder for hire and of violating federal regulations that protected exotic animals. Opening statements began on 25 March. The judge ruled that the jurors would be allowed to hear testimony about the zoo's financial troubles, over defence objections.

"Evidence regarding the lack of money to purchase food for animals is relevant to the jury understanding that Ms. Baskin's $1 million judgment against Mr. Maldonado placed significant financial pressure on the zoo," prosecutors told US District Judge Scott L. Palk. "Accordingly, this evidence is relevant to establishing Mr. Maldonado's state of mind toward Ms. Baskin – including the motive and intent to have her murdered."

However, prosecutors said they would not put into evidence allegations that the defendant embezzled zoo money to finance his campaigns for president and governor. In 2018, Jeff Lowe told the U.S. Fish and Wildlife Service that he discovered that Joe had been forging his name on cheques and using zoo income to finance the gubernatorial campaign, according to an affidavit.

The defence said that Joe had already been planning to leave the zoo he founded when new owner Jeff Lowe and his "hapless crony", Allen Glover, tried to set him up. "A lot of people don't know the truth, he was ready to go and he had started unloading his inventory," assistant federal public defender Bill Earley said in his opening statement. He had even "cozied up" to his long-time nemesis PETA as part of his strategy.

The defence attorneys also stated that Lowe tried to sell the zoo to Carole Baskin for $500,000 in 2017 to get her to back off and drop the damages case. When Carole didn't respond, they said Lowe then decided to get rid of Joe by setting him up in hope she would drop her case once he was arrested. Earley told jurors that Joe had become suspicious of Lowe and Glover, but played along with them to see what they were up to. The defence maintained the meeting with the undercover FBI agent where Joe talked about killing Baskin on 8 December 2017 was another example of the defendant "running his mouth" – something he had been well known for doing for years.

"No one took him seriously," said Earley.

He also impugned the wildlife counts against Joe, saying they were the federal government's attempt to assist "big money" animal rights groups close down small businesses that engaged in activities they didn't like. Joe infuriated such groups because his zoo allowed visitors to pet tiger cubs.

The first witness to testify was staff member, Erik Cowie. He told the jury about the night he had seen Joe select five tigers to kill in order to free up cage space for three circus animals. He told the court that Joe selected tigers that were not breeding and therefore of no economic value to him. One pair – Samson and Delilah – he described as healthy.

He talked about his particular affection for another of the five, the tiger named Cuddles, who he called "a clown". He spoke movingly about how he had watched as a new tiger was put into Cuddles' empty cage. Prosecutors then showed the court photographs of tiger carcasses that federal agents dug up at the back of the zoo. One Fish and Wildlife Service agent testified that they were stuffed in their graves like "hot dogs in a pack". This had a powerful effect on the jury and was a devastating beginning to Joe's trial.

Afterwards Cowie told reporters: "I knew what was going on. I'm not stupid. I knew cats were getting shot … Cage space. We needed three cages. He wiped out five cats. He came up [with] a 4-10 [shotgun] in his hand and … he just shot Cuddles. I heard it, and he comes up the hill and goes, 'Erik, if I knew it was going to be this easy to just walk right up the cage, I was just going to kill them all.'"

The defence noted Cowie was not a trained veterinarian, so could not know whether the tigers were healthy, and asked why he had not come forward sooner if the accusations were true.

Circus owner, Trey Key, testified he donated $5,000 to the zoo in October 2017 to board two tigers and a lion for the winter. He said: "Joe cares a great deal about animals" but had succeeded in aggravating trolls on social media rather than ignoring them.

Carole Baskin was in court. She sat in the back row. Still fearing for her life, she had federal agents escort her between her hotel and the courthouse. She testified as the prosecutors showed dozens of Joe's videoed threats. First there was the one where Joe shot the blow-up "Carole" doll, after asking his audience why Carole had better hope they never met face to face again.

In another video from February 2014 he held up a rattlesnake and talked of sending two to Carole Baskin for her forthcoming birthday. In a May 2014 video, he was shown pretending to dig a grave at the zoo and saying, "We're getting ready to bury Carole." The following year, he said: "When it's my time, she's going to die first." Then in a 2018 video, he said he was out to ruin her life.

Maintaining her composure on the stand, Carole pointed out that what the court had been shown was just a "very, very small sampling" of what he had said about her over the years.

"I believe he blames me for everything that goes wrong in his life," she said. "I felt like my life was in danger."

During cross-examination, the defence asked Carole Baskin if she had ever been physically assaulted by Joe or anyone on his behalf. She answered no.

"He never got the opportunity," she said. She had tried to get a restraining order and told the court that she had begun carrying a gun.

The defence maintained that Joe's "rants and raves" were just part of his persona. He was known for his inability to control his mouth and no one took him seriously. Earley asked her why she had not contacted the police each time they appeared if she was truly concerned about the videos "as crazy and as silly as many of them are".

"I don't think they're silly at all," she replied after the judge admonished the defence attorney for the form of the question. Her testimony ended there as the judge had ruled that there should be no mention of the disappearance of Don Lewis in the case.

The prosecution then called a string of other participants from the exotic animal industry. They testified that Joe had bought and sold exotic animals, often using fudged USDA paperwork.

James Garretson testified that Joe asked him "about a half-dozen times" between 2016 and 2017 if he knew anyone who would kill Baskin. In the fall of 2017, he began recording their phone conversations under the instruction of FBI agents. The tapes ran for nearly an hour and the jury repeatedly heard Joe say that he wanted Carole Baskin dead.

"She's got to go," he said on one of the tapes.

"Just roll that fat bitch into the ocean," he said on another.

Garretson testified about the set-up. He said he told Joe "one of my guys just got out of jail recently". This supposed hitman was the undercover FBI agent. A recorded conversation from November 2017 was played in court. In it, Joe was heard saying he was "tired of killing myself paying for lawyers", then asking "how much will this dude cost us?"

The defence noted that, in many of the phone calls, it was Garretson, not the defendant, who brought up the possibility of hiring a hitman, clearly opening up the possibility of entrapment. Also there was no evidence that any money had changed hands for employing the hitman. Nor had the burner phones or any firearms been purchased.

"The recording speaks for itself," said Earley. Joe had never been serious about going through with the plan.

When Allen Glover took the stand, he explained that he had wanted all along to take Joe's money and run. He said that Joe was a cruel man and that on occasions they had nearly came to blows. He let Joe believe his teardrop tattoo meant he had killed before, when really it was meant as a reminder of his late grandmother.

"To get that money from Joe, I'd let him believe anything he wanted," Glover said. "I said I'd cut her head off. He was fine with it."

He told jurors that Joe Exotic talked every day about having Carole Baskin murdered or murdering her himself.

"It was crazy," said Glover.

Glover said he accepted the cash but never intended to go through with the plan. He also testified that Joe got the cash by selling a liliger cub which he had bred at his zoo. When Joe only came up with $3,000 in November 2017 rather than the $5,000 promised, he didn't say anything.

"I didn't want to waste another minute there," he said.

Glover said he returned to his home state of South Carolina, then drove to Florida with the intention of warning Carole Baskin in person a few weeks later. He said he got drunk and high on cocaine and painkillers, and never made it to see Baskin.

"I just found a beach and found some people to party with. I had some money," he said.

He told jurors the defendant instructed him to kill Baskin as she walked along a trail near her home. Joe had sent John Finlay to get a fake Arizona ID from a shop in Dallas and gave Glover one of the park's cell phones. Glover said the defendant took a copy of an online photo of Baskin and saved it on the cell phone "so I wouldn't kill the wrong person".

The jury were played a recording where Joe said he was going to send Glover's cell phone to Lowe, who was in Las Vegas, to establish an alibi. On the tape Joe told Garretson: "Jeff is gonna text pics every once in a while back to the staff so that his phone registers in Vegas." The recording went on to capture Joe talking about his plan should Garretson get caught, telling him to claim that he had gone "off the deep end" having been fired from his job at the zoo.

In another recording Glover told Garretson: "I'm just a person that don't have a problem with it. I'm going to hell anyway. I'm not going to let this place fall. This is something that has to be done."

The final recording played to the jury was the one where Joe agreed to pay the undercover FBI agent, known only as Mark Williams, to kill a Florida woman and talked of using his gubernatorial campaign to create an alibi.

"Just like follow her into a mall parking lot and just cap her and drive off," he told the faux hitman.

The agent himself then testified that he had talked with the defendant in a cluttered office at the Greater Wynnewood Exotic Animal Park. He explained that the meeting had been set up by James Garretson who had, by then, become a confidential informant for the government.

"He agreed that I would commit a murder for hire for him," the agent testified.

In the recording, Joe brought up his gubernatorial campaign when the agent told him he would need to be seen out in public at the time of the murder. The agent promised to call from a burner phone from Florida and tell him "today is the day".

Joe said that Carole Baskin was evil and was trying to bankrupt them. The agent offered more than once to make Baskin disappear.

"I mean we can," Joe Exotic said on the recording. "The bitch has just got to go away. Got to go away." Joe was going to sell some of his tigers to raise the money, the agent confirmed. Joe also talked of buying the murder weapon from a flea market in Sulphur. The agent also acknowledged in testimony that after that meeting he never spoke to Joe Exotic again, never received a gun from him, never got any burner phones and never got the down payment.

The agent also said that the conversation went off at tangents, with Joe talking about politics and his forthcoming marriage. However, Williams denied the defence's suggestion that this indicated that the defendant was not serious. The agent was the last prosecution witness.

The case for the defence began on 29 March. Their first witness was Brittany Peet from PETA who had been subpoenaed to testify, though Joe was "someone PETA has long advocated against". She testified that Joe had said he would be willing to leave the exotic animal business, but only if Baskin dropped the $1 million lawsuit and the current owner – Jeff Lowe – also agreed to leave the business as well.

"Mr. Passage indicated that he wanted to get out of the business," Peet the told jurors.

Joe's defence attorneys asked Peet to support their claim that Joe was all talk and could not have been serious about murdering Carole Baskin as he was planning to quit the business. Peet recalled Joe talking about moving to Belize and she told the jurors that, at one point, Joe offered to share evidence he had against other people in the industry.

During cross-examination, the prosecution presented an email sent by Joe to Peet in January 2018 where he expressed his discontent with the draft agreement because it did nothing to "get rid of the judgment" or help in any way to pay off his legal fees. A deal was never reached.

The government then announced its decision to dismiss two of the wildlife charges that related to the Lacey Act due to insufficient evidence. The defence then argued that all of the remaining counts should be dismissed for the same reason. The judge rejected the motion.

Defence attorney Elliott Crawford said this case was "especially unique", as Oklahoma was not typically considered a hotbed for exotic animals. The case itself involved multiple moving parts. Mixing his metaphors, he went on: "It's kind of a recipe for a cake or chocolate chip cookies. You have to have certain ingredients. One of those big elements is the federal nexus. Either you have to show that the defendant travelled in interstate commerce or caused someone to travel in interstate commerce or used the mail or caused somebody else to use the mail or another facility of interstate commerce such as a cell phone to show that there was an intent to commit a murder." Witness credibility would be crucial, he said.

Joe took the stand on the sixth day of the trial, against the advice of his attorneys. The media gave him good coverage. They reported that Joe tried to convince the jury that his animosity for Carole Baskin had largely faded by 2017, when he began negotiating with Brittany Peet to begin getting rid of his animals and getting out of the zoo business for good. There was a deal in the works and he hoped to settle with PETA and then Baskin. It had been several years since he made his videos threatening Baskin. Why would he want, at that point, to pay someone to kill her?

In his rambling testimony, Joe claimed he'd been set up by Jeff Lowe, who was working behind his back to kick him out of the zoo. He accused Lowe, Garretson and Glover of conspiring against him and of running various criminal schemes from the zoo. He said Lowe told him to give Glover $3,000 so that he could travel to South Carolina to take care of some legal problems. He did it because he thought it would get Glover out of his hair. Meanwhile, Joe testified, Garretson and the fake hitman, Mark Williams, were so aggressive about the murder plot that he sensed that he was being set up and didn't take the bait.

Joe admitted to shooting the five tigers. He said it was because they were old and in poor health. Euthanasia by gunshot, he noted, was legal.

He said he made a deal with God while ill in 2014 to change his ways "if He let me walk out of the hospital". He began crying later when he told jurors about the death of his twenty-three-year-old husband, Travis Maldonado.

"The idea was to quit making all these animals suffer for money," he said. "I was done."

Joe also admitted making online threats against Baskin but characterised his statements – the more outlandish, the better – as a way to get donations. He said Baskin made him and others look bad on the website, 911animalabuse.com.

"Over the years, we probably made each other pretty famous," he said.

When confronted with his own recorded statements, he said he knew that Lowe and Garretson had been up to something and that he was playing along only to gather evidence. He accused Lowe of everything from drug use to sex trafficking. Lowe's name was mentioned repeatedly during the trial, but he was never called to testify.

Joe called the prosecution witnesses liars and specifically denied that he told zoo worker Allen Glover in November 2017 to carry out the killing along a bike path. He insisted that it was Lowe who talked him into sending Glover on to Florida.

About his 8 December 2017 meeting with the FBI agent posing as a hitman, Joe said he had a gut feeling at the time that the guy was an undercover cop so he never agreed to any murder and never did anything further to make it happen.

Before the verdict was brought in, Lowe and his wife posted on their Facebook page: "He's still delusional… We have had a lawyer in the courtroom the entire trial and that lawyer said Joe is done."

# TWELVE: Joe Takes the Stand

Throughout his career Joe had had the gift of the gab. He figured that he could talk his way out of any trouble. If he could not be on TV or addressing a political meeting, the stand in a federal courtroom would have to do. This was a high-profile case that had already attracted the attention of the media. He wanted his words to be heard, but his trial was not covered in the Netflix series *Tiger King: Murder, Mayhem and Madness*. So Joe's detailed testimony, taken from the court records, is given here.

While Joe had been charged as Joseph Maldonado-Passage and confirmed that was his name, he agreed to be referred to as Mr. Passage while giving testimony. He also gave his name as Joe Schreibvogel and spelt out the surname for the court reporter.

"So, Mr. Passage, what type of employment have you had during your adult life?" asked assistant federal public defender, Bill Earley, who was still representing Joe.

"When I was in high school, I worked at a nursing home as a nurse's aide," Joe replied. "When I graduated high school, I went through the Texoma Police Academy in Denison, Texas, and graduated as the youngest police chief in the state of Texas's history. In 1986, me and my brother and my first husband bought a pet store in Arlington, Texas. Did that for sixteen years. My brother got killed in 1997, and me and my parents built the zoo there in Wynnewood, Oklahoma, in memory of him. And we opened in 1999."

He confirmed that the zoo had been started by him and described how it started up.

"When my brother got killed – he was the biggest part of the pet store – so it was never the same. So me and mama and dad and Brian decided to sell the pet store. And mom and dad got $140,000 from the insurance company from my brother being killed in a car wreck. And my dad called it blood money, and he didn't want anybody making any money off of that. So he was going to donate it to charity. And you hear on TV how all the charities misuse money and stuff, so we all kind of agreed to build this rescue zoo in memory of my brother because one of his dreams was to go to Africa and see the animals running free. So we built the animal park there in Wynnewood, Oklahoma."

Asked to describe the park Joe said: "It's right off of I-35 and Exit 64. It's sixteen… started out with sixteen acres. It came with just an exterior fence and a roping arena and an old barn and an old farmhouse. And we started building cages, and animals started coming in and they never stopped."

What was the source of the animals?

"Most of all the animals come from people that re-homed them there because they had exotic animals, and they either couldn't take care of them anymore, or they got too big, or the city laws changed, or some state laws changed," said Joe. "And over the course of twenty years, we probably rescued and re-homed more animals than anybody in the United States."

The facility grew tremendously over the years.

"When we first started, we just had a gift shop and a few cages," said Joe. "In the gift shop we had a kind of a Subway shop where my mom would actually be the cashier and make the Subway sandwiches and stuff. And over the years we incorporated a travelling show where we did fairs and malls and stuff like that. And people built cages in memory of people that they have lost, so we called it a memorial park because animals got to live in honour of people that passed away. And there was actually three people buried underneath their exhibits there at the zoo. So it turned into 152 memorials as of when I left the zoo last year. And we turned it into a travelling magic show and tiger show for nine years."

There were educational programmes at the park.

"After we retired the magic show and the travelling educational show, we built a stage that had bleachers, and I did an educational show twice a day," he said.

Then a video production facility was added.

"I believe that started late 2011, maybe 2012," said Joe. "We had a TV studio where we videotaped everything going on in the park, and we broadcasted it on a website and called it *Joe Exotic TV*. And we brought animals on the show and taught people about animals."

*Joe Exotic TV* was broadcast on YouTube and the zoo's website.

"What other things were on the show?" asked Earley.

"We did online auctions," said Joe. "We raised money. And in 2008, I formed a corporation called the United States Zoological Association, where we went around and helped people rebuild their zoos instead of taking their animals away from them. We taught them how to fix up their zoo so they could keep their animals instead of always sending them to a sanctuary. So we raised money for that organisation. And then we had another thing online that we called the Animal Miracle Network, where we reached out to people that were terminally ill and dying, and we granted last wishes with animals for people all over the United States for one of their last wishes. So we kind of did all of that on our TV show."

Sponsors of the show included the Seth Wadley Ford dealership, the local Sonics and the local McDonald's.

In 2013, Joe created another show with a completely separate website called *Joe Gone Wild*.

"And what was the content of the *Joe Gone Wild* show?" asked Earley.

"It was pretty out there," said Joe. "I don't know if you have ever watched the movie *Jackass*, but we kind of incorporated it to be after the movie *Jackass* because the crazier you got, the more people watched it. We ended up with 64 million viewers. But the website had an age restriction where you had to be eighteen years old, and you had to verify your date of birth in order to watch the show. And the webmaster that designed the website had a chat room on one side, and people all over the world could chat with each other during the show, and then they could call into the zoo office and make requests or dare us to do different things on the show for donations for the animals. And, at times, we would raise $20,000 in two hours."

Bearing in mind the dignity of the court, Earley asked: "Now, if you would, just – and keep it as tame as possible – but what kind of outlandish material would you do on these shows?"

"We had tons of costumes underneath the desk. There was times that we dressed up like we were in Jamaica, and we had big drink glasses that we got at the state fair, and we put dry ice in them and made them look like bongs, smoking weed on the thing, even though I don't smoke weed," Joe said. "We had – I don't know if you have ever run into the diaper people on Facebook, but there's a huge community of adult diaper people on Facebook, and they called in and dared us to wear adult diapers one night. We did that for 500 bucks. We had blow-up dolls. It was pretty crazy."

"All right," said Earley. "Now, we saw a number of videos that the government played during their case in chief. Do you recall those?"

"Yes, sir," said Joe.

"All right. And, obviously, all of those were kind of centred on either animal rights or Carole Baskin, correct?"

"Correct."

"Where were those shows? I mean, were they within *Joe Exotic TV*, or were they on the *Joe Gone Wild* show?"

"I can't be exactly [sure] because they didn't play the entire video of the show," said Joe. "Every show was recorded live. And at the beginning of every show it had disclaimers saying it was for entertainment purposes only and viewer discretion advised and foul language would be involved and all that, and some would go to YouTube after they were recorded."

"All right. So were there shows that you produced or got yourself involved in that had nothing to do with Carole Baskin?"

"Thousands."

Earley asked Joe to give an example of a show that he'd made that had nothing to do with Carole Baskin.

"On *Joe Gone Wild* or *Joe Exotic TV*?"

"Both."

"On *Joe Exotic TV*, we had little kid shows, where we had little baby ducks and chickens and baby animals," said Joe, "and we taught kids about, you know, how long they stay in the egg and how they hatch and stuff like that. And then on *Joe Gone Wild*, I picked on Governor Kasich, I picked on PETA. I mean, we… it was about anybody that had issues with having animals in cages or zoos or anything or other facilities that thought that they could do things and we couldn't."

"So when these... these videos that we saw here in court, would you agree that there was some pretty outrageous stuff going on in those videos?" said Earley.

"There was some pretty outrageous stuff going on," Joe admitted.

"Was there a purpose behind those videos?" asked Earley.

Joe explained: "In the animal world, if I could make you look like you're an abuser... and Carole made this website called 911animalabuse.org, or .com, where she had ninety-two of us on this website. And her opinion, to get around free speech, was that it was her opinion that we abused baby tigers for allowing you to pet them. And the more that they can make you look bad, the more money they can raise because people think that you are going to stop them from doing that..."

So it was Carole who was making money, not Joe.

"... So I could take any one of you tonight and put you on my website and say you chained a pit bull to your tree in your backyard, and you never feed him, and by midnight tonight I bet I could raise $2,000 on something that you're not even doing wrong," Joe continued. "In the animal industry, that's the key way to raise money – they'll put stuff on each other's websites and bad-mouth people. And the more viewers you have, the more money you raise. And that's... so the bad thing about that, though, is the Humane Society of the United States, you know, sent in spies and made videos about us. The PETA sent in spies, and we have got four FBI records to verify some of this. And they would send in spies to make videos, and they would put a video online and edit it and make it look like the Humane Society videos that you see on TV right now. That's all pre-made videos. Okay? And we could do the same thing with tigers and lions. But what they do is they prey on the mentally unstable to carry out their crimes for them, and that is, to break into the zoo, cut the cages open at night. One morning – our manager, John Reinke, has two prosthetic legs – and a man drove all the way from Mustang, Oklahoma, down there to cut the animals out of their cages and kill John Reinke…"

So it was the animal rights activist who were out for the kill, not Joe. Reinke was unharmed.

"… And it took twenty-nine minutes on 911 to get the first officer at the park. So a lot of the stuff that we portray on TV and our videos is to look like these dangerous psycho mutts that you didn't want to break into our zoo in the middle of the night because we are armed, and we're not going to tolerate you coming in and cutting our cages open. And that was our simple line of defence."

"Now, in spite of the content of those shows, did you want Carole Baskin dead?" asked Earley.

"No."

"Did Carole Baskin and your ongoing dispute with her actually help you in some strange way?"

"I didn't know who Carole Baskin was until 2006, when I picked up a newspaper in Oklahoma City, and here's this article about this trashy little roadside zoo, and it was me, and the person that they interviewed was Carole Baskin," said Joe. "And over the years, I would say we both probably made each other pretty famous."

Earley then asked Joe about Big Cat Rescue Entertainment.

"Okay. Big Cat Rescue Entertainment, I believe that come about 2009 maybe, somewhere around there. We had growed into two road shows, two eighteen-wheelers and a tour bus. And one eighteen-wheeler was the animal show, and one eighteen-wheeler was my illusions, my magic show. And some of the malls – we always did malls because it was easy to market and you were guaranteed customers because people came to the mall. Okay. So some of the malls wanted just the animal show, and some wanted just the magic show, and some wanted both of them at the same time. So the animal show was Tigers In Need, and the magic show was Mystical Magic of the Endangered. Okay. And then whenever we both were at one location, instead of having two posters and confusing people and everything else, we came up with one name. Okay…"

Then he got into his war with Big Cat Rescue.

"… During that time, Big Cat Rescue had a program called Cat Whiz. Okay. And anytime you showed up somewhere, this programme would flood the mall with seventy- eighty-thousand emails and jam all of their computers up and their website up and everything else with this, 'Oh, these people are so horrible to these baby tigers and this is abuse and you shouldn't allow this.' Okay. So I had a marketing director named Darren Stone that came up with the idea – well, if she's going to send out seventy-thousand emails, let's make everybody think that it's her at the mall. So we called the Trade Commission and verified that she didn't own the three words 'Big Cat Rescue'. Okay. She had a logo, and she only owned it with the tiger jumping over the logo. So he created a logo with Big Cat Rescue, and we used the eyeballs from a facility we had permission to in Colorado called Serenity Springs. Okay. And when both shows were at one location, we used the word and the logo Big Cat Rescue Entertainment because it was magic, and it was with big cats. Made sense to us. And then everybody called back down to Florida and bitched at Carole. Was just a marketing way to pay back for flooding our clients with seventy-thousand emails."

"So as you were explaining that, my understanding would be that Big Cat Rescue, the Carole Baskin entity, they would contact the locations where you were doing a show and do this email flood; is that correct?" asked Earley.

"Yes, sir."

"Okay. So your purpose in forming this entity, Big Cat Rescue Entertainment, was to kind of throw them off their game, correct?"

"Correct."

"All right. Did you get sued by Ms. Baskin for that?"

"We got sued for trademark infringement, and then she testified the other day that she sued me for copyright infringement as well," said Joe. "And that had absolutely nothing to do with putting her face picture on anything. It was a picture that I got off of Facebook of three of her employees bashing rabbits in the head and bloody, dead rabbits to feed to the tigers and laughing about it. So kind of give her a little taste of her own medicine – and I sent that picture to every rabbit rescue in the country I could find, and she got a taste of her own medicine. So she went and bought the picture for $5 from the employee. Three months after I posted it, she filed a copyright and copyrighted it, and then she just out-moneyed me in a lawsuit."

"Now, did she get a judgment from you – or against you?" asked Earley.

"Our lawyers at one point just said, you need to just quit spending bad money after bad money, and just give her a judgment of whatever she wants. And so she got a million dollar judgment. And we didn't expect her to move that judgment to Oklahoma. So she moved that judgment to Oklahoma, and my lawyers recommended just filing bankruptcy on the judgment, and she sued the bankruptcy court as well."

"All right. So that initial lawsuit, the trademark and the copyright, those were being litigated in Florida; is that correct?"

"That's where it started, yes, sir."

"All right. And before the case was moved here for collection, were you required to litigate the case in the state of Florida?"

"Yes, sir."

"So did it become pretty costly?"

"We spent close to a quarter-million dollars."

"All right. Now, did that judgment affect you and the zoo at that time?" asked Earley.

"As in how?"

"Financially."

"We spent a lot of money on lawyers, but we kept operating."

"All right. Now, aside from the lawsuits and the judgment that Ms. Baskin has against you, what's your problem with her?"

Joe was typically forthright, accusing Carole Basking again of running a moneymaking operation.

"My problem is she's a hypocrite," he said. "You know, just like some of her other facilities in her... within her little organisation she's created. Her facility is in the middle of Tampa, Florida. It's right next to a major highway. She sells every kind of tour under the sun: Bone tour, feeding tour, kid tour, adult tour. It doesn't matter. I mean, I have taken one of her tours. Her animals are on exhibit. She can complain one month in public, writing that there's too many tigers in America, and then the next month she's rescuing one from Peru because there's none in America that can hold a good story to raise donations, so she's bringing in this tiger from Peru. And she'll drive clear across the United States to rescue a baby bobcat because baby animals raise money better because everybody likes baby everything, especially if you're going to rescue one. So there's absolutely nothing except petting animals – which she used to do before she made her millions – that we do any different than she does, except she wants to make every state illegal except Florida so she can corner the market on exhibiting tigers."

"Now, did you have any disagreements with her position on certain legislation?" asked Earley.

"I'm probably one of the biggest, most outspoken critics of her legislation push that she's continuing to push because – like the Big Cat Safety Act that they are trying to introduce right now, her organisation that she started, which is the global federation of animal sanctuaries, is the only one exempt from this law they're trying to introduce. And the way that they're doing this is by making political donations to different politicians in order to get these laws passed. But the big thing was in Ohio, when Zanesville, Ohio, happened with Terry Thompson, the guy that supposedly let all of his animals out and shot himself and killed himself in Zanesville, Ohio. And that right there is what started the controversy off – I knew Terry and that wasn't something Terry would have done, especially if you love your animals because you know they're going to be massacred the minute you open the door and let them run..."

Joe had claimed press credentials to cover this story.

"... Not to mention that I do investigative reporting because I'm a member of the United States Press, and I belly-crawled that farm to do my story. And to this day I don't believe that he killed himself. It was what they needed in order to make exotic animal owners look crazy and pass a law in Ohio to make it illegal to own exotic animals. So after they started that, I testified in front of the Senate and in front of the House to try and stop that bill that they were pushing through. And they got it pushed through, and they sent SWAT teams in peoples' homes and they took their animals, and Carole's organisation got quarter-million dollar contracts to move animals from Ohio to California, and from Ohio to Florida, to their facilities, which are absolutely no different than the facilities they were taking them from, except they came with quarter-million dollar contracts of taxpayer money. And that's why I went after John Kasich, Governor Kasich."

John Kasich was the governor of Ohio where the laws on owning exotic animals had become a good deal stricter. Joe was claiming that animal rights activists murdered Thompson in order to tighten Ohio's animal laws.

"So these disagreements that you were having with Ms. Baskin about legislation, about what you did, did those things get incorporated into your on-air shows, so to speak?"

"Absolutely. Big time," said Joe, "because we raised money for peoples' lawyers over in Ohio and everywhere else in the United States that were fighting laws. And we used the TV show to educate the general public, such as you, of what's going on. And you have a right under the Constitution of the United States to own personal property. And, unfortunately, tigers and lions and animals are personal property."

"You may have already spoken to this," said Earley, "but with respect to your on-air antics, did the viewership go up the nuttier it all got?"

"When we first started out, our viewership was pathetic because people just got bored with the same antics every day," said Joe. "And that's where we tried the *Joe Gone Wild* thing, and we started getting sixty- seventy-thousand viewers a night, and it went into the millions. And the last time I saw the counter on our YouTube was – we had sixty-four million viewers from all over the world that would sit up at 2 or 3 o'clock in the morning their time just to watch our show at seven o'clock our time. And the crazier it got, the more money we raised and the more people watched. And that flowed over even to my political – thing is – I tried to be serious in politics, and I got no support, and the more outlandish I got, the more real I got, the more support I got."

Earley directed his questioning back to the main issue – the Tiger King's war with the Big Cat woman.

"Now, as far as the park is concerned, did you discuss your difficulties with Ms. Baskin at the park?" he asked.

"I never spoke to Carole Baskin at the park," said Joe. "The only time I have ever spoke to Ms. Baskin was face to face in Ohio at one of the hearings, and I never even spoke to her during any of the depositions. It was always Mr. Howard."

Earley asked: "But as far as your problem that you were having with her, either legal or philosophical, did you talk about those things with people at your park?"

"Oh, every... every day."

"All right. So who would be involved in those conversations?"

"You know, the staff, at morning meetings or night meetings or the management in the office. It was no secret that, you know, we're being sued, we're being watched. And you never know which employee is a plant because she had a bad habit of hiring spies, and she had no problem bragging about that on her website. So we discussed, you know, what was right and what was wrong going on at the park that we needed to be careful with."

Now to the nub of the matter.

"Did you ever mention to park employees that you wish Carole Baskin was dead?" asked Earley.

"You know, there was never a time that I wished she was dead," said Joe. But the question seemed to have knocked him out of kilter. "There was many times of – and I say this about a lot of people – is I don't understand why – you know, I was – I was raised to believe in God, and I don't understand why little kids have to suffer so bad, and people that treat people like that just get to live on and on and on without ever being in a car wreck or something like that, and – and why so many little kids have to suffer."

"Did you yourself get death threats?"

"I had many death threats," said Joe, "and I turned them in to the sheriff's office. We sent them in to the FBI. I actually have the FBI agent's number on my cell phone from the Norman office."

"All right. Now, was your ability to run the park impaired somewhat in 2014?"

"I was extremely ill. I threw up for 188 days. And I went to the doctors and my T-cell count was off the chart, and my white blood cell count was off the chart. So they automatically thought I had AIDS. And I took nine HIV tests within probably four months, and every one of them came back negative. So the next step was to think that I had cancer. And so they did several tests, and we never got to a PET scan, but they did prostate surgery on me on October 21, 2014. And all of my... I did that at Baptist Hospital, and two days later all of my organs quit. I went into kidney and liver failure and spent almost thirty-seven days in ICU and in the hospital there. And the doctors actually gave me... because I would not take dialysis, the doctors gave me two days to live. So they did all they could with IVs and stuff..."

This was when Joe cut a deal with his maker.

"... And I sat there and made God a deal because I had a really bad break-up with John Finlay, and I was just an ugly person at that time. And I made a deal with God that if he let me walk out of that hospital, that I would completely change my attitude. And He let me walk out of that hospital, and I practically raised John Finlay's daughter. And to this day, me and her are connected at the hip. And from that time on I... we quit the *Joe Gone Wild* show, and I tried to do what was right."

But things were going wrong at the zoo.

"Did that cause you to reflect on whether or not you were able to run this park by yourself?" asked Earley.

"Well, it was no secret on social media that I was in rough shape. I was on IVs for the next year. While I was at work, I carried an IV bag with me. I did my shows with IVs in my arms…"

Then the problems began.

"… And a gentleman by the name of Jeff Lowe contacted me on Facebook. He had tigers in South Carolina. And we got to talking, and he ended up buying a baby tiliger from me. So him and his original wife, Cathy, came to the park and picked up the baby tiliger and stayed for an hour or so, and then they left. Okay… And then I get this phone call from this reporter out in South Carolina that said that Jeff Lowe said that he owned tigers in Wynnewood, Oklahoma, and in Colorado. And I was like, there is nobody that owns tigers in Wynnewood, Oklahoma, except me. So we kind of had a little disagreement there. And then he started to buy a facility out in Colorado. And that was when me and Travis Maldonado got married. And Jeff flew us out to his place to see his house and the facility that he was working on buying and we went skydiving for our honeymoon. And he had this gigantic house. I mean, it was a mansion, and it had an indoor swimming pool in it and a Ferrari in the driveway and a Hummer and flashing money…

"And he asked me if I wanted to sell the zoo. And I didn't exactly want to sell the zoo, but I said, 'Hey, I'm open for a partner, you know.' And I had IVs in my arm at the time when we flew out there and he knew I was sick, and I was concerned whether or not I was actually going to make it or not. So we had talked about Carole and the lawsuits. And my mom and dad were adamant that my brothers and sisters were not going to get possession of that property in order to sell it, and tear it apart if something happened to me or mom and dad. So Jeff talked me into putting his name… having mom put his name on the deed of the land, a quitclaim deed. And then through the lawsuits with Carole, she had always said that… my life insurance policies were being paid by the zoo, so she had a judgment against the original zoo. So if I was to die, the judgment should get my million-dollar life insurance policies, Okay, to pay off the judgment, since they were paying the premiums. So Jeff talked me into putting him on as twenty-five per cent of the life insurance and he would pay the premiums, so that way, the zoo was out of my life insurance, and it was in Jeff's hands…"

Joe clearly felt he had been taken for a mug.

"So, yeah, I thought… I just took him for face value, and I thought, you know, this man's got all this money. He can take care of the animals if something happened to me, and he was going to buy this place out in Colorado and help the place in Oklahoma. And so we went home. And he called me again and asked if we wanted to come out for a Halloween party. So we flew… he flew us back there for a Halloween party. And by then his name was already on the land, and his name was already on all the health insurance and all that. And that's when I got the first taste of how he treated his original wife."

## THIRTEEN: The Only Person on this Planet

Public defender Bill Earley was concerned that he was losing the jury, so he sought clarification.

"Let me back up for one minute because I want to go back to something you said a little bit earlier," said Earley. "When you originally met him, you said that he purchased a baby tiliger."

"Correct."

"What's a tiliger?"

The court needed to know. And it was an opportunity for Joe to big himself up.

"Amongst everything else I do, I am the only person on this planet who has produced a liger, a tiliger, a liliger and a tigon," he said. "And I worked very closely with the scientists of the National Institute of Health and Texas A&M, providing DNA testing and umbilical cords so they can study big cats and how they evolved and how they're going to handle the climate change and stuff. And a tiliger is a tiger – and you can do it in different colours. You can use a white tiger; you can use an orange tiger or a tabby tiger or a snow tiger – and you breed that with a female liger and you get a tiliger. And the colour variation depends on what colour of father you use. For years it was believed that ligers are sterile, and it's only male ligers that are sterile, not female ligers.

"But the trick is you can't put two adults together or they're going to kill each other, so you have to raise them together.

And that takes five years before they become fertile enough and adult enough to breed, but the discrimination between the two species is gone. And that's why nobody does it because there's no money in it because you have to wait five years in between each step. And I'm the only person in America that has made that fourth step – actually, I'm the only person in the world that has made that fourth step, because after you hybrid them four times, the males are no longer sterile. It's just like a Bengal cat or a Savannah cat that's bred with exotic animals. Okay.

"The theory that the animal rights people like to use out there is they outgrow their bones. I think you have heard that in here before. Okay. Or they're deformed or they're too big for their parents. There has never been a recorded incident in our world of a hybrid cat born with a genetic flaw. A lot of people confuse genetics and birth defects, okay, as the same thing, and it's not. A birth defect happens from being cramped in the womb or something like that versus a genetic defect that is actually passed down a bloodline."

Earley asked Joe whether he had sold a tiliger to Mr. Lowe.

"I did," said Joe.

"Was it legal to sell that?"

"It's absolutely legal to sell any hybrid."

"Now, Mr. Lowe has managed to kind of get into your business at this point; is that right?"

"Yes, sir."

"Were you still in the process of litigation with Carole Baskin?"

"Yes, sir."

Earley asked: "Were you, at this time when Mr. Lowe starts to get on the scene, still in settlement talks with the Baskins?"

Joe could fix the moment in his mind.

"When we were out there for Halloween, for his Halloween party, when we flew back to Oklahoma City, we stayed in Oklahoma City that night because the next morning I had mediation with Howard Baskin, and we spent ten or eleven hours in mediation. And me and Howard actually had it worked out to where he was going to allow me to continue for the year, and then we would stop cub-petting and we'd stop breeding and we would simply slowly close the zoo down.

"But I needed to make sure that we could pay our outstanding bills, you know, throughout that period. And he understood that. So at the end of the day, we had come to an agreement to do all of this until he picked up the phone and called Carole. And part of that was a $5,000 payment every month toward the settlement, okay, toward the judgment. But the thing that we were worried about was we are cutting our funding of play cages and everything else to make that $5,000 payment. And in case we couldn't, Carole wanted my mom and dad's house and property that was completely paid for. And that's when the lawyer stepped in and said, absolutely not. So that kind of went to crap."

"About what time period is this going on?"

"November of 2015."

"All right. So in early 2016, who took over as the owner of the park?"

Joe said that, in late February of 2016, Lowe created three companies.

"One was the Greater Wynnewood Exotic Animal Park, which operated the zoo; one was called Big Cat Institute, which was supposed to be a non-profit that trained interns to do what we do – it turned out to be nothing but a way to hide payroll. The third one was the Greater Wynnewood Development Group, which was in charge of the land."

"All right. So who actually owned the zoo after February of 2016?"

"Jeff Lowe."

Then Earley addressed the change of the name of the park.

"Now, did the name of the park change?" he asked.

"It did," said Joe. "It was the Garold Wayne Interactive Zoological Park until February when they – the board – voted to dissolution and close it."

"Was there a reason behind the name change?"

"Well, in order to shut one organisation down and escape another judgment, it closed and had to, by law, change the name to open up another organisation," said Joe. "So Carole would have to start the lawsuits all over again."

"At least that was the thought?" said Earley.

"That was the thought."

"Now, had Lowe already got his name onto the insurance policies at this time?"

"Yes, sir."

"Who all was on those policies?"

"It was Jeff Lowe; in 2016, it was my husband, Travis Maldonado; and then twenty-five per cent went to John's little girl, Kimberlin."

With the change of ownership, Joe's role changed.

"All right. What was your role at the park after Lowe took over?" asked Earley.

"Entertainment director."

"And what did that mean as far as your daily work?"

"Well, the park had been basically branded with my face for twenty years, close to twenty years. So I put on all the shows. I did the big tours twice a day at 11.30 and 2.30 every day. I did the ordering. Most of the merchandise was all private labelled with my picture on it and my name. The bad part was my licence [to own big cats] was there, along with Beth Corley's licence and Trey Key's licence and Ryan Easley's licence…"

These were other keepers at the zoo.

"And Jeff didn't have a licence there at that time because his licence was still in South Carolina, but his cats were there. So we put all of his cats under my licence, not Beth Corley's licence. They were under my licence. And the reason for that was… is because he knew that I wanted to quit. Okay. So it didn't matter how many noncompliant citations we got from the USDA under my licence, it wasn't going to affect anybody else because I was going to turn my licence in eventually because I wanted out of it. So almost everything that we did had to be under my licence, whether I owned the animals or not."

"So how close in time to when Jeff Lowe took over had you started having these thoughts about 'I'm on my way out'?" asked Earley.

"Well, they moved to Wynnewood the last part of November of 2015, and they didn't have a place to stay…"

They, in this case, were Jeff and Lauren.

"… They left Cathy in Colorado that time because Jeff got arrested for beating her up. So they had to rush out of Colorado. Okay. So they moved in my house with me and Travis, and they stayed there for probably two, three months. And that's when I found out everything in Colorado was rented. He didn't own nothing. He was behind on his payments on the Ferrari and the house was rented. He skipped out on the lease of the house. And by that time it was already too late because his name was on everything in Wynnewood…"

For Joe, that was the time to move on.

"… So I went to Tampa, Florida, to do a music video. I think it was in March of 2016. And I did a music video with elephants there at the Two Tail Ranch, and then I was a speaker at a convention called 'Take Back the Conversation', there in Tampa. And then I had a political rally at the same time, then I came home. And I came home and sat in the office and wanted to quit. I was just going to walk away at that point. And he [Jeff] talked me into staying there. Okay. So he builds this little cabin out of storage buildings for him and Lauren to move into. So they finally move into their own cabin. And by that time the criminal side started coming out, and I started seeing what kind of scams they're running and they turned the park into a front for his criminal side. And then it turned into their own little private hunting ranch of young girls, and it just escalated from there until I just couldn't stomach it anymore."

"Now, about this time did Allen Glover show up on the scene?"

"Allen showed up, I want to think it was probably April of 2016. He came from South Carolina. He had worked for Jeff out there with some liquidation companies or some liquidation stores or something. But anyway, he came to work at the zoo as a yard guy."

"All right. Was he your employee?"

"He made it very clear he wasn't my employee," said Joe.

"Okay. Now, was Lowe at the park on a daily basis?"

"They lived on the park, and he was pretty much at the park all the time through 2016. And that's where they started. They had a little old lady in town that made clothes for the funeral home. And Jeff, in his liquidation history, somehow or another got a hold of some of the singer Prince's outfits and got sued by Prince."

Assistant US Attorney Amanda Maxfield Green, for the prosecution, then asked if she could approach the bench.

"You may," said US District Judge Scott L. Palk.

The attorneys had a bench conference out of the hearing of the jury.

Maxfield Green for the prosecution warned the judge that Joe was keen to make a lot of criminal allegations against Jeff Lowe. These allegations were, she said, "totally unfounded" and that there was "no evidentiary support for" them. She insisted that were Joe to continue down this line of answers that would prejudice the case.

Judge Palk considered the matter.

"Well, what immediately comes to mind is the question 'Was Mr. Lowe at the park very often?'," he said, "and then I don't know how that got to Prince, but – all right." The judge gave Bill Earley a chance to respond and he confirmed that he would rephrase the question.

Judge Palk instructed Joe to listen carefully to his counsel's question, stick to the point and if further details were required they would be asked for. The objection was sustained.

Earley continued: "All right. I believe you did answer that question, that he was there pretty much daily. Would that be fair to say?"

"Through 2016, yes, sir," said Joe.

"All right. And during that period of time was there an off-site business with respect to either animal petting or a show that Mr. Lowe was involved with?" asked Earley.

"That started, I believe, along about March of 2017," said Joe. "He had a place in Oklahoma City called the Neon Jungle."

"All right. And was that basically just an offshoot of the business down there in Wynnewood?"

"It was set up in a mall there in Oklahoma City to play with baby tigers, yes, sir."

"All right. Now, as far as Mr. Lowe is concerned, and his activities, did he eventually move out of state for long periods of time?"

"March, April – March through June is when the Neon Jungle was there. And he hooked up with this lady from Las Vegas in the middle of that and started human trafficking in Las Vegas."

Judge Palk reprimanded him once again.

"Mr. Passage, again, the question was, did he eventually move out of state for long periods of time?" said the judge. "I want you to listen to the lawyer's questions and answer those questions."

Joe confirmed that Lowe had been out of the state for long periods.

"And where did he go?" asked Earley.

"Las Vegas," said Joe.

"All right. And as it concerns the park's business, and I mean animal business, what was your understanding of what Mr. Lowe was doing out in Las Vegas?"

"He was supposed to go out there and open up a company called The Jungle Bus and—"

"And what was that supposed to be?"

"It was supposed to be where people could pay to get on this bus with the animals on the bus and go on, like, an hour or two-hour drive and play with the animals on the bus, kind of like you would a party bus."

"All right. Now, as far as his business interest out in Las Vegas, was that contributing substantially to the park's income?"

"It didn't contribute at all."

Earley then looped back.

"Now, I think you testified that you considered leaving the park after Lowe got ingrained in it in 2016. Is that correct?" he asked.

"Yes, sir."

"Did your desire to remain at the park change in 2017?"

"It did."

"What changed?"

Joe had more veiled accusations.

"The more that they used the park as a front for everything, the more the meaning of it being a memorial park and representing people that have died went away. And it just – the whole morals of what we worked twenty years for was gone."

"So you were even more inclined to get out of the business at that point?" said Earley.

"Absolutely."

Earley then wanted to get into the technical side of the case.

"All right. I want to switch gears with you for just a moment and address some of the specific counts in the indictment. Okay?" he said.

"Okay."

"And the first set of counts I want to address are counts eight, and then nine through eleven. So, count eight, if you recall, concerns an offer for sale to, I think it was Darlene Cervantes; is that correct?"

Darlene was an animal trainer.

"Correct."

"Do you remember that testimony?"

"Yes."

"All right. And with respect to that particular text exchange you had with Ms. Cervantes, explain that to the jury."

"Well, I have nineteen Facebooks because they limit you to five-thousand friends," said Joe. "So my office people would run all of my Facebooks and answer my messages for me because I had to be out on the park most of the time. So I was in the office one day and Darlene, who is kind of out there anyway, asked me if she could buy a tiger. And that's when I asked her if she had a USDA licence and asked her which state and all that. And I went to work and Amber continued that conversation via a radio because we carried radios. So it was between me and Amber. But the easiest way — and I probably have done this a thousand times in the history of this park and being on the road — is somebody always walks up and says, how much would a tiger cost me? And the easiest way to end the conversation is jack up a price to where you know they can't afford it, and the conversation ended right there and you didn't have to go through all of the legalities and spend thirty minutes with everybody that wanted to buy a tiger. So, you know, I would... I told her a thousand bucks because she was homeless. She didn't have a thousand dollars and I knew that conversation would stop. No different than a conversation at a magic show when I tell people it was $20,000, because you know they ain't got it, and the conversation just ended right there."

"So was it your intention to offer these cubs for sale to Darlene Cervantes?" asked Earley.

"No. It was my intention to just say a price and she'd go away, which she did."

"Now, counts nine through eleven concerned a number of what Mr. Finlay, I think, determined were sales. Count nine, November 16, 2016, a male tiger cub to Brown Zoo in Illinois. Do you recall that?"

"I recall that."

"All right. Was that a zoo-to-zoo transfer?"

"It was."

"What kind of licence do you have?"

"I have a Class C exhibitor's licence by the United States Department of Agriculture, the Animal Welfare Act, which allows me the right to exhibit, breed, sell and transfer," said Joe. "Because they only have three licences. And it's an exhibitor's licence, which does it all; a breeder's licence that only allows you to breed and sell; or a broker's licence so you can be the middleman in between all the sales."

Earley said: "Mr. Finlay testified that, I guess in his opinion, the transaction or this zoo-to-zoo transfer was a sale. What is your testimony with respect to this transaction?"

"I don't remember every transaction, but, I mean, it could have been. But can I explain the forms?" said Joe. "Under my licence, I had peoples' animals that were from Louisiana; I had Jeff's animals; I had some of my animals; I had some of the circus animals because, in order for them to be at the zoo and us be open to the public, it doesn't matter who owns them, you could bring your bobcat to my zoo, and I could exhibit it and it still remain yours, but it's got to be on my inventory in order to be legal.

"So anytime an animal or a baby tiger or anything was taken off of my inventory, it has to come from Joe Maldonado. Okay. It can't come from you in Louisiana, because you're not an exhibitor. I'm the exhibitor, even though it's under my licence and you own the animal. So it's got to be from me to the Brown Zoo. All right. And I don't sell that. I didn't sell that. Jeff, the owner of the zoo, sold those. So that's why they say donation on there, because I transferred them off of my licence to someone else for no charge, and he made the sale between them and him. And from day one, when I knew what he was all about, I kept ledgers of my own to verify every dollar and every sale. And I logged in QuickBooks; I earmarked every deposit that was made from cubs so I could defend myself one day."

"With respect to count ten, that is a tiger female, eleven weeks old, to 'TS' in Indiana. Do you recall that transaction?" asked Earley.

"That one would be Tim Stark, and I remember that one very well."

Stark was another big cat exhibitor Joe tried to have a partnership with.

"All right. So was that the sale in interstate commerce?"

"That one was actually free. Depending on your inspector… our inspector allowed us to use cubs between four weeks and sixteen weeks. Tim Stark's inspector's only allowed him to use cubs up to twelve weeks old. And that's the problem with the vague laws is every inspector can read into what they want it to read in. So the zoo made him a deal, if he took this one that was eleven weeks old that he could only use for one week, we would give him a younger one for free, and that would get a bigger one out of our zoo that we didn't have to grow up and feed for the rest of his life… So that was not a sale."

"And then also count eleven is March 6, 2018, tiger, female, six weeks old, again to Brown's, which is referred to as Oakridge Zoo in Illinois. Is that the same Brown's?"

"It is the same folks."

"So the same as count nine. Do you recall that?"

"Without looking at my notes in QuickBooks and verifying that deposit, but I would probably say it probably was," said Joe.

He confirmed that this was probably a sale, but by the zoo, not by him personally.

"So if I'm understanding you correctly – and, of course, we don't know what Brown's or Tim TS, whoever that is, has to say about this, but you are simply passing them off of your inventory to another zoo's inventory by creating the paperwork that's associated with this; is that correct?"

"Yes, sir. And we did that with Beth Corley's inventory as well."

"All right. And so whether or not this was being sold or someone was providing a donation back for the animal, that was between Mr. Lowe and that entity; is that correct?"

"Correct."

"All right. So that's the substance of your testimony as to why you're not selling anything, correct?"

"I didn't sell anything and I didn't collect a dime for myself, no. It all went in his bank account."

Earley decided to follow the money trail.

"So if Mr. Finlay, after one or all of these trips, came back with cash or cheque or however these people may have been paying, what… and he handed it over to you, is that what happened?"

"He would either give it to me, or if I wasn't there he'd give it to one of the girls in the office."

"What would happen to the money from there?"

"It would be put on a deposit slip for the park, and on the very bottom I would write 'Jeff' so I knew where the money come from, and I would put it in the bank and I would log it in QuickBooks as 'cash Jeff'," Joe said.

"All right. I want to talk a little bit now about counts twelve through twenty, and these are labelled in the indictment as Lacey Act false labelling of wildlife charges. Do you remember the substance of the testimony concerning these allegations against you?"

"Is that the vet certificates or the forms?"

"The forms and the certificate of veterinary inspection," said Earley.

"I believe I do."

Earley needed to explain the details to the jury.

"Now, I don't really plan to go through each one of these individually with you," he said, "but, in substance, with the exception of one of the counts, which involves a CVI form and we'll talk about that separately. But these are all counts dealing with what is alleged to be a falsification of those delivery and receipt forms. Do you understand that?"

"Yes, sir."

"All right. So with respect to those particular allegations, tell us about your understanding of the forms and the information that's required."

"The form is simply, like I explained before, to get it off of inventory," said Joe. "That's all the USDA cares about is where the animal ended up. Okay. We were supposed to get where it's coming from, where it's going to, both of our licence numbers, the animal information of what species it was, what sex it was, approximately how old it was and what condition it's in, and then who transported it and how it was transported, if it was transported. And that's all they required. And we got some of those on napkins from people. I mean, they didn't even put them on actual pieces of paper."

"There were forms that were introduced. Do you recall these?"

"I do."

"Were those your forms?"

"The ones... okay. Which ones are you talking about that were introduced?"

"For example, the delivery form that went to Brown's Zoo."

"Okay. Those were the zoo's forms, yes."

"All right. So the delivery forms would have been developed by who?"

"Whatever secretary was in the office that created them on Microsoft Word."

"All right," said Earley. "Now, there are... on some of the forms there's little boxes to check for sale, donation, exchange; on others there's nothing, but there appears to be something written on them about it's a donation. Explain how that happens."

The situation was confusing.

"It depends on..." began Joe, "– it was like whoever works in the office, gives themselves the title as the office manager, redoes everything. Every time you hire one, they had to redo everything. And some of the forms would come out with the boxes on there. But what never made sense was if you put 'sale' on there, it never asked you how much you sold it for. And it wasn't required on the official form for the USDA, so nobody really paid any attention to that. And the reason why it was always written 'donation' on there is because the person that had the licence never got the money. So the people whose licence it was actually did donate it."

"Do you know why those options were even provided or why that word was written on there if it wasn't required?" Earley asked.

"I think Jeff and Lauren had done one inspection one time while I wasn't at the zoo, and the inspector talked to them about something, and they had the office girl redo the forms."

"All right. To your knowledge, is that information – whether it was a sale, an exchange or a donation – is that information required by the United States Department of Agriculture?"

"No."

"Now, count eighteen is the certificate of veterinary inspection. Have you seen those forms before?"

"I have."

"And how are those forms created?" asked Earley.

"Those stay at the veterinarian office and either me or Reinke or one of the girls in the office would call the vet and give them what... you know, the animal, the sex, the species, how old it is. And then either Reinke – Reinke done most of it, John Reinke – as far as running the animal over to the vet so Dr. Green can see it and then finish the exam, and bring back the pink copy that we give the receiver at the other end. So after the transaction is completely done, we don't even have a copy of the certificate of veterinarian because the vet keeps one to send to the state, she keeps one for her records, and the pink one goes to the people to prove that they got it at that end. There was times that we would be actually in a cage with an animal and we would be calling on the radio to the office the information for them to call in to the vet. And in twenty years, I don't ever remember telling a vet whether it was an exchange, a donation or an exhibition or transfer. We never even discussed that ever."

# FOURTEEN: Count Down

When it came to the charges under the Lacey Act and the Endangered Species Act, Earley was eager to rebut every count in detail.

"With respect to count eighteen, the June 12, 2018, form that Dr. Green testified about, did you advise her to place 'donation' or any other type of exchange on that form?" he asked.

"Which animals are on there?" Joe said.

"It's an African lion, male, eight years old. And an African lion, female, eight years old."

"I did not even call that one in. I had nothing to do with that one or the transfer form."

"All right. That was in June – specifically, the form is dated June 12, 2018."

"Correct."

"Were you at the park that day?"

"I was at the park, yes, sir."

"But you don't recall having anything to do with the information?"

"I know I didn't."

"Now, finally, with respect to the false labelling allegations, there's count twenty-one," said Earley. "And you may recall that is a form that you were asked, by Mr. Garretson, to generate. Do you remember that?"

"Yes, sir."

"Do you remember that particular interaction with Mr. Garretson?"

"I don't remember it except for watching the video."

"Okay. So tell us about what you remember, why you created the form, what the situation was with that."

"Apparently, by watching the video… and to this day, all I can do is be honest, I don't even remember that video. But he had asked for a copy of a disposition form for his lemur. Okay. And at that time he had a gentleman work for him that stole all of his records and a bunch of other equipment, and he was having trouble finding all of his receipts from where his animals came from. And he had previously purchased a lemur from us, and that's why on the video I say, is this one the one we lost, because I thought he was needing one to replace the one that we lost. And so apparently he said, no, it's the one from Omar. And I wasn't even thinking about an animal coming across state lines being an endangered lemur," said Joe. "I was more thinking because he was in a hurry, because he claimed that he was going to be inspected by the USDA, and he just needed to show that he had a lemur on a disposition form. It wasn't to get around the Fish and Wildlife or anything, because in twenty years I have never seen them people. So it was just for that form. And then I walked over, on the video, and Xeroxed it so we had a copy of it, which even confuses me more because my inspector knows exactly how many animals I got and what animals I got. And I would have not figured out how I would have covered having a lemur, because he has the same inspector. So the whole damn thing was confusing to me. I can't really answer why the hell I did that. I'm sorry about my language."

"Well, did you create that form to create a false record to try to fool the USDA somehow?" asked Earley.

"Apparently, I did."

Having disposed of some of the minor charges on the indictment, Earley wanted to set the scene before tackling the rest.

"Before we get into the remaining counts in the indictment," he said, "I want to talk to you a little bit about late summer of 2017 and then going into the fall. What was your relationship with Mr. Lowe like at that time? How would you describe it?"

"He was in Vegas primarily, most of the time," said Joe. "And it was really rocky because we got to know him and James [Garretson] real well. They talked to each other, and James comes to the park and they just constantly are tape-recording each other and tape-recording everybody they talk to, and it's just like a big circle of drama. And every time I would talk to James about how bad I couldn't stand Lauren and what was going on with all of the illegal stuff – and Vegas draining that zoo and money, he would play that to Jeff. And within a couple of hours of talking to James, I would get a phone call getting an ass-chewing from Jeff of why I'm talking about his wife or why I'm bitching about money and so forth. So pretty rocky."

At this point the court recessed for lunch. When the court reassembled, Earley continued his questioning.

"Mr. Passage, I think we left off with your relationship with Mr. Lowe, but I want to back up just for a moment to go back to what we were discussing before, and that's counts twelve through twenty-one. Now, with respect to Government exhibit twelve, I believe this deals with count nineteen in a delivery form. Do you recognise that?"

"Yes, sir."

"All right. Now, is this your handwriting on the form?"

"Yes, it is."

"And were you involved in the transaction itself?"

"Yes, sir."

"All right. Tell us about that."

"This was right at the time that I was actually leaving the zoo for good," said Joe. "And I had this pair of lions that we were donating to the Animal Haven Zoo up in Wisconsin. And we... what I done was I billed them for the two drivers and the gasoline and the truck to take them up there, and, if I remember right, it was $3,200. And we ended up blowing an engine on one of the trucks and we had to send another truck to go get that truck and another driver to go up there and rescue the other drivers. And we finally got it all done.

"But anyway, by the time it was all over with, we didn't even make any money to pay the gas and stuff to get it all done. And that is part of what our licence allows me to do. It's the same as if I had FedEx do it or American Airlines or anybody else. They would have charged the people for the gas and the trouble to go up there and back because they couldn't come get them."

"So was this form inaccurate with respect to any information on it?" said Earley.

"Absolutely not."

"Could you pull up Government exhibit thirteen? Now, this is count twenty, which deals with the form associated with the delivery to Branson Wild World, correct?"

"Correct."

"Do you remember the testimony about that?"

"From who?"

"Mr. Finlay, I believe," said Earley.

"I remember him saying that he's the one that delivered these, yes, sir."

"And that there was some money that was counted out – I think by his girlfriend at the time. Do you recall that?"

"Yes, sir."

"Okay. What about this form? Is that your handwriting?"

"No. This is not mine," said Joe. "And actually, I wasn't even in the state of Oklahoma when this transfer was done."

"Did you have any participation in getting this transfer arranged?"

"I did. Before I left the state – and we'll probably get into that later because I was threatened is the reason why I left for a few days. Branson Wildlife Park wanted to purchase the serval and the African cat and the bats and everything else. And because I was leaving the park, we had a bunch of babies that I had to get rid of because Jeff couldn't take care of them without killing them, and nobody else at the park could raise them being that little. So I told Jim with Branson Wildlife Park on the telephone that I had some baby lions that I would give him because they were illegal to sell baby lions. Since he was buying the bats and everything else, if he would take these babies because the rent house that I had up in Yukon at the time ready to go to, we couldn't have the tigers or lions up there in the rent house. So technically, if you really want to complain about this form, it should have said donate and sell instead of whoever filled this out and just hit the donate box, because everything on there was sold except for the two lion cubs.'

Earley looped back again. "All right. Now ... in the summer of 2017 your relationship with Mr. Lowe was pretty rocky."

"Very rocky," said Joe.

"All right. What was your relationship with Mr. Garretson like at this time?"

"Me and James was never friends or close friends. And I referred to him as a giant Chucky Doll because he's just eerie all the time. He's always up to no good. Everything he done was criminal. And him and Jeff were tight, they were very tight in everything they did. So mine and his relationship, there was none."

"All right. Now what about Mr. Glover? We haven't really talked about him. What was your relationship like with Allen Glover?"

"We hated each other."

"Was there any time that you all, kind of, got along?"

"You know, he helped me with Travis's memorial for a few days, and that's probably about the only time we got along," said Joe.

"All right. What was your problem with Mr. Glover?"

"Well, I mean, constantly drunk, would not come to a staff meeting, sleeping with my mother-in-law, both of them doing meth," Joe said. "I had to fire her from smoking meth in the commissary. He just wouldn't listen. And he came with Jeff and they don't know anything about the Oklahoma weather, and he just starts chopping trees down and bamboo down, and this is protection that the animals need from the wintertime, and it was October. And he just wouldn't listen to anything."

"Well, why didn't you fire him?" asked Earley.

"I couldn't fire him. He was… they made that pretty clear, that he worked for Jeff. And in his testimony you heard that he had nobody to save him all the time, like I was going to hurt him or something."

"Now, during this time period, did you believe that maybe there was something going on between Lowe and Garretson as far as it affected you and the park?"

"It started out that they were manufacturing fake Prince clothes in the office and… I mean, all of that is why we didn't get along, everything they done criminal at the park."

"Okay. But did you think that they were spending a lot of time together?"

"They spent a bunch of time together," said Joe.

"All right. And with respect to, you know, anything that subsequently happened, were you aware that they were talking with each other about ways to get you out of the park?"

"At first, in late 2016, it didn't affect James, but Jeff – at that time I was taking CBD oil without THC in it because I don't like smoking weed because I just can't handle the high. So I would open up a capsule of amoxicillin. This is real important to—"

Assistant US Attorney Maxfield Green interrupted and asked to approach the bench again at this point. Out of the hearing of the jury, she said: "Your Honour, again, we have already gotten Prince clothes back in, which seems apropos to nothing that was asked. He's now attempting to insert a story I know very well that he wants to get out there about, again, totally unfounded accusations, things we have no evidence for other than his accusations … I don't think that defendant can just give a rambling narrative of every terrible thing he thinks someone who is not subject to cross-examination has done."

"The question was is he aware about these two talking about ways to get him out of the park, which I understand has been part of the context of all of this," said Judge Palk. "But, Mr. Earley, where are we going? It was getting a little far afield."

"What I anticipate Mr. Passage testifying to is a couple of occasions at the park," replied Earley. "One where he believed that someone, I think he thinks it was Lowe, had put some hash oil into his medication. He was doing a show inside a tiger cage with some tigers in there. It affected him and it could have resulted in him being seriously injured or killed. The second thing that I anticipate he'll get into is that there was at some point some perfume placed on his boots. Tigers react very aggressively to certain smells and the time that he went into the tiger pen, he was basically attacked by a tiger. This is actually on a video. So there is a basis for it, at least the tiger attacking his shoes. And he believes that Mr. Lowe, with the assistance of someone else, had put that into motion so that they could, you know, have him seriously injured, somehow removed from the park based on that."

"But is that not all just rank speculation on his part?" said Judge Palk.

"Mr. Passage would testify that Mr. Lowe actually admitted on Facebook or social media that he had switched out his medication," said Earley. "I have seen a video where the lions did go after his boots and after him, or at least one of them. He actually had to fire his weapon to get the lion to get away before he could get out of the cage."

Maxfield Green objected again. "Your Honour, number one, hearsay. Whatever Mr. Lowe may have posted on Facebook about it is clearly hearsay. Any admission he made to anybody about it is hearsay. I will concede, on the Government's side, we have seen a video of him being dragged by his foot by an animal, but there is just simply no way... we can't have a trial of every perceived wrong that Mr. Passage believes is attributable to Mr. Lowe."

Judge Palk agreed. "Mr. Earley," he said, "I think it's well established in the evidence, at least the jury could believe or disbelieve that there's ample testimony that Mr. Passage and Mr. Lowe were at odds at various times on various ends of the extremities. And I don't think it is a mystery, and it's clearly established that there's testimony that Mr. Lowe wanted him out of the park. I think it's getting a little far afield to get into all these other things in terms of these individual steps that he may or may not have taken. It seems a little tenuous to me, so I'm going to sustain the objection."

"May I just sort of do a very summary question to move him off this topic and move on?" Earley asked.

"Well, it's hard for me to know what the question's going to be," said Judge Palk and he consulted Maxfield Green.

She said, "I think that it has been established, and maybe one more question would establish to his satisfaction that he believed Mr. Lowe was out to get him or trying to get him off the park in a variety of ways. If that's his belief, that's his belief, but all of this specific detail that cannot be substantiated is irrelevant and prejudicial."

"I think that's fair," said Judge Palk.

Back in open court, Earley asked Joe: "Mr. Passage, was it your belief that Mr. Lowe was trying to get you off the park?"

"Yes."

"All right. Now, with respect to Fish and Wildlife Service, you had frequent inspections by the USDA. Is that correct?"

"Very frequent," Joe said.

"About how often did they come out to your park?"

"Sometimes every month, sometimes you didn't see them for a couple of months. The inspectors have to show up every time somebody calls in a complaint on you. So that's another thing in this industry, it's fun for one facility to keep calling in fake complaints to another facility because it keeps the inspectors coming and it just ties you up with paperwork."

"Now, they would come at whatever frequency they would, but did Fish and Wildlife ever inspect your premises?"

"The Oklahoma Fish and Wildlife – I had to have an exhibitor's licence from them for native animals, like raccoons or black bears or mountain lions and foxes and stuff like that."

The Federal Fish and Wildlife were a different matter, Joe said. "In twenty years I never seen a person from the Federal Fish and Wildlife. And that goes down to the Endangered Species Act. For twenty years nobody was concerned whether or not I had a purebred Siberian tiger or a Sumatran tiger. And we sold tigers up until 2016, and then they put on this generic thing, which is really just a policy. It's not even a law by Congress. And to this day, they still don't have a form to tell how many tigers you have, how many are born, how many die, where their bodies are after they die. In twenty years, I have had probably fifty-plus tigers pass away or euthanised, buried in that back pasture, and nobody gives a damn. Nobody."

"I want to change the topic here to the fall, now, of 2017," said Earley. "Did anything happen during that time frame that changed your entire way of thinking?"

"I went to town to get my car fixed, and I got a phone call that my husband shot and killed himself inside the gift shop," said Joe.

"When did that happen?"

"October 6, 2017."

"May sound like a silly question, but how did that affect you?"

"My entire soul died," Joe said.

"In the days following, did you get a chance to stay by yourself and grieve your loss?" asked Earley.

"I held a press conference the very next day, and I did my show at 11.30, just like I was supposed to. And I never took a day off. And I was even his preacher at his funeral."

"Did you ever contemplate harming yourself?"

"Yeah," said Joe.

"Who helped you get through the first few days of that?"

"John [Finlay] and his daughter."

Again Earley returned to the meat of the wildlife case.

"Now, we have heard testimony, a lot of testimony, about these five tigers being put down in October 2017. Do you recall that?"

"Yes, sir."

"Did you do that?"

"I did."

"All right. Tell the jury why you did that," Earley said.

"After Travis died, I walked through the park every morning looking at the clouds trying to see his face because I couldn't dream about him or anything. And I walked through and checked the animals every morning, and I would have to ask myself what the hell am I doing because I have all these crippled animals that I am making suffer to be on display to suck donations out of people. And I was no better than the facilities that we talk bad about, or the people that we took the animals away from. Me and John Reinke talked about it. We owed the vet so many thousand dollars already. To tranquilise a tiger so a vet can give it a shot takes forty-five minutes sometimes, and it takes several hundred dollars' worth of medicine, and then the animal is just convulsing and throwing up and seizing until the vet can even get to it. And the shotgun was a half a second and it was twice as fast. And I had legal right, according to the state of Oklahoma and the USDA, to do that."

"How many years have you dealt with tigers and big cats?"

"Close to twenty-five."

"Do you consider yourself very familiar with that species?"

"I consider myself one of the world's experts in tigers," said Joe.

"You had a veterinarian associated with the park, correct?" said Earley.

"Yes, sir. Dr. Green."

"And you and Dr. Green, through your agreement, had developed a euthanasia protocol, correct?"

"Yes, sir."

"And that protocol required Dr. Green to euthanise any animal that needed it, correct?"

"For the USDA licence, yes."

"All right. Did you violate that protocol in October?" asked Earley.

"The USDA licence – I would have gotten cited by the USDA as a noncompliance for not calling the vet. Wouldn't have been anything criminal, but I was giving up my licence anyway, so I didn't care if I got wrote up. The idea was to quit making all these animals suffer for money."

"Did you violate the law by euthanising those animals?" asked Earley.

"Absolutely not," said Joe.

"Now, explain why you think you did not violate the law by euthanising those five tigers."

"Because the state of Oklahoma says that you have the right to shoot or euthanise your own livestock as long as it doesn't... 'instantaneously' is the word that they use for it. And this law that they have charged me with is absolutely a law that is extremely vague because Congress didn't enact this right, and that's why the Trump administration is working on redoing this law right now. The word 'take' is to pursue, harass, harm, shoot, kill, wound, capture, or collect an endangered species. That is, for something in the wild, that's not something born in a zoo or every zoo owner would be arrested by now, and every circus owner would be arrested for harassing an animal to make them jump through a hoop. This is for animals in the wild... has nothing to do with this. And if it did have something to do with animals in captivity – I had fifty born, according to the last testimony you heard the other day, and I euthanised five, so I should be getting credit for forty-five more."

"After Travis died, what did you decide you were going to do?"

"I was done," said Joe. "I called Brittany Peet several times, crying because of what Jeff put me through and James always holding my teeth over my head because I have stolen teeth in my head thanks to them two."

"Now, had you met Ms. Peet before?"

"Not before the Dade City Wild Things thing."

Joe had, however, talked to Brittany Peet on the phone.

"What was it like for you to meet Brittany Peet?"

"I wished I'd have met her ten years ago."

Earley asked him why.

"Because she was nothing like we all portray each other to be," Joe said. "She was a real human being with real feelings, and she understood what position I was in, and she wasn't about just killing animals like we all think PETA is about."

"Did you think that she was someone who could help you get yourself out of the park?"

Joe agreed that she was helping him leave.

"All right. Now, as far as your arrangements with Ms. Peet, tell the jury what you had in mind," said Earley.

"Me and my mom had a plan," said Joe. "It was going to take a little while because we had to jump through all of the civil litigation hoops to do it. But Carole was suing my mom for illegal transfer of assets of the land because we changed the name from the first park to the Garold Wayne Interactive Zoological Park. So the transfer of the land was an issue. And we came up with the idea and the plan, and we ran that by Howard Baskin – through a third person because we couldn't talk direct to him because of the lawsuit – that mom was going to quit fighting it and quit paying the lawyers. So that way, Carole could win the judgment on the illegal transfer of assets, which would void the land deed that Jeff was on and it would go back to hundred per cent of my mom owning the property.

"Because Jeff never paid the lease like they had a contract, she was going to evict him. And that would have got Jeff off the park. And we were working out a deal with PETA to work out with Carole to move all the animals out, and let John Finlay cut the cages apart and sell them for scrap iron in order to have us some private money to move because Carole would have owned the land with that deal. And that was our plan."

"So effectively shut down the entire operation?"

"Correct."

"While this was going on, you're trying to work with PETA and resolve issues with Ms. Baskin, was there still a lot of drama going on at the park?"

"It was constantly drama going on at the park," said Joe. "I couldn't even go to town. I couldn't even go home and eat lunch. My house is inside the zoo. And I would go home and eat lunch, and I hear this screaming on the radio. And I run out in the park and here's one of my female workers laying there without an arm and everybody standing there just looking at her like she has some kind of disease. And I kill myself trying to train my staff for medical emergencies and animal emergencies, and then they let the chimpanzees out, then they let the tigers out, then they let the leopards out. And then I go to town and my husband dies. I just couldn't take any more."

"Now, during this same period of time, even prior to Travis' death, did you become involved in some outside activities?"

"I ran for public office, yes."

"What did you run for?"

"In 2016, I just… I write a lot of letters to senators and congressmen, and you never hear anything back ever. You get a form letter if you're lucky. And I laid in bed one night and I was like, how do a normal person, like me and you, ever get heard in this country. And I woke up the next morning and I filled out my federal papers to run for president against Donald Trump as an independent. I didn't know what I was getting into really. And we didn't do it as a joke. I was very serious about it. I probably learned more in eleven months running for president than I did in twelve years of school. An independent is not recognised in this country, so you have to go to every state and get 140,000 signatures in order to get access to the ballot, and pay a fee. And

I was the first person to ever make thirty-seven ballots when it come election time in November.

"So after that, the night of the election, the Libertarian Party that had Gary Johnson running for president against Donald Trump called me and asked me if I would change parties and run for 2020. And I thought, hell, yeah, if they're calling me from the national Libertarian office to run for president, I'm game. So the next morning I changed my parties and I was like, I don't know if I can keep my mouth shut for four more years. So the governor race in Oklahoma was up because she had termed out..."

The incumbent, Mary Fallin, had completed her eight years in office and could not stand again.

"... So I signed up to run for governor of the state of Oklahoma. And for a year and a half they had to put up with me on that stage with fifteen others debating them. So we, as American people that normally pay taxes and work out here for a living, had a voice."

"Were you kept busy during the fall of 2017 with that as well?"

"I was in, I believe, six parades between Thanksgiving and the first week of Christmas. And I had Amber, John's girlfriend at the time, and her three kids living in my house to keep me alive. And, you know, a lot of people give me a hard time about getting married so soon, but I studied regression and I was looking for every reason for Travis to come back. And I believed that God gave me Dillon to keep me alive."

It's fair to say that Joe's testimony about his private life cannot have gone down well with the conservative, Christian people of Oklahoma City and the God-fearing members of the jury.

214

## FIFTEEN: Big Cat Rescue

In his years fighting Carole Baskin, Joe had never confronted her face to face. However, he had been to Big Cat Rescue.

"Now, I believe you testified earlier that you have been to Tampa, Florida, correct?" said Earley.

"Many times," said Joe.

"Okay. Tell me what years you have been in Tampa, Florida."

"The entire time that we were fighting this litigation, we went down there for depositions several times. I flew down there and went shark fishing and parasailing. I took John and another kid on a trip down there deep sea fishing. I flew down there to do the music video. I actually flew down there to do a protest in front of Carole's road that goes to her place."

"When was that?"

"Maybe 2012, somewhere around there."

"Okay. How about 2015 or '16, had you been down to Tampa?"

"I think '15 – I think '16 is when I did the music video and was running for president. I did a presidential rally there in Clearwater."

"During those visits to Tampa, Florida, and particularly the visits after the lawsuit and things started getting acrimonious between the two of you, did you ever try to approach Carole Baskin?"

Although he had visited Big Cat Rescue, Joe never saw the Big Cat woman herself.

"I even went on a tour," said Joe. "I paid to go on a tour at her facility to see what it looked like compared to ours. I never even saw Carole Baskin. And I have never emailed her. I have never called her. I have never sent her a message on social media."

"Have you ever called her and threatened her?"

"Absolutely not."

"Have you ever delivered or sought to have delivered a threat in writing?"

"No, sir."

"Prior to the fall of 2017, had anyone ever approached you about hiring someone to kill Carole Baskin?"

"Not that I can recall."

Earley then addressed the charges at the top of the indictment.

"Let's talk about count one of the indictment," he said. "Count one charges that in November you inquired of Allen Glover if he would travel to Florida to murder Carole Baskin in exchange for some money. Did you do that?"

"I never talked to Allen Glover about this," said Joe.

"It also says that you told Glover that – or that Glover told you he would go to Florida to murder Carole Baskin in exchange for some money. Did he ever say that to you?"

"No, sir."

Earley then got down to the details of the charge.

"Now, the indictment charges that on or about November 6 you caused Mr. Glover to travel to Dallas to get a fake ID for use in this proposed plot for him to go to Florida and kill Carole Baskin. Tell us about this ID situation."

"In October, the last week of October, Jeff called me from Las Vegas and told me to call James and get the address of where he goes and gets these fake driver's licences that they make to

216

go lease fake addresses, and have Allen go down there and get a fake driver's licence because he needed to get a bus to go back to South Carolina and fix all of his legal problems and everything else he had back there. And Jeff said, 'and I may send him to Florida to take care of my problem.' That was his exact words."

"Was that in October?"

"That was in October. And we all forgot about it. Jeff and James never responded to me. I – we just forgot about it. And then Jeff called about a week, week and a half later and said, 'Did you ever get Allen that address?' So I called James again and James sent me the address. And I asked John if he'd take him to Dallas because I didn't want anything to do with Allen in a car for five hours, and I didn't want any part of whatever they were up to because I had already received a tip through the little canary grapevine there at the park that they were up to something. So that's when I called John on his way to Dallas and told him to keep at least a block away from that place and do not go in."

"Now, according to your testimony, you were aware that Lowe wanted him to travel to Dallas and get this ID, potentially for going to Florida, is that right?" Earley asked.

"That's what Jeff said, yes, sir," said Joe.

"So did you provide Finlay a vehicle to go down there?"

"That's the vehicle he always drove."

"All right. And did you tell him maybe find a different vehicle, don't take one associated with the park?"

"No. We didn't have any other vehicles."

"All right. So it didn't bother you that there was a bumper sticker or something on that vehicle that would associate the vehicle with the park?"

"No."

"All right. And what was your intention of keeping Mr. Finlay a block or so away from the business?"

"Because whatever they were up to, I didn't want John being implicated in that. And I think I said that on one of them videos too, that we didn't want any part of it because mom's nurse told me that they were up to something."

"What did you think they were up to?"

"You know, between him and James, you never know what they're up to because, I mean, they'll look on social media, at each other, like they're fighting and they're best of friends. It's a constant game between them two."

"Did you question in your mind, why is Jeff telling me things?"

"I questioned in my mind why Jeff was telling me things all along because on September 30 he sold a tiger in Las Vegas to Paul Logan, the YouTube star. And I got him to wire $2,000 back to the park so I would have a receipt of him selling that tiger. And he did. It was just the craziest thing because everything that they did – they kept providing me with exactly what I needed, copies of leases and the whole nine yards."

"I believe Mr. Glover said something to the effect that he thought you were trying to gather information or something like that. Do you recall that testimony?"

"I remember him saying that I was fishing, and that's exactly what I was doing," said Joe.

"So when you provided the information that would allow Finlay and Glover to go down to Dallas and pick up an ID, did you do that with the intention that Allen Glover used that to assist in a plot to murder Carole Baskin?"

"I didn't exactly know what they was going to use it for because it was a toy ID. I didn't even know if he could get on a bus with it."

"The indictment also alleges that, as part of this plot, on November 25 you used the mail to send a cell phone out to Las Vegas to conceal Glover's, I guess, participation or involvement in this plot. What do you recall about the cell phone?"

"Okay. Before all that… there was a lot that happened before that. Jeff had called me several times, talking about him going to South Carolina and him going to Florida and—"

"Who's 'him'?" asked Earley.

"Allen."

"All right."

"Okay. And then Jeff gets arrested. In between that all, I think, was – if I have got my timeline right – I don't remember when he got arrested. It was close to Thanksgiving he gets arrested. And I had talked to James, and I repeated exactly what Jeff told me because I know they're talking to each other. And that made them both feel like, yeah, they got me in this little web, but I was also consulting a police officer that drove for me and was my bodyguard. And he kept telling me, just don't cross the line. You can fish all you want to get the information, but don't cross the line. And I thought crossing the line was actually hiring a man to go do this, you know. I didn't think asking questions was crossing the line because I just wanted to know what the hell they were up to. But they were like high-pressure salesmen trying to sell you a vacuum cleaner with extra parts. Just non-stop. It was all about Carole, Carole, Carole, Carole. And then Jeff said, 'give him three' – I mean, at that time I was texting Jeff and saying, the man won't work for me, he won't come to a meeting, he won't do this, he won't do that. And I guess Jeff… Allen was bitching at Jeff too about the same thing. He didn't want to work for me anymore. He wanted to go home. So Jeff calls me and says, give Allen $3,000 so he can get his ass back to South Carolina and get his legal mess cleaned up, and he'll be out of your hair."

"So we're covering a couple of extra things here. So hang with me," said Earley. "We'll just cover that while we're on it. Did you give Allen Glover some money?"

"I did."

"And you did that because you were told to?"

"I was directed by Jeff to give him three thousand bucks to go home so he had travelling money and living money because Jeff had retail stores out in the east coast and he was going to go work for Jeff out there."

"All right. So where did the money come from that you gave to Glover?"

"Out of the night deposits, just like Jeff told me to take it out of the night deposits."

"And what do you mean 'night deposits'?"

"Every night, and especially during the holidays, we just kept every day's income in an envelope in the safe until the end of the holiday, and then combine it all together and put it in one deposit."

"So, are these like park admission fees and things like that?"

"And the pizza restaurant money and both gift shops' money, uh-huh," said Joe.

"So the cash that you provided came from the business, correct?"

"Correct."

"All right. Now, along with that there's this allegation about the cell phone. Tell me what your participation was with respect to this cell phone allegedly being mailed to Mr. Lowe as part of this plot."

"After I gave Allen the money, a couple hours later he walks over into the office and he lays his cell phone on the desk, and to this day I swear it didn't have a charger. It was just a cell phone. And he says, here, we're supposed to mail this to Jeff. And

I carried it in, and I give it to Brenda because I didn't have his address. And I said, 'Brenda, Jeff wants you to mail this cell phone to him.' And that was the end of it."

"Was there any other discussion between you and Allen about this cell phone?"

"No."

"Any discussion with Jeff about this cell phone?"

"No, sir."

"Now, there was testimony from Mr. Glover that you gave him another cell phone."

"That was all a lie."

"Did you give him another cell phone?"

"Absolutely not, especially a company phone that we just advertised several thousand dollars to order pizza with."

"So did you see a phone on the day that he was leaving town?"

"No, sir."

"Did you use a phone that belonged to Glover to take screenshots of information about Carole Baskin and her place?"

"No, sir."

"When did you know that Allen Glover would be leaving the park on November 25?"

"I didn't even know he left."

"When was the first time you figured out that he actually left the park?"

"Probably two or three days later."

"Did you have anything to do with him making arrangements to fly back to South Carolina?"

"I didn't even know he took an airplane until this all started."

"Did you hire Allen Glover to kill Carole Baskin?"

"Absolutely not."

Having disposed of the first count, Earley moved on.

"Well, let's talk about the second count," he said. "Do you recall the recordings that were played between Mr. Garretson and you in which Garretson is talking to you about this guy that he had that could do things? Do you remember that?"

"Yes, sir."

"Do you remember those conversations with Garretson?"

"Pretty much."

"When did you first hear from Garretson about this guy that he supposedly had?"

"I don't even remember exactly, maybe mid-September."

"All right. And so how did that come up?"

"Can I back up just a little bit and fill you in on that?" said Joe.

"Well, if it has something to do with how this topic came up, go ahead," said Earley.

Joe recalled having toothache.

"That's the reason why this topic come up in late June or August, or July, I had a horrible, horrible toothache and I needed two root canals and two crowns. And James says, I have a CareCredit card that's about to expire…"

Maxfield Green stepped in again.

"Your Honour, we object," she said. "Same objection as before as to relevance and hearsay and prejudicial."

Judge Palk: "Sustained."

"Okay, Mr. Passage," said Earley. "What I need you to do is talk about how this topic of Mr. Garretson's guy came up and when it first came up."

"We were on the phone talking about my teeth."

"Okay. And that's fine," said Earley. "And when was that?"

"August–September, August. August, I think."

"So that's the first time that you heard Mr. Garretson bring up some guy that he might have to do something. What was it that this guy could do?"

"Well, he called me; I didn't call him," said Joe. "And every time he called, it was about Carole or Jeff. So it was – what information you know about Carole, or what, you know, is Jeff paying any bills, or what's Jeff doing in Las Vegas. And if I remember right, he just said, is Carole still effing with you. And I said, yeah, obviously, she never stops. And he says, well, I know a guy that can take care of it. And through this entire process, you can watch these videos. Every time I use the excuse I have to sell a cub or I ain't got no babies born, I ain't got no money. It was the easiest way to get rid of the man."

"Just thinking back, maybe including the recordings and maybe non-recorded contacts you had with Garretson, how many times do you think he brought up his guy during the fall of 2017?"

"Probably ten or twelve, at least," said Joe.

"Did those remarks continue into December?"

"Yes, sir."

"All right. Were those conversations that you started or was the topic brought up by Garretson?"

"It was always him calling. And I believe one of them in early December even. I even lied to him and told him I had a photo shoot in Dallas to get out of even the conversation, but I was actually at a parade in Davis, Oklahoma."

"When he was contacting you in December and November about this, were you still in discussions with Ms. Peet about extricating yourself from the park?"

"We were still moving tigers out and cutting cages apart."

"Your decision to leave the park, how did that affect your thoughts about Carole Baskin?"

"You know, after Travis died and dealing with that and dealing with PETA's lawsuit to come get them first nineteen tigers – and having three kids that I'm not used to in the house screaming and hollering and meeting Dillon on the 28th and six parades to do and running for office and doing debates at the same time, Carole Baskin didn't even enter my mind unless one of them called and brought it up."

"Did you ever agree, whether it's recorded or not, to meet this guy before this December 8 meeting?"

"He only had one recording of that, but he called like two or three times, hey, I'm going to bring my guy up tomorrow. And he never shows up. I'm going to bring him up Thursday, and he never shows up. Well, hey, you going to be around Friday? You know what, it's the same as always. The man never done what he said he was going to do. So I just said, sure. And I'll be damned if they didn't show up."

"Well, let's talk about December 8," said Earley. "Did you plan on meeting with this person?"

"No."

"Now, he obviously did show up at the park."

"Yes, sir."

"What were you doing at the time that they popped in on you?"

Joe didn't recall, but he was sure he was working in the park doing something.

"Were you continuing to do your daily duties and do tours and take care of animals and all that other stuff?" asked Earley.

"Yes, sir."

'Was that in addition to your concentration on your campaign?"

"It was during the concentration on everything," said Joe. "I mean, that was the first day actually that… well, no, Dillon had already moved in and even he was… I mean, everybody was in and out of the office the entire time."

"Now, where did most of that conversation take place?"

"In the office away from the gift shop."

"Is that sort of a secretive, closed-off place?"

"No, it's open. Everybody had access to it. It's just a portable building that we had next to the big gift shop office because we outgrew the gift shop office."

"Now, what was your gut feeling about this conversation?"

"I had a gut feeling it was an undercover cop."

"Why?"

"Because they were so high pressure. I mean, it," said Joe. "First of all, they blocked the door. I couldn't get out the door. They stood in front of the door. I don't recall anybody ever sitting down. And you have got a giant Chucky and a guy that looks like hell blocking the only door to get out of the building. And they're like, 'Oh, we can kill her, we can do this, we can drop the price down to 5,000 bucks…'."

Joe claimed he had had his doubts.

"…You're really going to drive to Tampa, Florida, and stay there and kill somebody and come back on 5,000 bucks? I can't even deliver a tiger that cheap."

"Did you think it was a set-up?" said Earley.

"I believed it was a set-up," said Joe.

"Now, there was a discussion about getting some money together. Do you remember that?"

"I do."

"Did you ever get money together?"

"No. And I told them on the recording that I had to sell some cubs to get some money, but I kept telling them the same thing I heard from Jeff during his little set-up because at the same time he's trucking around with an undercover FBI guy using stolen credit cards."

"Did you ever provide Garretson money for the services of Mark [Williams]?"

"Not a dime."

"Now, there was this discussion about getting a gun for purposes of carrying out this plot. Do you remember that?"

"That was their idea."

"All right. So did you ever try to go get a gun for Mark?" asked Earley.

"No," said Joe.

"Now, there was also some discussion about getting some phones – a phone for you and a phone for Mark so that you two could communicate, and it wouldn't have anything to do with the park. Do you remember that?"

"Yep."

"Did you ever go and purchase any phones for you and Mark?"

"Never even thought about it after they left."

"So did you hire Mark to kill Carole Baskin?"

"Absolutely not."

"Did you take any further steps, as far as collecting money, making inquiry about guns, inquiry about phones, anything that would suggest you had any interest at all in carrying through with what Mark and Mr. Garretson had proposed?"

"Nope."

"Now, we heard a little bit of testimony from Ms. Peet about her trying to intervene and perhaps reach some sort of settlement that would, you know, basically take care of not only them but also the Baskin situation. What was your understanding of what she was trying to broker for you?"

PETA wanted to close Joe's park down.

"PETA had a separate contract of their own where I had to get rid of all of the animals, and I could not ever own an exotic animal again, couldn't have anything to do with anybody that had exotic animals," Joe said. "So I couldn't go to work for anybody that had exotic animals. And we were going to move all the animals. We were going to allow John Finlay to move into the main house and cut the cages apart, and that's where we were going to get our extra money. Plus she had no problem coming up with $100,000 to replace the money that mom paid for the land, but they didn't want Jeff Lowe making a dime. And that's what broke the deal was Jeff wouldn't agree to anything because he wanted $400,000 to walk away from it. So we couldn't get Jeff out. So that's why we needed mine and my mom's plan to work on through. And that's what we were working on. Between the lawyers and PETA and me and mom, we were actually working on that plan up until I got snitched out of having them investigated."

"All right. So there wasn't a settlement?"

"No, sir."

"And at least from your view, was that because Jeff Lowe wouldn't sign on?"

"It is because Jeff Lowe wouldn't sign off on it."

"So after the first of the year, going into February, March of 2018, what was your plan as it pertains to the park?"

"Well, January 2, 2018, I got my first traffic ticket in my life – running a stop sign – and broke my neck and my back and my right leg. And I was in OU Medical Center for a few days there. And then I get home and I'm in braces. And the whole thing of leaving the zoo was still priority on my mind. So we move some bears and some monkeys and some more tigers, and then because Allen was finally out of my hair. Every time I moved an animal before Allen left, he'd call Jeff and Jeff would call and say, what are you doing moving this animal or getting rid of this animal. So I couldn't get rid of most of the animals that were under my licence until Allen was gone. So after Allen was gone, and after I got out of the hospital after having my wreck, we moved almost every primate in that zoo to other facilities, except for the two chimpanzees and the one primate pigtail macaque that John Reinke, the manager – actually, it was his monkey. So we got rid of all the primates. We got rid of almost all the bears. We only had three bears left…"

By then Joe was cooperating with PETA and the authorities – to no avail.

"…We were still placing tigers at different private facilities. And Brittany was helping me organise all this, but we were having troubles finding sanctuaries that had room for 200 tigers. I mean, moving 200 tigers is a process, you just don't do it overnight. And in June they come up with this Carole thing, you know, a couple more times. And then May he got in some more legal trouble out there and I was feeding information to Brittany. I was feeding information to the district attorney in Las Vegas. I was feeding information to another man that was piping it up the USDA to – Bernadette Juarez is the top USDA for us, and she was supposed to be giving some of this stuff to the FBI because he was selling skins and teeth and everything out in Vegas from tigers. And so I have got these screenshots and all of the information I needed. If somebody would have just come and ask me, we could have avoided this whole thing."

"Well, did anybody ever come and ask you?"

"To this day, nobody has."

"Now, we heard a recording of a phone call that you had with Mr. Finlay while you were being held in custody. Do you recall that?" Earley asked.

"Yes, sir. Yes, sir."

"And during that phone call you suggested that he had told on you. Do you remember?"

"Yes, sir."

"Do you remember what you said?"

"I asked him who he's been talking to and he said the FBI. And I... John, the only thing John knew was he was taking Allen to Dallas to go to Florida. Because if he'd have told John the truth... John has a very low self-esteem, so he always attaches himself to the wrong people because they become his friend fast. And he just wouldn't keep his mouth shut if I would have told him the truth, so that's why I told him to park a block away from the damn place so he didn't get implicated in anything. And what's he do, he walks right in the damn building."

"So what did you mean during this conversation when you accused him of selling you out, or whatever the exact words were?"

"Well, I mean, he knew that the direct orders came from Jeff. And I wanted to make sure that when he talked to the FBI he didn't say it was just my sending him down there – that I wanted to make sure that he told them that Jeff is the one who told us to send him down there."

"All right. Now, at any time did you intend for someone to kill Carole Baskin in exchange for money or any other thing of value?"

"No."

Judge Palk then took a fifteen-minute recess, saying: "My intent is that we power through and – and finish at least with testimony today, even if that means we may end up having to stay just a little bit late."

He didn't think they could wrap up the case before 5 p.m. that day, but he intended to dispose of the rest of Joe's testimony.

## SIXTEEN: Selling Your Life Story

After the break, Assistant US Attorney Amanda Maxfield Green began her cross-examination. She immediately attacked Joe's Achilles heel – his evident craving for fame.

"Good afternoon, Mr. Passage," she said. "Mr. Passage, since you have been in jail, you have been working on selling your life story to several different members of the media, correct?"

"I have been working on selling some of the footage from the zoo and the past," said Joe. "One of them I had a contract with in, like, 2017."

"Rebecca Chaiklin is one of your filmmakers, correct?"

"Correct."

"And what about Eric Goode, he's one of your filmmakers, correct?"

"They're together."

"Rebecca and Eric work together?"

"Correct."

Eric Goode and Rebecca Chaiklin were the directors of *Tiger King: Murder, Mayhem and Madness* broadcast on Netflix in March 2020.

"Is Rebecca in the courtroom today?" Maxfield Green asked.

"Eric is."

"So Rebecca and Eric, they're working on a film about your life, right?"

"We started a documentary way before Travis died," said Joe.

"Okay. What about Teresa McCown? She's one of your filmmakers, correct?"

"She used to be my producer before my studio burnt down."

"And is she making a film about you as well?"

"She hasn't asked for any footage or anything yet. She hadn't done anything. I don't know what she's doing," said Joe.

"Well, you have gotten several thousands of dollars already from Rebecca and Eric, correct?" asked Maxfield Green.

"Correct."

"And have you gotten several thousand dollars from Teresa McCown for your story?"

"I haven't gotten a dime from Teresa. My husband has."

"Okay. And that's up into the several thousands of dollars, correct?"

"Correct."

"And you have been negotiating with them ever since you have been in jail, correct?"

"Correct."

"And it was Rebecca Chaiklin and Eric Goode who paid John Finlay for an interview about you, correct?"

"From my understanding, they paid a lot of people," said Joe.

Finlay had testified that he had agreed to the interview because "talking about what happened in my life is helping me move on."

"And this is all in connection with a film about your life, correct?" Maxfield Green asked Joe.

"Correct."

Then she moved on to the substance of the charges.

"Now, you and Mr. Earley covered a lot of stuff. So I'm going to try to go a little bit in order … Now, Mr. Earley talked to you about Darlene Cervantes. Do you recall that?"

"Yes, ma'am."

"And he talked to you about Government's exhibit twenty-one, which is that text exchange with her, correct?"

"Yes, ma'am."

"Now, your testimony was that you told her that the cubs would be a thousand dollars just to get rid of her, correct?"

"Correct."

"Okay. But you saw that text exchange in the Government's part of the case, right?"

"I saw it, yes, ma'am."

"Now, that text exchange went on from October to February, correct?"

"That should explain that it wasn't a very serious sale, was it?" said Joe.

"But that whole text exchange was all about selling a couple of tigers for a thousand dollars, correct?"

"Correct."

"Okay. Now... you have got to forgive me, I have got a lot of notes here."

"You're all right."

"So you told... you said on direct that in 2014, in October of 2014, you got extremely ill; is that right?"

"Very ill."

"And you got so ill, it sounds like you were on your deathbed; is that right?"

"I was."

"And you made a deal with God, correct?"

"I did."

"That if you walked out of that hospital you were going to be different and, I can't remember what words you used, but you were going to 'do better', I think you said."

"I was going to try and change, yes, ma'am."

"And that was in October 2014?"

"That was. October 21, to be exact."

"Okay. So do you remember when we were talking to Ms. Baskin, and during the Government's case, we looked at a lot of posts and videos of yours, correct?"

"Correct."

Maxfield Green called up Government's exhibit ninety-seven.

"Now, that's a post on your Facebook page, right?" she said.

"It's a post on one of my Facebook pages."

"And you had several, correct?"

"I had nineteen of them."

"So this is one of them, correct?"

"That is one of them."

"Is that a photo of you standing at a coffin?" asked Maxfield Green.

"That is."

"And now, as I recall, this one says, 'I bought my good friend Carole in Florida a Christmas present. It even came with me singing a farewell song.' That was posted on December 28, 2014, correct?"

"Mine says twenty-one hours," said Joe.

"Okay. I think if you look in the lower right-hand corner that shows when that screenshot was."

"Oh, when the screenshot was taken. Well, I mean, that shows when the screenshot was taken, but that don't show when the post was put up," said Joe.

"Okay. Well, you heard the testimony on direct that Ms. Baskin believed it was posted on about December 28, 2014?"

"I heard a lot about what Ms. Baskin believes."

"So December 28, 2014 would have been after you made your deal with God, correct?"

"Would have been a long time after that, but may I elaborate on that?" asked Joe.

"No," said Maxfield Green. "I just… December 2014 is after October 2014, correct?"

"I was way too sick to be on top of that casket in December 2014."

Then Maxfield Green called for Government's exhibit 100, another video clip showing Joe making a death threat, to be played to the court. The court and the jury watched as Joe appears on screen saying of Carole "when it's my time she's going to die first."

"Okay. So that video was posted on September 17, 2015, correct?" said Maxfield Green.

"All right," said Joe.

"And that would have been after October 2014, correct?"

"Correct."

Joe then asked: "Can we play the music video?" Joe wanted to play the video he had made to accompany the song, *Here Kitty Kitty* for the court.

"I don't think we need to," said Maxfield Green.

"Well, it shows that—"

"Mr. Passage," Judge Palk intervened. "Mr. Passage, please just answer the questions. Mr. Earley will have the opportunity to ask you additional questions if he wants to elaborate for some additional information, but please just answer the questions before you."

"Yes, sir," said Joe.

"Okay, Mr. Passage," Maxfield Green continued. "The best as I understood your testimony on direct, you're telling us that you never sold a tiger across state lines, right?"

"Up until 2016 I sold a bunch of them," said Joe, correcting her.

"Okay. Let me get this right then," said Maxfield Green. "Your testimony is that after 2016 when the generic tiger loophole closed—"

"And I didn't own a zoo at that time," Joe interjected.

"So your testimony is that, after that point, in 2016, you never sold tigers, correct?"

"I did not."

"Okay. Is your testimony also that you never, in the same regard, would have never falsified any documents to cover up a sale like that, correct?"

"I mean, all of the... all of the documents that we fill out are transfer forms and those are donated from whoever owned the animal," said Joe.

"Now, Jeff and Lauren Lowe were back at the park by May 2018, correct?" said Maxfield Green.

"Yes, somewhere around there."

"And you had a conversation with the two of them when you were sitting at a desk in their house at the zoo, correct, on about May 3, 2018?"

"I think that conversation started in the office... and overflowed through the house."

"So you recall that conversation?"

"I think so, if you're talking about the same one."

"Okay. And you're aware that conversation was recorded, correct?"

"Yes, ma'am."

Addressing the bench, Maxfield Green requested the judge admit further exhibits into evidence. These were recordings of conversations between Joe and Jeff Lowe.

"Is there any objection from the defendant?" said Judge Palk addressing Earley.

"Well, we haven't actually seen these exhibits, Your Honour," said Earley. There followed an exchange at the bench, out of the hearing of the jurors. Earley raised questions about how the recordings had been edited.

Earley said: "The only concern was that this particular video covered a lot of territory, to include allegations of campaign finance…" The prosecution had agreed that these details would not go into evidence.

"There is nothing in this exhibit about campaign finance, embezzlement," Maxfield Green pointed out. "The comments that are being offered are being used to directly impeach what Mr. Passage has said. He is talking about sales of tiger cubs to Mr. Engesser that had clearly happened at the few months prior and his falsification of documents to cover that up."

Robert Engesser was the proprietor of Jungle Safari, aka The Zoo Pat (formerly known as Engesser's Exotic Felines, Luce Enterprises, The Zoo and Endangered Species, Inc.), a privately-owned travelling petting zoo which spent nine months of the year exhibiting big cats and their cubs in the parking lots of malls and shopping centres.

That matter was resolved and the proceedings resumed. The video clips of Joe's discussion with Lowe were played for the jury.

"That conversation was on May 3, 2018, correct?" Maxfield Green asked.

"I guess, yes," said Joe.

"Now, Mr. Passage, again, it was your testimony that you never sold endangered species – cubs, lions or tigers, correct?"

"According to this video right here, he was accusing me of stealing his money from selling a cub," said Joe.

"Okay. Were you intending to broker the sale of a litter of lions from your jail cell?"

"Do what?" asked Joe.

"Were you intending to broker the sale of a litter of lions from your jail cell?" Maxfield Green repeated.

"Broker a litter of lions from my jail cell? I don't have any lions," said Joe.

"You made phone calls from jail, right?"

"Made a couple hundred."

"Okay. And you're aware that those calls are recorded, right?"

"I am."

Maxfield Green then moved to admit exhibits into evidence which were recordings of Joe's phone calls. Judge Palk asked the defence if they had any objection.

"If Ms. Green's representing that they're phone calls from the jail and that Mr. Passage is on them, I have no reason to disbelieve her," said Earley.

The recordings were admitted in evidence and played in open court.

"Okay, Mr. Passage, on direct you testified that Jeff Lowe was selling tiger cubs, correct?" said Maxfield Green.

"At the zoo."

"Okay. And that you even kept a ledger where you kept track of his tiger cub sales, right?"

"I did."

"Okay. Now, so you knew – you know – back last year that Jeff Lowe was selling tiger cubs. Is that your testimony?"

"Yes."

"Why didn't you report that to law enforcement?" asked Maxfield Green.

"I tried to report a whole bunch of stuff," said Joe.

"Who did you report the fact that Jeff Lowe was selling tiger cubs to?" Maxfield Green asked. "Did you report it to the U.S. Fish and Wildlife Service?"

"I didn't report it to the U.S. Fish and Wildlife Service because I have never seen one of them guys," said Joe. "And when you call the U.S. Fish and Wildlife, nobody ever knows nothing. They transfer you ten different times. So I told the Garvin County Sheriff's Department, I told the USDA, and—"

"Who did you tell at the USDA?"

"I told the guy that was sending everything to Bernadette Juarez. And I told the investigator and the district attorney out in Las Vegas because I had screenshots of him selling cubs out there."

Joe then asked if he could comment on the prosecution's video.

"I didn't have any questions about that," said Maxfield Green, effectively muzzling Joe.

Resuming her cross-examination, Maxfield Green asked: "Now, and just to understand the timeline and everything, so Jeff Lowe... it was your testimony that Jeff Lowe was in Las Vegas from about May, June of 2017. Is that when he left for Las Vegas?"

"Somewhere around there," said Joe.

"Okay. And he sounds like he came back and forth a little bit, correct?"

"Whenever he run out of cubs."

"So he came back in about April 2018, correct, or came back…?"

"For a little bit or for good?" asked Joe.

"For good."

"I think it was closer to May," said Joe. "I'm not sure."

"And that would have been 2018 when he came back for good?"

"Well, he came back, supposedly for good, and then he left again."

"Now, you talked about this proposal from PETA, correct? You talked about that on direct?"

"Yes, ma'am."

"And you were here for Ms. Peet's testimony last Friday, correct?"

"Yes, ma'am."

"Okay. And so you heard her testify that any negotiation with you that she was proposing did not involve Carole Baskin. Did you hear that testimony?"

"I forget exactly what she said," Joe said. "But the negotiations that she was working with me was with PETA, and Carole would not agree to anything unless I agreed to PETA's thing first. That's what was going on."

"Okay. But Ms. Peet testified that the Baskins were not part of a draft proposal she was giving you in January 2018, correct?"

"The draft proposal was PETA's draft, PETA's side of it," said Joe.

"Okay. And you saw the email between you and Ms. Peet from January 24, 2018, correct?"

"I don't recall we saw that email."

"Well, it's Government exhibit 160," said Maxfield Green. "We can just look at it. It's already been admitted. Okay. Now, this is an email from you to Ms. Peet on January 24, 2018, right?"

"Yes, ma'am."

"It says, 'Brittany, unless I'm blind or stupid, this does not get rid of the judgment.' And it was Ms. Peet's testimony that that judgment meant the litigation between you and Carole Baskin. Did you hear that testimony?"

"Yes, ma'am."

"Okay. And it says, 'nor help in any way to pay off our legal bills and to make any money'. And that's what it says, right?"

"Yes, ma'am."

"Okay. And that email was from you to Ms. Peet in January 2018, correct?"

"Correct."

"Okay. And you also testified that, as part of your working with PETA through the, I guess, winter of 2017, 2018, you gave up forty tigers, correct?"

"Nineteen the first time and twenty the second time," said Joe.

"Okay. Now, that first nineteen, those were the Dade City tigers, right?"

"Yes, ma'am."

"The ones that came in on the cattle trailer in July 2017?"

"Yes, ma'am."

"Okay. Now, you gave those up because PETA sued you to force you to give them up, correct?"

"Correct."

"And then you gave them an additional twenty, twenty-one tigers at some other point?"

"After I met Ms. Peet in person, yes."

"Okay. Now the tigers you gave them, those were your non-breeding males, right?"

"No. We gave them some pairs… I believe we did."

"Okay. And we spoke about the passing of your husband on October 6, 2017, correct?"

"Yes, ma'am."

"That was Mr. Maldonado, correct?" said Maxfield Green.

"Correct."

"And you're currently married to Mr. Passage, correct?"

"Correct."

"And you married him [Dillon Passage] on December 11, 2017. Is that correct?"

"Correct."

"So is that about eight weeks after Mr. Maldonado died?"

"Couple of months."

"And, in fact, the conversation that we listened to between you and James Garretson and Mark Williams, the undercover agent, that was just a few days prior to your being married, correct?"

"Correct."

"Okay. So you testified on direct with Mr. Earley that James Garretson kept telling you that he could get you a hitman. Is that your testimony?"

"Yes, ma'am."

"And you kept telling him that you needed to sell a cub to get rid of him. Is that your testimony?"

"That is my excuse to always get rid of him, yes."

"Now, when James Garretson kept coming to you and offering you a hitman, you didn't report that to law enforcement, correct?"

"No."

"You testified on direct you had an FBI agent's phone number in your phone, correct?"

"Correct."

"But you never reported it to him, right?"

"Never got any good response out of the last four things we reported to him," said Joe.

"Okay. And you're saying… your testimony on direct was that James Garretson brought Mark Williams to the park to meet you. We heard that whole recording, correct?"

"Correct."

"I understand your testimony to be that you knew that he was an undercover officer, correct?"

"I had a gut feeling," said Joe.

"Okay. And you didn't contact law enforcement about that, did you?"

"No."

"You didn't confront James Garretson about it, did you?"

"No, because I still needed to get some information of where these girls were being held." It's unclear what Joe meant by this but it's likely that he was again trying to insinuate that Lowe was involved in some criminal activity.

"You didn't try to... you didn't blow the undercover cop's cover, did you?" asked Maxfield Green.

"No. He was still using stolen credit cards hauling that cop around. Why would I tell him I knew anything?"

"Okay. And so the best I understand the remainder of the testimony you did with Mr. Earley is that, essentially, pretty much all of the Government witnesses were lying about something, correct?" said Maxfield Green.

"They were definitely lying about Robert Engesser," said Joe.

"Okay. And Allen Glover's lying about pretty much everything?"

"He's protecting his boss."

"Okay. And James Garretson's lying about pretty much everything?"

"About... all I heard him testify was to the recordings that we heard."

"Okay. John Finlay, is he lying?"

"John Finlay was pretty on point except for he said we delivered a hundred cubs over state lines, which is probably right, but they weren't all after 2016," said Joe. "But other than that, John was probably your most honest witness you have had so far."

"Okay. Including the part where he said you called him when he was on the way to Dallas and told him that the fake ID was so that Glover could kill Carole Baskin? Was he right about that?"

"He had that backwards," said Joe. "I told him that first, and I called him and told him to stay away from that building on the way."

"Okay."

"And Carole Baskin was lying," Joe said.

"Okay. Thank you. But you're telling the truth, correct?" said Maxfield Green.

"Yeah. The… the…" Joe stuttered.

"That's my question, Mr. Passage. You're telling the truth?" Maxfield Green asked.

"Yes, ma'am."

"No further questions, Your Honour."

On redirect, Bill Earley asked Joe how long he had been working with documentary filmmakers.

"Since probably 2009, 2010," said Joe.

"Okay, let's just use the time frame of 2009 up until you left in 2018," said Earley. "In the spring of 2018, was there anybody there filming you or trying to document what you did at the park?"

"The last part of 2017, we documented when Travis died," Joe said. "I had to re-act spreading his ashes and the whole bit. And then, in 2018, they were out filming other people for the same documentary. And then when it got close to June and all hell broke loose and I hid some animals out in Tulsa at a facility over there, they videotaped me moving and hauling the animals there and spent all day there. And then I… I ain't got nothing to hide… and then the next day they took me to a motel, and we did a little bit of soft porn for the same documentary in my underwear…"

This was a surprise turn, but all part of Joe's growing media portfolio.

"So I've filmed with Allison Eastwood [host of short-lived, National Geographic reality TV show, *Animal Intervention*]. I've filmed with Japanese people for a Japanese film. I have filmed a lot of films."

"Apparently some news outfit, CNN or somebody came and talked to you, right? We saw a video clip of that."

"Years ago."

"Has that continued throughout the years?"

"I have been all over the world on TV, yes. Yes, sir. And talk shows."

"So is the fact that someone is collecting footage that you have from the park, is that something unusual?" asked Earley.

"Not at all," said Joe.

## SEVENTEEN: Documented

While Joe's own TV efforts had been hampered by the burglary and fire at his studio, other filmmakers were still interested.

"So what is somebody working on right now, to your knowledge?" Earley asked.

"Well, Eric Goode and Rebecca are still working on the same documentary we started two and a half years ago," said Joe. "And after I left the zoo, they downloaded several computers with probably thirty-thousand hours of video because we filmed everything at the park. I have got the girl [Kelci 'Saff' Saffery] losing her arm on tape. I have got it all. Everything that happened at that zoo is on tape. And I signed a contract back in early 2016 – '17 with Mr. Goode. And he owed me twenty more thousand bucks, and that's what my husband has been living on since this all started because they bulldozed my house; they bulldozed everything I own. I lost my car. We have nowhere to live. He's living with his mom and his sister in Texas. And, you know, Mr. Goode even has Ms. Baskin on videotape that he has offered once or twice to show she was lying about that assault in Tampa, Florida. That happened in 2006 before I even knew her."

"So this business about you collecting money or what have you from people, that's old news?" Earley said.

"It's from people that owe me money, yes, sir."

"All right. And I guess you have already said this, you have nothing?"

"I have nothing. If I walk out of here today, I have got to give this suit back."

This was lucky as Joe had earlier vowed never to wear a suit.

"Now, Ms. Green asked you about Government's exhibit 97, which was this photo that was supposedly posted on Facebook December 28, 2014. You had some disagreement with the date?"

"Well, first of all, Joe Schreibvogel's Facebook page was being run by somebody out of the office. Okay? I run the Joseph Maldonado-Passage page. Second of all, we quit the magic show in 2011. We retired the magic show. And that's me standing on top of a casket in one of our main illusion shows, and they're trying to tell me that was in 2014."

"So, to your recollection, even though some screenshot may show that it's in 2014, you believe that photo was actually from 2011, or thereabouts?"

"Or thereabouts."

"All right. Now, Ms. Green showed you a video clip from September 17, 2015, suggesting that you broke your deal with God and you weren't changing your ways. You were going back to your old ways…"

That is, hurling threats and accusations at Carole Baskin.

"…Do you remember seeing that?" Earley asked.

"I do."

"Is that what that represents?" asked Earley.

"No, it doesn't."

"What do you think it represents?"

"It represents a very, very professional music video that we put out that she hates, and it's about her feeding her husband to the tigers." This was Joe's chance to speak about the music video that Maxfield Green had refused to play to the court and keep Carole Baskin in his sights, even though Judge Palk had ruled that there should be no mention of the disappearance of Don Lewis.

"So this is a music video?"

Joe confirmed that it was a music video.

"All right. Is that all that follows that introductory comment by you?" Earley asked.

"That is all that follows."

Earley went back to the wildlife charges.

"Now, your testimony is that up to 2016 you probably sold a bunch of tigers; is that right?"

"Yeah."

"And it wasn't illegal then?"

"Nobody ever DNA tested them to see if they were purebred Siberian or Bengal."

"Well, if they did would they have found that out?"

"If they had something to compare it to."

"All right. So after 2016, your story is that, 'Hey, I never sold any tigers.' Why are you saying that?"

"Because Jeff claimed everything, whether he touched it, whether he used it, whether he bought it, it became Jeff's. And I tried to get some of those animals out of there, and he told me I owed $4.6 million for boarding, and that was through my legal team."

"Now, we saw that little video, or actually three little clips of that video that Lauren Lowe had recorded. Do you remember that?"

"Yes, sir."

"Okay. Do you remember that day?"

"I do remember that day."

"What do you remember about that day?"

"That day started in the office," said Joe, "and he was throwing shit around and hitting file cabinets. I thought they were going to beat the hell out of me because I have seen him beat up an employee before. And we finally got out of that office, and then I took the paperwork and the bank statements down to his house to prove to him that he didn't know what the hell he was talking about, and it escalated there until I left."

"Now, you said something to the effect that you had sold something to Mr. Engesser – a cub?"

"I do remember saying that, but I made that up just to get out of the situation."

"Okay. So had you, on behalf of the zoo, had any transactions with Mr. Engesser?"

"Yes, sir."

"Okay. Let me ask you this: Whatever transactions you may have had with him, did they occur in November 2017?"

"I don't believe so at all, no, sir."

"And I want to just go back. Is it your testimony that you did not receive any money from Mr. Engesser in November of 2017?"

This was alleged to have been the money that Joe handed on to Allen Glover for the assassination of Carole Baskin.

"I know I did not," said Joe.

"The money that Lowe asked you to give to Glover came from where?"

"The cash register deposits."

"So if Mr. Engesser testified – and you heard him – that he hadn't been there and he didn't buy a cub from you in November of 2017, would that be true?"

"That would be true."

"Now, Ms. Green asked you about some phone calls that were recorded where you're brokering the sale of a litter of lions. Did you hear that?"

"I heard that."

"All right. So the first one, Government's exhibit 162, had something to do with Charlie somebody and some lions. Tell the jury what the conversation is about."

"Okay. Dillon was living at his mom's and his sister's down in Belton, Texas," said Joe. "And Charlie [Carmel 'Charlie' Azzopardi who was indicted in 2006 on three felony accounts of illegal trafficking of animals including clouded leopards and tigers] over in Amarillo, Texas, used to have a zoo open to the public, but PETA harassed him to the point that he lost his USDA licence, and he closed to the public, but he still has his animals. And every time he has a litter of baby lions born, they end up dying because he don't know how to take care of them. So he would call us and Reinke would... because Reinke lives in Texas, he would run over to Amarillo and pick them up and save them. Okay. And we'd take them back to the zoo. So he was expecting a litter of babies, and we're all gone from the zoo. So I was going to have Dillon go pick them up over there. And it's perfectly legal; we're not selling anything across state lines. And I would have found a buyer for them from jail in Texas so Dillon had some money to live on. Simple as that. You don't even need a USDA licence because you're in the same state."

"So there really wasn't anything illegal or underhanded or anything having to do with that."

"Absolutely not," said Joe, who went on to explain the legal situation as he saw it. "If he would have got some cubs and came to Oklahoma to stay and start... because the laws in Oklahoma are better, he still wouldn't have been breaking no laws because he's not going to be open to the public. So he doesn't need a USDA licence. And he doesn't need any licence from the state of Oklahoma because in 2006 we did have licences here. Okay. And you had to have a $50 permit to have a bear or a cat that grew to weigh over fifty pounds to keep or maintain on your premises. And in 2006 I was doing magic shows, and the game wardens wrote me some tickets for leaving my property with my animals because they thought it said keep them maintained on premises. You couldn't leave your premises with the animals. So I hired a law firm in Pauls Valley, Oklahoma, and I filed a lawsuit against the state of Oklahoma because in 1952 they wrote a law that said they own all wildlife. So, if they're going to own it and sell you a deer hunting licence for a deer on your property, they're going to pay to take care of it. And I filed a $380,000 boarding lawsuit against the state of Oklahoma and they wrote me a $20,000 cheque and told me to go away, and they got rid of all the laws. And that's why we don't have any laws here."

"Now, Government's exhibit 163 was some reference to Charlie and Greg Woody," said Earley. "What was that about? Do you remember that call?" Joe claimed he had donated six lions and two adult bears to Woody. A white tiger cub loaned to Woody by Joe had died in Woody's care.

"It was the same conversation... It's just they cut it apart."

"All right. Now, I want to make sure I understand what this situation was and what your testimony is with respect to PETA. Now, this email, what were you talking about as far as the proposal from PETA?"

"She sent me the draft, okay. And it didn't have any dollar figure in it. It was just to close and quit doing all this and that. Okay. And I sent that email back to her. And PETA, in order to get a place to close in Texas, paid the man six – and all he had was two bears – paid the man $60,000 for those bears, okay, and some of his circus equipment to move to their facility, which is the Black Beauty Ranch in south Texas. And that was... I was referring to, because Jeff just wouldn't do anything without any money. So I put in there, I'm like, hell, you paid 60,000 bucks for two bears. I said, you're getting an entire zoo, the property and everything. And I needed some money to pay off the bills so we didn't just stick everybody, owing them money."

"So if I understand correctly, you had to agree to PETA's proposal, correct?"

"Before we moved on to Big Cat Rescue's proposal," Joe added.

"All right. So unless you and Mr. Lowe agreed to that proposal that was sent to you by Ms. Peet?"

"Correct."

"Ms. Baskin wasn't going to enter into any negotiations with you to resolve your problem with her?" said Earley.

"You are right."

"All right. Now, Ms. Green asked you about the transfer of tigers, the second transfer. The first one had to do with the Dade City tigers, correct?"

"Yes, sir."

"So the second group that went out, that was you getting rid of your own, correct?"

"Yes, sir."

"You weren't paid for that?"

"No, sir."

"And you thought that there were some pairs, correct?"

"I believe there was, yes."

"But what else was included in that transfer?"

"Three bears, I believe," said Joe. "Three black bears and some baboons. I think there was a trio of baboons."

"So, as far as reducing your inventory, did that lead to you almost getting rid of all of the primates on your property?"

"That got rid of the big primates, and then we sent a bunch of littler primates over to Tulsa."

"Who assisted with that?"

"Just the park staff that helped catch them," said Joe.

"So was that part of your agreement with PETA to try to reduce your inventory?"

"Well, I told her that I was going to, and she was having troubles finding a place to send everything. And to this day, because of the litigation, I haven't spoke to her directly. We have been going through somebody."

That was the end of the redirect. Then it was Maxfield Green's turned to cross-examine Joe again.

"You just testified that the filmmakers that you have been communicating with, those were people from your past, correct?" she said.

"Yes, ma'am."

"Okay. And people that got in touch with you prior to all of this, correct?"

"Most of them, uh-huh."

"Okay. But you have been soliciting to shop your story around to people since you have been in jail too, correct?"

"I haven't been soliciting nobody because I can't reach out to nobody. There's been a whole lot of people email me to the jail, yes."

"You have been sending and receiving emails in jail, correct?"

"Yes."

"And you're familiar that all those are logged, correct?"

"Yes, ma'am."

"Okay. Government's going to introduce… well, first let me lay a little more foundation here. Do you know Manuel Oteyza?"

Oteyza is producer and production manager, known for *Joshua Tree* (1993), *Stuff Happens Hosted by Bill Nye* (2008) and *Blackfish* (2013).

"I do," said Joe.

"Is he in the courtroom today?"

"He is."

"Have you emailed back and forth with him?"

"Not as much as we have talked on the phone."

Maxfield Green moved to admit exhibit 165. There was no objection.

"Now, this is an email from you to Manuel Oteyza, correct?"

"It is."

"And are you familiar with Mr. Oteyza's other films?"

"*Blackfish*."

This was controversial film about the captivity of killer whales and its dangers for both whales and their keepers that won several awards and numerous nominations. The 2013 documentary sparked a public backlash against SeaWorld and led the theme park company to end killer whale shows. Oteyza was seen in the courtroom, taking notes.

"That's one," said Maxfield Green.

"Yes, ma'am."

"And this was on November 17, 2018, correct?"

"It looks… appears to be."

"Does it say, 'Manuel, just curious if you ever buy material for your film. I am desperate to get a rent house before my bond hearing so I can go home until trial. I have thousands of hours of footage on computers from my studio at the zoo and on hard drives, along with over seventy pages of my diary from the age of five until now and after this experience. I will make the biggest advocate for animals you have ever seen. I'm in need of $7,000 for deposits and rent to cover me until trial, or until I can get home. Just curious, Joe.' Is that what you wrote?"

"Yes, ma'am."

While he acknowledged negotiating from jail with the filmmakers, Joe bristled at the suggestion that he'd been paid several thousands of dollars already by filmmakers for his life story, claiming that he hadn't got a dime.

"Now, Mr. Earley asked you about that conversation with the Lowes that we saw earlier, right?"

"Yes, ma'am."

"And your testimony, when Mr. Earley asked you about that, is that I believe you said that you made that up to get out of the situation. Is that what you said?"

"I did. And it started in the office and I made up one in there too."

"That was my only question," said Maxfield Green. "Thank you."

Joe was allowed to step down. There were no more witnesses.

In her closing statement, the lead prosecutor Amanda Maxfield Green urged the jury not to believe Joe's story. "The Tiger King: that's how he has marketed himself and lived his life," she said. "But here's the thing with kings – they start to believe they're above the law."

She replayed for jurors part of Joe's phone conversation with former boyfriend John Finlay, after his arrest the previous September in Gulf Breeze, Florida. In the conversation, Joe expressed shock when Finlay revealed that he told the FBI he drove to Dallas to get Glover the fake ID for the Florida trip.

"Oh, so… so, you hung me out to dry? Huh?" Joe said.

Maxfield Green told jurors that, again, Joe's mouth "became his own worst enemy."

For the defence, Bill Earley said: "Keep that in mind and consider who has a motive to snare Mr. Passage."

He also dismissed the testimony of Allen Glover, saying it "was impossible to corroborate" because he did not take a cell phone with him to Florida and admitted on the stand to being under the influence of drink and drugs at certain points during his trip.

"These murder for hire allegations were manufactured," Earley told the jury.

They were not swayed. After six days of testimony from more than a dozen witnesses, the jury went out to consider its verdict at 11 a.m. on 2 April 2019. At 2.55 p.m., they unanimously brought in a guilty verdict. Joe was convicted on all counts – two for the murder for hire scheme and seventeen of violating the Endangered Species Act, wildlife trafficking and killing multiple tigers. Facing twenty years in jail, he accepted the verdict silently, staring straight ahead into the distance.

Carole Baskin wasn't in the courtroom it see it. She left after three days of the trial. Clearly she did not want to waste her time listening to Joe defending himself. Back at her sanctuary in Tampa, she was relieved when the verdict came in.

She posted: "I am grateful that justice was served and Joe Schreibvogel-Maldonado-Passage hopefully will serve time in prison and no longer present a threat either to me or to his former big cats. While media attention regarding this trial has primarily focused on the murder for hire charges, there is a much larger significance to the wildlife charges. For years, a network of big cat owners like Passage who have engaged in cruel cub-petting schemes and the exhibition of big cats have also been engaging in the illegal sale of tigers and other animals back and forth among themselves simply by checking the box on the USDA transfer form that says 'donated' instead of 'sale' and quietly paying cash for the animals."

She went on to list some of those mentioned in the trial who did this. They included Bhagavan "Doc" Antle, Tim Stark, Bill Meadows, Mario Tabraue, Kathy Stearns, Robert Engesser, Jeff Lowe and Omar Villareal.

Joe's attorneys had announced beforehand that they would not be commenting or releasing a statement regardless of the outcome. However, First Assistant US Attorney Robert J. Troester had prepared a statement. It read: "The self-described Tiger King was not above the law. Rather, the jury only needed a few hours of deliberation before finding him guilty of engaging in a murder for hire plot to kill a rival and violating federal laws intended to protect wildlife when he killed multiple tigers, sold tiger cubs and falsified wildlife records. We are thankful for the jury's careful attention, deliberation and verdict in this case."

PETA President, Ingrid Newkirk, also put out a statement, saying: "Joe Exotic has been on PETA's radar for years as a notorious animal abuser and as the primary supplier of big cat cubs for the cruel cub-petting industry, and PETA already succeeded in getting thirty-nine tigers, three bears, two baboons and two chimpanzees out of his hands and into reputable sanctuaries. The world will be a safer place for all living beings with this man behind bars where he can no longer harm animals or the animal advocates he hanged in effigy."

Leif Reigstad, a reporter covering the story for *Texas Monthly*, went to visit Carole: "We spoke a week after the trial, in the living room of a small ranch house at Big Cat Rescue, surrounded by wall art depicting exotic cats," he said. "She hoped that if Joe were handed a strict sentence, it might deter others in the exotic animal industry from operating zoos like his. Yet it troubled her that Joe, even from jail, had remained involved in the exotic animal business. In a recording that was played during the trial, he appeared to be brokering the sale of some lion cubs through Dillon."

Carole posted a video again saying that Joe was not simply "one crazy bad apple" and calling out several other roadside zoo owners. And she continued to update 911animalabuse.com.

"For Joe, it was very personal," Carole said. "Whereas for us, it was just another one of these bad guys that we are trying to make people aware of."

Another one of them, Carole said, was Jeff Lowe.

Lowe called the verdict "justice for the animals." He also said that Joe had committed other crimes including embezzling $88,877 in zoo funds to pay personal and political campaign expenses. He told *The Oklahoman*: "Joe lies every time his lips move."

Meanwhile Allen Glover told the *Daily Mail*: "My only plan the entire time was to drain every dime I could get from Joe, I hated that guy. Joe's plan would have never worked, even if he had hired a legitimate hitman."

His motives were clear: "I just couldn't stand being around Joe anymore and I wanted to get out of there and go back to South Carolina. But I didn't have any money to leave, I was only making $150 a week."

A veteran convict, Glover said he didn't believe Joe would last long in prison.

"He's not going to ever set foot alive outside of prison again, he won't do his full sentence, I give him five years at most before he's dead," said Glover. "I should know the mindset it takes to survive, I've spent a long time in prison, and Joe doesn't have what it takes."

Glover's criminal record continued. In 2018 he was arrested twice for driving under the influence. He pled no contest to both charges, was given a one year suspended sentence and paid a fine.

Joe's former park manager and long-time friend John Reinke was more forgiving. He said: "Did Joe do wrong? Yeah, I'm sure he did wrong. He did sell cubs. He did transport cubs. The murder for hire thing? I don't think it ever would have went this far unless someone pushed it."

The conditions at G.W. Exotic Animal Park did not improve after Joe left, but Lowe told reporter Sean Williams, writing from the *Daily Beast*, that he'd had "five consecutive perfect unannounced USDA inspections", spent $4,000 a week on food and confirmed that the big cats were "happy". However, Williams found conditions squalid. He talked to employee Taryn Walker, who said the new owners are incompetent, and fed the cats chicken rather than more expensive and nutritious red meat. When Taryn reported the park for mistreating its horses, Lowe called her a "c*nt" on his Facebook page, claiming that she tasered tigers. "Show your face here again you bitch, I have a rake and shotgun with your name on them," he said.

Lowe told Mark Lewis, editor of the *Wynnewood Gazette*, he was installing a drive-in theatre at the park. He'd convinced Joe Barth, a neighbour in Beaufort, to move his theatre there, then reneged on the deal. Barth claimed Lowe stole the movie equipment and still fears for his safety.

Leif Reigstad also visited the zoo the day after Joe was convicted. It was 11.30 on a Wednesday morning and he was the only visitor there. Every few feet signs warned of surveillance cameras and armed guards. Many of the cages were empty. The ones that weren't, held cats that paced aimlessly inside their small enclosures. There were piles of dried faeces in some of the cages, he noted.

Tacked on to many of the enclosures were faded placards from donors, often memorialising the dead. "This compound is in loving memory of Grace Maples. We loved you best. Robbie, Tena and Cameron Wilson, Ft. Worth, TX," one read. "This Tiger Complex was Built in Loving Memory of Jarrod 'Willis' Hurley," read another. "May your spirit be free."

"It was a reminder of what the zoo could have been and of what Joe once supposedly wanted it to be: a living memorial, a sanctuary from the tragedies in life, both animal and human," said Reigstad. "One person not memorialised anywhere at the zoo was the Tiger King. Joe's face had been scrubbed from the property. Even the billboards on I-35 had been taken down. Somewhere in the back pasture, there were more than fifty dead tigers. There was no memorial for them either."

*Tiger King: Murder, Mayhem and Madness* directors Eric Goode and Rebecca Chaiklin told *Entertainment Weekly* of their concern for the animals during the coronavirus lockdown in Spring 2020.

"No one is going now and there's no source of income, and that's been going on for a long time," said Goode. If the zoo fails, the outlook for the animals would not look good. "Some will be placed but I would suspect a lot of them will die from starvation, and probably be put down. And this is probably true for a lot of operations around the country right now that keep exotic animals. And even big zoos are struggling right now to keep their animals."

The directors also discussed how Joe has been handling life behind bars.

"Eric and I keep in touch with him and he has now been in prison for a year and a half – going on like a year and nine months or something," said Chaiklin. "He has a really different perspective on what it means to be in a cage and really has done a lot of thinking about that."

She also condemned Joe as a racist after a clip emerged of him ranting about not being allowed to use the n-word. He was filmed mouthing off in a bizarre clip about a perceived injustice of not being able to use the racial slur while black rappers can use the racist insult in their music.

Chaiklin told *The Hollywood Reporter*: "Joe is a racist, I would say categorically. He said things when we were filming that were very unsettling."

## EIGHTEEN: Fame and Misfortune

There may be more disruption for the zoo to come. Jeff Lowe said locals told him that there may be human bodies concealed in the park. One of the staff got drunk one night and told him that, several years earlier, they were out on the property getting high with another zoo employee when two protestors tried to climb the fence.

The employee apparently shot both of them, with one protestor supposedly dying on the fence and the other falling to the ground choking on his own blood, only to be shot again.

"It was about 3 a.m. at the time," Lowe said he was told. "After they were finished off, they told Joe what happened. Joe allegedly instructed them to put the bodies into the cavity of the big construction tires they have out there that weigh about two hundred pounds each.

"He then told them to throw gasoline on it and light it on fire to burn the bodies. Joe thought the dead protestors were working with PETA and they were UK citizens, which is why they never showed up on a missing person's report."

Lowe said he told the authorities about it.

"They came out and searched that particular area of the property bringing a bone specialist from the FBI out of Quantico. They walked around and dug in certain areas," said Lowe. "The problem was it was the area where Joe had thrown animal bones at for years. There were already hundreds of bones buried there from the animals that they fed to the cats."

Lowe said the feds decided at the time to wait and see how long Joe was going to be sentenced for to see if it was worth the estimated $1 million needed to excavate the entire area. But the prognostications of doom were premature. The zoo's fortunes revived after the Netflix series *Tiger King: Murder, Mayhem and Madness* was released in March 2020. Thousands of people, ignoring social distancing and without face masks, thronged to the zoo, then renamed Tiger King Park, at the beginning of May 2020 after it re-opened following the coronavirus shutdown. Jeff and Lauren Lowe were still there to greet guests.

Clearly Joe still has his fans. *The Oklahoman* said: "Even in disgrace, Joe Exotic remains somewhat of a media darling." The newspaper itself filled its pages with coverage of the trial and splashed the guilty verdict across the top of its front page.

Later, from jail, Joe was said to be negotiating his own radio show to be broadcast from inside prison. Dillon said: "I know he absolutely loves the attention. He's got a load of really good feedback, a lot of letters, a lot of emails."

Lowe said he was asked by a *Dateline* producer for an interview for a one-hour "prime time report about the case once it is adjudicated", according to a post on Facebook. Later he announced he had made an agreement with a "certain media outlet" and will be dealing with them exclusively.

"Some very interesting stories will evolve from this, I promise," Lowe wrote in a Facebook post. However, Lowe declined to talk to *Texas Monthly*, saying that he had sold his exclusive life rights to Netflix. He hadn't.

*Texas Monthly* did speak to Joe's ex, John Finlay. He was then living in a Motel 6 off I-35 in Oklahoma. He said Joe had ruined his life. But he'd found work as a welder and was optimistic about having the chance to start over.

"This is going to be the beginning of my life without him in it," he said.

He had a girlfriend and said that having a daughter had helped him focus after his years at the park. He would never set foot there again. Lowe had threatened to shoot him if he did.

"Trespassing animal abusers will be shot and killed," Lowe had said.

"He's as bad as Joe, if not worse," said Finlay.

His eleven-year relationship with Joe had left scars.

"Whether he knows it or not, he did mentally abuse me and he controlled me," he said. "But I've actually got it figured out now."

The mother of Finlay's daughter later filed a petition for a protection order. In it she claimed that Finlay told her "he would put a bullet in anyone who stood between him and his child". She also claimed Finlay had "told numerous people he wanted to leave the state with [their daughter], and he was headed to Florida before he faced prison".

An emergency order was granted, but weeks later it was rescinded because the police couldn't find Finlay to serve it on him.

Despite the coverage, the full story about Joe Exotic had yet to be told, said Finlay.

"A lot of people don't know the truth," he said. "And a lot of people don't care to know the truth… they want the nice story about the guy with the tigers."

The media lapped up Joe's lies – a drunk driver killed his brother, he rescued a meth addict who became his husband – keen to buy into his quirky, animal-loving character.

Meanwhile, with Joe behind bars, a darker side of what went on in his zoo came out. It was said that Joe controlled and abused the zoo's staff, accused them of being traitors and threatened to throw them back on the streets. He hooked some on drugs. All of them witnessed animal abuse on an astonishing scale.

At least twice a week he ordered staff out in a white delivery truck, with "NO PETA" written on its side, to collect expired meat and vegetables from Walmart stores across Oklahoma. Sometimes the crew worked until 2 a.m., cutting food out of its packaging for use the following day. Oftentimes they ate the meat themselves: Joe joked it was a miracle nobody got sick. Other times crew killed and butchered the zoo's "hoof stock" – low-value horses, cows, and goats – to be "fed out" to the exotics, his breadwinners. Some crew went to local auction to bid for horses and bring them back, to kill them and feed them to the animals.

Staff said Joe was bent on control. He was abusive – sometimes physically and sexually – and as predatory as the animals he loved to breed. Joe could be kind one moment, spiteful the next. Some of the more enthusiastic crew members took his abuse as collateral damage, knowing that a regular park would never allow them to have such close contact with the animals. Many felt they could never leave. Some who did said they'd escaped a cult.

When journalist Sean Williams contacted Joe in prison, Joe asked if he could pass a message to Donald Trump. He claimed he's been set up like Terry Thompson from Zanesville and was a political prisoner. Joe himself also wrote to President Trump, begging for a pardon.

"I am being sent to prison for a form being filled out wrong by my vet's secretary under the Endangered Species Act," he wrote. "I am being sent to prison for forms filled out wrong by the zoo manager while I was over a thousand miles away… under the Endangered Species Act.

"I am being sent to prison for euthanising my own tigers that were born and raised at my zoo to keep them from suffering because Congress did not put in the wording the word TAKE was meant for animals in the wild not in America."

Joe's contention was that he had not taken any animals from the wild. His animals were bred in captivity. But his defence had fallen on deaf ears.

"My trial was not about the truth, it was about the win for the prosecutors," he wrote. "All my proof was turned over and completely ignored just to push an animal rights agenda to ban owning exotic animals."

He signed off his letter to Trump saying: "I know by seeing your passion and conviction regarding our rights as American Citizens that this isn't what you meant by your belief to 'Let's Make America Great Again'.

"Mr. President, I am pleading with you to please have this looked into. I am currently incarcerated at the Grady County Jail in Oklahoma and facing twenty to fifty years in prison for doing the same thing every zoo and sanctuary owner has had to do at one time or another."

He also complained about conditions in jail, saying humans are treated worse in American jails than animals under USDA regulations. Apparently without irony, Joe wrote from prison: "Do you know why animals die in cages? Their soul dies." Adding: "Go sit in a cage with your animals for a week. I mean, when I left the zoo and I sent my chimpanzees to the sanctuary in Florida and imagined what my chimpanzees went through for eighteen years, I'm ashamed of myself."

Though still married to Joe, Dillon disappeared. He refused to speak to the press and Joe would not reveal where he was. However, in May 2020, he surfaced on Fubar Radio blaming Carole Baskin for the Covid-19 pandemic.

"There is only one person that we can blame for this and that is Carole fucking Baskin," he said, offering no further explanation. Meanwhile he was still in touch with Joe.

"It's not always easy and there's always gonna be something that's kind of there to bring us down," he said. "Some of the things that really help me is I have a group of friends that are constantly messaging me and we talk all day long. We send each other videos of previous festivals and pictures of stuff of when we would hang out. It's the little things that'll brighten your day."

Joe and Dillon had up to five calls a day, but this was cut down due to the Covid-19 pandemic when inmates had to stand further apart when they queued for the phone. Joe was then move to the Federal Medical Center in Fort Worth, Texas, where he was quarantined for fourteen days as there were cases of Covid-19 in Grady County Jail. Dillon said that Joe was still optimistic that Carole Baskin would be caught for the alleged killing of her husband, Don Lewis. The case had been reopened, though it was not clear how this would help Joe's situation.

"I think his main goal though once he gets out of jail is to rebuild his reputation because it was totally tarnished and torn to pieces once he got arrested," Dillon said.

There were others who also cut Joe a bit of slack.

"Despite his lies and manipulation, I enjoyed speaking to Joe," said Sean Williams. "He's charming and an engaging speaker. He made me feel I was his best friend, telling me that, as a British writer, I could stick it to the American press who 'make everything look horrible'. If he thinks you're a potential enemy, everything changes. When he discovered I was reporting his true story, Joe called me a 'bully' via his jail's commissary (fittingly called Tiger). He told others I couldn't be trusted."

During their conversations, Joe expressed no regret.

"Am I going to take the fall [for stuff] that everyone did wrong?" he asked.

Not only was Joe not remorseful, he was downright belligerent.

"Kiss my ass right here from jail," he posted to Facebook. "None of you will ever come close to knowing the stress it took daily to deal with keeping hundreds of people alive, just so a bunch of people, that their own families threw out, could not appreciate a job and a home.

"I am proud of what I did in my life and any loser that says otherwise had the same chance – they just fucked it up. That zoo is closing and the new one will never open. I promise you that, 'cause a bunch of people are going to jail. I am making sure of that."

Reporter Leif Reigstad also got in touch with Joe by phone at the Grady County Jail, where he was awaiting sentencing.

"At first he was reserved. He hardly resembled the bombastic man I had watched on the witness stand and in his many videos," Reigstad said. "He told me of his childhood, about his loveless family. He told me he was sexually abused when he was five. He spoke fondly of the early days of the zoo and seemed proud of the animals he had rescued."

Reigstad asked Joe if he regretted posting any of the things he had about Baskin. He said no, explaining that he had to act tough online in the face of hostile animal rights activists. He reiterated his claims that he was framed, and he questioned the motives of the prosecutors.

"Am I in jail until they can shut down this industry, or am I taking the rap for all these other people?" he said. "Come hell or high water, at some point, I'm gonna make world news, okay? Something's gonna change in the name of Joe Exotic."

Joe refused to explain what he meant.

"This is a recorded telephone, so I'm not gonna tell you that," Joe said. "But at some point, bet your ass, I'm gonna make world news."

Around a dozen letters asking for a lenient sentence were submitted by Bill Earley ahead of his sentencing. Earley's own sentencing memorandum complained that Joe had been "painted as a liar, thief, animal abuser and homicidal maniac".

"Sadly, this court has been exposed only to the worst that the government and animal rights groups can assemble," Earley wrote. "The truth is that hardly a day went by that Mr. Maldonado-Passage did not touch someone's life in a positive way. The lives he touched include terminally ill children, terminally ill elderly people, souls lost to alcohol and drug use, others suffering from broken hearts, the poor, the homeless and societal outcasts. These were the people that kept Mr. Maldonado-Passage grounded and what gave him the energy and desire to keep his park open."

Another ten submissions came from friends asking the court to consider their experiences they've had with him.

"I believe Joe has a good heart," one supporter, Rebecca Paradis, told the judge in a handwritten letter. "It's been long enough. Please let Joe come home."

Joe himself posted on Facebook on 4 December 2019: "This will not be swept under the rug forever. At some point during this course of action, this is going to be exposed."

Joe still said he believed that he would be vindicated on appeal. Between his letters to the President and the judge, he posted on Facebook: "It may take me a month or a year to see the light at the end of this dark tunnel but we will have another place full of animals that will give you a place to spend your holidays open every day of the year."

In court at the sentencing hearing, wearing an orange jail jump suit, Joe hurried to the podium as fast as his ankle chain would allow. During a rambling ten-minute statement, he cried, apologised for his past mistakes, talked about his two "incurable" diseases and pleaded to be set free so he could go home and look after his ailing dad.

"I know that I've done wrong," he said. "I know that. I will never be here again."

Again he complained that Jeff Lowe had set him up and that government witnesses had lied about him at trial.

Judge Palk admonished him for repeatedly trying to blame others and for his "doing as you please" attitude to life.

"Despite what you may believe, you are not the only in-step person in an out-of-step world," the judge said.

Palk sentenced Joe to twenty-two years in prison. He was unbowed.

"I still maintain my innocence and looking forward in the upcoming days to my attorneys filing my appeal and moving onto the next step in this nightmare," Joe said in a statement posted on his Facebook page.

He vowed to sue the federal government for false imprisonment and accused the US Attorney's office and FBI agents of perjury.

In his statement Exotic said he was "punished for taking advantage of my Constitutional Rights to not plead guilty to their very well-orchestrated frame job of murder for hire, so they superseded my indictment with eighteen wildlife charges".

He continued: "I will also be looking forward to the Civil Suit I will be filing pro se in the upcoming days against the US Department of Interior, The Federal Wildlife Service and its Directors, and agents involved for $84,840,000.00 for the reasons of false imprisonment, selective enforcement, malicious prosecution, discrimination, loss of eighteen years of research, loss of personal property, mental anguish, pain and suffering and the death of my mother, along with a few other counts."

There was a conspiracy against him, he said.

"If I wasn't living this for real, I would never believe that in America the Government could actually take part in such lies to further an animal rights agenda. But again, look what they are doing to our own President. Our Justice System is so broken," he wrote.

After the sentencing, Carole Baskin said: "The evidence showed that over the course of many years, he has tried to coerce others into killing me, and in the end, resorted to hiring others to kill me. Because of his constant threats to kill me, I have found myself seeing every bystander as a potential threat. My daughter, my husband, my mother, my staff and volunteers have all been in peril because of his obsession with seeing me dead."

In an interview with the *Daily Mirror*, Carole talked of the effect Joe had had on her.

"Due to Joe's constant threats to kill me, my life changed beyond recognition," she said. "There was nowhere that I felt safe. But more worrying was the threat he could pose to those around me. I was suspicious of everyone and carried a gun everywhere. One time, I nearly doused an innocent supporter of my work in gas as I filled my car up because I thought he'd been sent by Joe to kill me. So many of his threats involved blowing me up so he could thrill over seeing me burn to death."

There were others who thought that a sentence of twenty-two years in prison was not enough. His niece Chealsi Putnam said: "If it were up to me, I would have sentenced him to life behind bars. He wouldn't have ever seen the light of day."

She condemned calls for her uncle to be pardoned and has slammed celebrities who are calling for his freedom. People were making her uncle into a cult figure and jumping on the "Free Joe Exotic" bandwagon. She said she hoped that the celebrities such as rapper, Cardi B, really investigated the person they were supporting because "Joe is an evil, maniacal person" and their calls to pardon him "makes them look like idiots".

"He's caused a lot of pain to a lot of people," Chealsi said.

She had no regrets on helping the FBI find Joe, saying: "I'd do it again, he needed to be caught."

Joe was evil, she said, preying on the weak and taking advantage of people who were down and out in their life. He deserved every year of his twenty-two-year prison sentence and claiming he had done many more illegal things.

"Joe's a liar so I was worried that the jury may fall for the show that he puts on, but fortunately they saw through his BS and convicted him of all of the charges," she said. She had not spoken to Joe in almost two years, but she had only one thing to say to him: "Hope you rot in hell."

Indeed, Joe could be looking at more time behind bars. Chealsi said she had been told that Joe is being investigated by the IRS and the fraudulent use of campaign funds when he unsuccessfully ran for governor of Oklahoma in 2018.

Her voice was joined by one of the jurors, named Kristin, who condemned the TV coverage Joe was getting, which, she said, "made him out to be almost a victim", "lovable" and a "good guy".

"It just wasn't even the same story," she said. "It did a huge injustice to the jury because now people think that we convicted him based on absolutely nothing."

But she was adamant that the jury had reached the right verdict.

"We could have convicted on both murder for hire counts based on one sentence that Joe said, which was 'the first guy that I hired to kill her ran away with my $3,000. Now we're going to try this again'," Kristin said.

Undaunted, in an interview from jail, Joe said: "I'm done with the Carole Baskin saga. It's now time to turn the tables and

Joe gets out of jail – a free man and exonerated from all these charges." Adding later: "When I walk out of here am I going to be as crazy as I was before? That will never change!"

Netflix series *Tiger King: Murder, Mayhem and Madness* was released on 20 March 2020 and was soon the streaming giant's top-trending title worldwide during the lockdown. *Vanity Fair* called it the "perfect social-distancing binge". It was watched by 34.3 million people over its first ten days of release, ranking as one of Netflix's most successful releases. Dillon said that, without watching a single episode, Joe was an instant fan. Now Joe Exotic had the fame he always craved.

"You know it would be nice if I could actually see me being famous out there, but I've seen these same four walls for a year and a half now," he said.

He was so famous that, at a White House press conference on 9 April 2020, a journalist asked the Tiger King's former rival and current idol, President Donald Trump, whether he would pardon Joe Exotic. Trump said: "I know nothing about it… What did he do? I'll take a look at it."